OUT of IT

Para a Lélé.
com carinho antigo,
algo da literatura palestina,
algo concernente a direitos humanos,

Tadeu

Doha, em 24.4.12

OUT of IT

Selma Dabbagh

First published in 2011 by
Bloomsbury Qatar Foundation Publishing
Qatar Foundation
Villa 3, Education City
PO Box 5825
Doha, Qatar
www.bqfp.qa

ISBN 9789992178744

For my parents Claire and Taysir for teaching me
how to observe and to feel respectively.

PART I

GAZAN SKIES

Chapter 1

These were terrible times, but the email changed everything.

The night before the flares had started at around eight, Rashid was sure of that much. Before them, there had just been the insistent tattering of gunfire somewhere in the background. His perception was cushioned and brightened by Gloria's leaves by then, so that when the flares actually kicked off, he had been stoned making the dry air fill with toxic smoke and the falling lights squirm around on his eyeballs long after they had faded.

By the time the heavy stuff (*Baadoom! Baadoom!*) had pounded in on them he had been well and truly blitzed and in that state he sometimes found himself almost willing those bottom-of-the-stomach explosions to burst forth after all that stuttering gunfire: *Just do it, why don't you? Go on, come out with it!* There had been a missile with a light so bright it lit up the whole strip, right up to the fence. Smoke had blown back at the sky and seeped along the ground close to the lights.

The strike on the hospital was possibly half an hour after the flares, maybe more. It felt as though it had taken out his guts with it. That could have been when he had really lost it. There was a vivid point of being where he had let himself go. It was imprinted on his mind, an instant of reaching in his soul, when he had found himself leaping up on the roof next to the water tanks, teasing the locust heads of the helicopters. *Hey you! Can you see me? Here on the roof! Can you see me?*

That was the moment. He could not remember anything after

that. That was it. Blank. Stoned, utterly stoned. The thickness of it was still there like a fungus under his forehead.

He had awoken with his legs splayed out under his bed in imitation of a shot man, face and floor tiles sealed together by a membrane of spittle. He came to with a headache, that told him that he should suffer as he was a disgrace, was good for so damn little and so on and so forth.

This had been when he woke up.

But now, fifteen minutes later, he was something new and somewhere different. He no longer cared about any of the indignity that could be associated with passing out under his bed. All that was before he had logged on and downloaded. Before finding it there. Having it here.

The email had changed everything.

He had been transformed.

Now he stood in front of the bathroom mirror, bare to the waist, face wet, arms spread. Supreme.

Here he was, reflected back at himself: the eternal man in a body of youth. His forearms, face and neck were darker than the rest of him, but Rashid ignored the sallow skin that created the ghost of a T-shirt over his chest, the one that cut across his arms. He disregarded the underdeveloped muscle tone and there were days when he would think the word wasted, *wasted*, and feel his flesh shrinking under the surface of his skin. This was a morning when he saw only his collarbones that framed it all, the swoop of biceps and triceps on his arms, the stomach definition that needed no work for it to stay like that and the scrub of dark hair from his navel down to his jeans. 'Pathway to heaven,' Lisa had said tracing along it with her fingertip, 'pathway to heaven.'

And at the thought of her, her laugh, *Lisa!* It exploded within him again and he could feel himself fly, up, up, out of all of this.

4

See himself fly, an Olympic diver in reverse, Icarus in the sky, Jesus on a hill – it was all confused – fly up, out, over all this.

All this what?

All this *bonery*. He knew how the earth would look from up there: like dried-out coral, ridged, chambered and sandy. He knew as he had traced his finger over the satellite pictures of it when dreaming of escape. From up there it was hundreds and thousands of habitations reduced to scratches on a bone. At that height, the line that fenced them in would barely be made out, nor would the checkpoints, not from up there, but even from that stratospheric distance, the contrast with the other side would be stark. On the *other side, that* side, the place they came from, that had been *theirs*, the one that they weren't allowed to even *visit* any more, it wasn't bones, but a blanket: an elaborate blanket of modernist design. It was patterned with rows, circles and stripes, each shape coloured absolutely as though painted with the tip of a cursor and the press of a button. Mud brown here, a dash of hunting green there, some rust-coloured lines for border definition. That side glinted. Solar panels and swimming pools twinkled in the sun.

To hell with them.

To hell with them.

He was out of there.

Flip, flip, flip for he doesn't fly, he is flipping now over the sea, the White Sea, *al bahr al abyad*, the Mediterranean, and it's so blue and alive with fish and dolphins leaping, leaping like him: over, up, out of it all, into the sky and away.

Right the hell out of there.

Out of here.

For ever.

Well, at least for a year.

Chapter 2

The comment came from nowhere, but after it was said Iman had been unable to treat the meeting in the same way. The chairwoman had smiled approvingly at her notepad and that was that.

'But you've just turned up here,' was all the woman had to say, 'you're new to this.'

Which was where it was. Where, Iman felt, it had always been, although no one had said it before. Iman was the outsider, the returnee and as a result she did not deserve to so much as comment on what was going on there.

'*Swisra*,' someone was saying behind her, Switzerland. They were talking about her schooling. That was completely unacceptable. Iman turned on the woman who had spoken, but instead of being intimidated by Iman's stare, the woman was now explaining Iman's background to the women near her. 'Her father was with the Outside Leadership,' the woman was saying. 'She teaches at a school. Only been back for a year or so.'

'But what if I have? That doesn't exclude me does it? Maybe I have something to add anyway?'

She had to handle herself as though he was watching her, she thought. '*This is how I dealt with it*,' she would tell him if he were to ask later, if she saw him again. '*I stood there and I told them*.' But told them what? They were watching her now, not all of them hostile, some of them encouraging, most of them curious, but none of them seemed to appreciate the magnitude of the insult. Didn't they see that she was being pushed out?

'I may not have been here long,' she strained to be dignified rather than haughty, to be calm rather than hysterical, 'but I am here now and I am not planning on leaving. I should still be able to have my say.'

'*Sah!*' Umm Nidal, who Iman and her twin brother Rashid, referred to as Grande Dame, now usefully decided to deploy her clout, '*Sah!* She's right. She should have her say.'

'Your point?' the chairwoman asked, scratching between her roots at her scalp with the end of her chrome pen and squinting. She always needed to squint to take Iman in.

'My point is that we can't keep waiting for one great opportunity to present itself, because it won't.' Iman took a breath *calm, calm.* 'We need to decide on small, manageable steps that are realisable and doable. It is better to do something, no matter how small—'

'Thank you,' the chairwoman said. 'Thank you, Miss Mujahed.' She nodded at Iman for her to sit down.

The Women's Committee's fortnightly meeting was being held in an unfinished, windowless basement room in one of the newly built universities in the city and they had been there all night. The walls were bare breeze blocks, the floor uncovered cement. It was the type of room you would find in a holocaust museum, Iman thought. The plan had been for the seven o'clock meeting to last no longer than two hours, but the bombing had started unexpectedly at eight and the decision had been for them to stay. And to stay. And to stay some more.

Iman had, for the most part, embraced being stuck there. She had gone upstairs and found the caretaker's wife in a closet-like room on the second floor, and, armed with a bag of keys, they had together found a couple of rugs in one of the offices that they brought down for the Committee members to sit, lie, or sleep on. They had boiled water in a saucepan and found cups for tea and sugar (*Bravo, Iman! Bravo!*) which she had brought in on a tray. She had helped with the sharing of the working phones between the women. She had complimented a couple of the women, joked with others. She had done so much. She did not deserve that comment (*You've just turned up here*), that reminder of who she was. That she was not wanted.

It was now nearly dawn, and sitting down, Iman realised how depleted the women looked: dread had dulled them. Most of them had barely participated in the meeting. Many had just followed the movement of the planes overhead with their eyes. Others had slept. Only the chairwoman had not let up for a second.

Iman coiled up her hair to form a rest against the wall. What would Raed say about the Committee? She couldn't stop thinking about him. Raed, who was so interested in what she had to say, who found a wryness in her that others missed, who had opinions on everything and every opinion seemed to intrinsically, magically concur with her own.

To escape from the Committee's pettiness and the bombing's complete lack of pettiness, Iman found herself retreating back to thoughts of Raed, to the sensation of the touch of his arm against hers. It had happened months ago now, in a flat in the Beach District. There had been a party and the sofa had been too small for the number of people on it and she had been pushed up against him. She had, of course, heard of him before and he was the older cousin of one of her students, but that had been the first time that they met. At one point he had pushed the side of his foot close against hers and left it there. She was sure of it. And then a look had followed the touch to show that it was not an accident. Just the thought of his look, his touch, even months later, could change her breathing pattern.

If it all became a bit too much, she went back to sitting on the sofa. Or she went further forward and thought of a kiss that had not happened yet, but one that would surely stop the world when it did.

It was emotional distortion by boredom. She could not even remember his features any more, they seemed to have become worn down by the number of times she had gone over them in her mind.

She needed to get over it.

But two weeks ago he had been injured and ended up in hospital and she did not know him well enough to visit and her brothers didn't know him at all. She asked his cousin about him, but there was a limit as to how much information could be got out of a seven-year-old. *He's good, Miss. He's healing well, Miss. Do you like my picture, Miss?*

What would he say of her participating in a group like this? Would he condone it or think it a waste of time? Her older brother, Sabri, thought it important, and she normally went through the conclusions and recommendations with him afterwards. She never bothered to discuss the Women's Committee in any seriousness with Rashid. *No, Rashid, they're not getting any better-looking in case you were going to ask.*

When she had first moved to Gaza and joined the Committee, she (*Fool!*) had been so keen. She had brought home agendas, written out topics and underlined them: *Role Models or Empty Mascots? The Role of Women in the Front's Hijacking Operations of the 1970s, Embracing the Other? Determining the Women's Committee Policy towards the Islamic Resistance Movement.* She had made pages upon pages of notes. But in meeting after meeting, the same topics had divided the floor into the same factions and the same excuses had been given for the same inaction. But what can we do in this situation? With these circumstances?

Damn the circumstances.

The circumstances would never change if they didn't do anything.

But do what? 'We should,' Raed had said, in such a simple way, as though describing how to play backgammon to a child, 'fight them with what they fight us with. It is the only way. The religious movements understand this. We are being too soft, which is why we are not getting anywhere. Our strategy makes no sense.'

Making tea during a bombardment had made her feel like she was part of a meaningful movement. And that was where it was at. She was too soft was where it was at.

Iman noticed that Manar was watching her from across the room. Diligent, devout Manar. And what did that understanding smile mean coming from her? That slightly greasy face in that tightly bound headscarf. *What, Manar? Do you have something to say now? Why don't you say in then?*

The chairwoman had started her summation. Iman leant over her knee and her hair fell in matted clusters down her back. Not one point, Iman realised, not one word, let alone one *idea* that Iman had said was in the conclusions.

The chairwoman declared the meeting over and left. As soon as the door shut behind her it was as though the room's centrifugal force had been released and a panic spread through the women: *Where did they strike? North? No, east from here. Of course, the south, they always do the south. They say they are using new planes, different bombs . . .*

Within seconds the previously docile Committee members were all clamouring to leave, waking up the others, picking up bags, someone took the tray with empty glasses. Manar came forward to help Iman fold a rug. *Troubled girl*, Iman thought as she looked at Manar, hoping that by doing so she could dispel the hold that Manar seemed to exert over her, as she did on the rest of the Committee.

Manar joined Iman in rolling up the other, larger rug. Despite her overexaggerated humility, Manar definitely had airs. Iman had noticed that she did not, for example, even deign to read the agenda when it was circulated, instead she just waved, almost imperceptibly, to indicate that it could not be of interest to her although she found it charming that it was to others. What gave someone the confidence to feel that sense of entitlement and superiority? No one knew anything about this woman. She hardly spoke and yet since she had arrived at the Committee everyone seemed to have changed. No one joked about not fasting in Ramadan any more, instead many women said that they did, and rather than discussing that old topic of how the veil objectified women, they now spent their time having heated discussions about the oppression of women in the West.

Iman studied Manar: she didn't have a bag and wore no make-up. The only sign that she cared about her appearance at all was her eyebrows that were badly plucked. There was a general beige-ness to her, an asexual studenty casualness under her long floor-length dark coat that she had buttoned back up. With it on she was back to being an oval of plain features edged in black.

'I'll come with you,' Manar said, indicating the door as they picked up a rug each.

Outside, the crackling amplifier had started the dawn call to prayer. *Prayer*, the muezzin cajoled, *is better than sleep. And sleep*, Iman thought, *is better than meetings*.

'Aren't you going to pray?' Iman asked.

'I'll do it later.' Brown dust and crumbles of concrete from the rug stuck to Manar's outfit. 'I'll help you with these first.'

They found the caretaker's wife and returned the rugs in silence. Coming down the stairs, they didn't speak to each other either and Iman felt a rush of foreboding come over her, like the realisa-tion of a childish superstition. Today would be the day, Iman thought with a lurch of fear that felt like taking a step to nowhere in a dream, when something truly awful would happen to her family. It would occur to spite her for refusing to acknowledge the severity of the bombing. It would get her back for trying to shrug the whole thing off. They could have got them. They could have hit the house. Iman realised that her hands were stiff on the banister and that her teeth were clenched against each other in her mouth.

In the entrance hall the caretaker's daughter was already mopping at the creamy floor tiles with a mop. The reassuring sound of water, mop hitting plastic bucket, water being spread across tiles, was echoing around the walls, up to the high ceilings. Iman took in the rectangular gilt clock, the enlarged photograph of the President and the boxed-in noticeboard displaying students' results. These were all comforting – the girl would not be able to continue mopping the floor if Iman's family had been hit in a strike, surely?

It was at the doorway that Manar turned to Iman. 'It's not what you came back for is it?' she asked. 'You didn't come back for this.' It was getting light outside and through the glass doors Iman could see the smoke. The girl with the mop no longer seemed particularly reassuring.

No shit, Iman could hear Rashid saying. *You think someone would come back for this?* 'What do you mean?' Iman asked.

'You wanted a role.' Manar chose her words studiously. 'They are not giving you one are they?'

'I have to find my own role.'

'Exactly.' Manar did not move, but nodded. 'Exactly. But I think I could give you some help with that. There are people—'

'What people?' Iman asked.

Manar did not reply but closed her eyes slowly as though they had together chosen to listen to the swish and slop of the mop on tiles and dragging back of the sea on the sand.

'Manar, maybe we can talk another time? I want to get home. I don't know what's happened to my family. And besides, you heard the chairwoman, she reached her conclusions and I am not part of them.'

'You can do better than this. There are people who asked me to talk to you.'

'Who can want to talk to me?' Disquiet came over Iman together with a sense that she needed to listen to everything in order to be able to recall this conversation verbatim for Sabri who would be able to tell her what it all meant.

'It's OK Iman. I have been listening to what you say in there. You are right about making a difference.' The statement was delivered with significance, like a medal dropped around Iman's neck. 'You *were* right to come back to Palestine. You *do* have a role here.'

'And what is my role?' Iman's bag rattled on her arm. Her house keys, a lighter and some children's bangles that a girl she taught had given her knocked together, 'Who are you talking about when you say "we"? I don't get this "*we*".'

'A group. A serious group.' Manar replied. 'We don't *meet*, not like this. It is a question of being *contacted*. It just depends whether you are ready.'

'Ready for what?'

'To make a difference. To *really* impact the situation.' Manar's pretty ringless hand rested on Iman's arm. 'They think you are capable of it. Only you. Of all of the Committee, they asked me to speak to you, Iman Mujahed. They chose you.'

'They *chose* me? Who did?' Exam-result expectation flushed to Iman's hands. She always did well in exams. Behind her water sloshed out of the bucket on to the floor.

'Yes, they did and I am here to ask you. You need to think carefully about what you do and say, because once you have been contacted, then you cannot change your mind. Our group is, as I say, *serious*, and we have to be – how will you understand this? –

strict. Yes, we have to be very *strict*.' Her eyes challenged Iman. 'With anyone who changes their mind. So if you decide to do something that will make a difference,' she gestured in the direction of the room they had just been in, 'rather than all this, you know, *talk*, then you need to let them know. That's all.'

A jet struck through the sound barrier. The slam of it seemed to pull up the floor, shaking them and the contents of the room. It appeared to gloat that theirs was a world that rested only on a sheet. *Boom!* Iman's ears split. Down the corridor someone – the caretaker's wife possibly – yelled out for the mercy of God. The jet returned. *Boom!* Somewhere a pane of glass slid and smashed to the floor.

You see? Manar's lids said. *What did I tell you?*

'The question is, are you ready?' Manar's smile signified that the conversation was coming to an end. 'We knew that you were,' Manar continued, as though Iman had replied to her, 'We just wanted to be certain.' She nodded before she left, leaving Iman standing by the main entrance with nothing but the sound of the sea shooting on to the beach and the residue of a limp hand on her arm.

Chapter 3

The emails were like certificates of release in Rashid's hand. He'd got as far as the door with them where he waivered, undecided as to who to tell and how to tell them. It wasn't really the morning for it.

He looked back at the room that he was now destined to leave. Brown corn bent in the wind along the hem of his curtains. Half-drawn, the curtains let in the light, but kept out most of the view. Between them, in the middle distance, two smoke spirals were pulled and twisted by their own clouds. A darker stretch of smoke stemmed out of the hospital. Black clouds spumed across the sky.

Rashid went to the window for a closer inspection of it all. Was it possible that the building teetering on concrete legs across the wasteland had tilted further since the day before? He leant his head to one side. Maybe it was his vision that needed altering. Three cars crouched beneath the building in cloth covers. There were days when everything needed to be checked. The trees with the sea beyond them, were all *aadi*, normal. The cars were *aadi*, too. The tents with his neighbours in them were the same as ever. The odd thing – and it took a while to figure out what it was that he hadn't identified yet – was not so much the smoke, nor was it the building, the sea, the trees or the cars, all of which had their place and were in their place, but those men. The men coming around the building were not *aadi* at all. Not at all. There were two of them. Two of them and they were armed.

Oh, piss off. Just get out of here for today.

15

But the men neither pissed off nor did they get out of there. One fat, one thin, they moved around the garage pillars. The thin one leant against a car. One looked left, the other right, then both looked up at Rashid at the same time.

He stepped back and drew his curtains across the smoke, the buildings, the sea, the men, their guns.

There were days when brown corn was preferable.

But the emails were still there in his hands. *Yes!* Again he flew. He was above it all. Levitating, aloof. Was off. To London. To Lisa! Nothing could take that news away. Nothing. He would not let it. Not anyone. Not anything.

Chapter 4

Iman found a changed world around her when she came outside. The sea was still ahead of her, the university building behind, the city curling around to her left. A hut next to the corniche that sold beach balls and puffy orange crisps still had its placard with prices screwed on to its side. Everything was where it had been the night before, but the air was now thick with the smell of metal filings. Smoke leaked out of the places where the earth had been hit, as though the horizon itself had been punctured; whorls of it twisted and expanded, walling them in. She could not place herself in that landscape. It seemed ominous, extreme, almost fake. *It had been a visitation*. The thought of Manar now made her panic. Manar was a *visitation* and now it was all over: the voice, the face, the darkness, the smoke and then the end. *Over*.

The peachy campus buildings were not where she thought she would be when she saw all of this: the beginning of the end. A disembodied face in cheap, dark fabric. *A role for you. We have a role for you*.

She was seeing things. Hearing things. She had been up all night and now the weird high of fatigue was making her delusional.

The strikes were far from her home. She had taken that in at first glance. The smoke was far from their place. Her family would be OK. She found that she was breathing again, albeit cautiously, as though it was something that could only be done with deliberation.

But there, under it all, below the smoke, the air was soft, almost balmy. The clouds were ruffled over the sea and the scratches of jet trails were already dissolving up into the atmosphere. Close around her it was quiet, still, fresh. The streets were empty.

It was not over. It was not the end. Her family was safe. She was being melodramatic.

She walked towards her home, past buildings that without the daytime crush that normally surrounded them appeared serene. The workers who had permits to pass through tunnels of wire and cattle gates to jobs on the other side had already done so. The rest, the unemployed and the underemployed, still slept. The streets without their people were new, foreign, hers. Graffiti spread over the walls and the shuttered shops. Tree trunks were wrapped tight with posters of the dead.

There really was no one around at all. The curtains of smoke had created a veiled world around her that she had never been in before.

Iman sat on the playground wall away from the signs of donors promising reconstruction. A ginger cat strutted out in front of her and lay on its side, making a show of its belly, before it gathered that Iman was no fun at all and gave her its back. It leapt up on to the wall further down, lifting its head to squeeze its eyes at the growing light.

This was her lot. This was her life, the life of her father, her mother, her brothers. This was their lot, their country, their place in the world. This was what she had come back for and it was for her to find a meaningful role within it. At the time she had decided to join her family in Gaza there had been change, hope, peace agreements, agreements that, however faulty, had enabled what before had always seemed impossible. And she had returned valiantly, triumphantly to find that there was no role offered to her at all, except for that of wife and mother, both of which were pushed at her constantly.

The religious lot gave her the creeps though. Superior as well, that Manar. *We have a role for you.* Who were they? What group? They *chose* her? For what exactly?

It was quiet enough for her to smoke, right there in public, sitting on a low wall in the street. No one would see her. With her cigarettes, she pulled out a creased brochure for a centre for the disabled that she had visited months ago. The walls for the centre had been covered with pictures of bandaged children holding up their stumps and smiling at the camera, their mouths full of tubes. The brochure provided double, triple and quadruple digit figures of amputees in loopy script together with advertisements for pros-thetics: *'Liberation 2000 Lower Limb Range'*, *'Empowerment Arms and Hands'*.

'A disaster,' the receptionist had said when Iman had visited. 'My boss, he doesn't think. An organisation for the disabled on the third floor with no lift?' She had plied Iman with paperwork. 'You can help us – you were educated abroad, write us a proposal, get us moved. Up and down the stairs all day I am, the entrance jammed up with wheelchairs, the neighbours complaining.'

That was what she would do, Iman thought, smoothing out the brochure. Something small. She could write a proposal. It was a start. Forget Manar and her group.

She hurried with the lighter and the flame, on too high a setting, leapt up to singe a strand of curls, creating a stink in her nose.

She realised as she sat there with the knowledge that the house was all right, that it had really got to her, the extent of her agitation about her family. Now it had passed, she felt the calm, the cigarette, the morning air, the sense that the world hadn't completely exploded, that the destruction was only partial. The type of elation that followed on from despair was lifting her out of it.

Someone was watching her. She could feel it as she sat there.

She looked up at the buildings. The shutters were blank. There was no one on the street. Iman got up, dropped her cigarette and paced across the road pretending that she had purpose, somewhere to go, that she hadn't been sitting, smoking on a playground wall in the aftermath of a bombing. There was mud on the road, the paving slabs broken. She took a small leap over some cracks around a tree's roots then, sensing again with the sickening pump of a lost heartbeat that someone was watching her, looked up.

It was her brother Rashid . . . but it wasn't. The same profile, height, slimness, but not the same stance or clothes, nor the same look.

The man was wearing a rough green jacket with large pockets and toggles like those on a child's jacket, and was propped up, shoulder blades resting against the wall, as if this was New York or Paris and he had just come out for a smoke in a back street. He looked stuck on to the scene; everything close to the ground was sunken and sepia, but to Iman the jacket's green was somehow out there with the sky in this other world where trees were allowed to respond to light, a world where Mediterranean sunrises were allowed to just *be*.

He rocked on to his feet as she approached and gave her a familiar look, although she was sure she had never seen him before. Long and gaunt like Rashid, he had the high-cheekboned looks of a North African and the posture of a foreigner. He also had a gun.

By taking a step backwards he indicated that she could pass in front of him on the dry pavement. As he did so, his gun hit against a shutter sending a metallic judder down the street. She stepped so close to him that she would have been able to smell him, had she inhaled any breath at all, and then she was past him and he had not moved. He made no effort to follow her but he was still watching when she turned back to check.

* * *

20

Iman's family lived in the upstairs apartment of a two-storey block that had been one of eight of the same style. The buildings stood on a road that could, with a little imagination, once have been described as leafy.

Now the Mujahed home, unclad and progressive in style, with its long, triangular wall on its flat roof, stood alone in the middle of a tented wasteland. To Iman, it appeared to sit in an elephant's graveyard of arched steel and clumps of concrete. Bent strands of metal twisted up, catching the pink light of dawn, and appeared like the legs of buried flamingos. Light caught on fragments of sheets and toys held down by slices of painted walls.

The army had come one night months ago to destroy their area. They had demolished the neighbourhood's structures, pulled out its roots, and dug up its foundations. Soldiers had rollicked over their mess in yellow bulldozers, chasing the newly homeless. The trees had burnt for days.

Iman's neighbours' tents did not have groundsheets. Triangular constructions pulled to by wooden sticks, they sprouted limbs and blanket corners. That morning the Mujaheds' home, standing alone among the tents, seemed to protest that it was the bit that had been forgotten. *Knock me down with my friends. Let me lie with them.* Bougainvillaea bulged over the wall. The one remaining olive tree stood like a fig leaf across the door. Not even buildings should be singled out for survival.

Iman tried not to look too eager to cross the threshold into her building. It was essential that she concealed her desire to put a gate, a path and two metal doors between her and the mess outside, out of respect to those who were forced to live there. She strained to talk to the neighbours, to ask after their children, and to find something to chat about with those who were open to it. She could not offer help, she kept telling herself, because if she did, there was no knowing where it would end. But whatever she did, they always watched her and she always heard them in her head, commenting on her clothes, her foreignness, her virginity, her marriageability, or her lack thereof.

And then she was through. The gate would close and she could forget them and their mile-long walks for water (the Mujaheds' own supply was too intermittent to be shared), their haggling for cement and building materials, their tempers lost on bored, hungry children. She could close the gate behind her and walk down the stretch of tiles leading through the narrow, underutilised garden, past the entrance to Abu Omar's apartment and upstairs into her own home with its smells of jasmine air freshener, cardamom, bleach and cigarette smoke.

But today one of them had got in. There was someone from out there inside the gate: a bundle of an old woman with a tattooed leathery chin sat on their doorstep. She had pushed back a clump of vegetation to find the parts of the tiles that were still coloured and was running her finger over the traces of patterns on the Nablus tiles, proprietarily almost, it seemed to Iman. She was stroking them.

The woman stood as Iman entered, but standing made little difference to her. She was still bent and lumpy. There was so much stuffed into the internal chest pocket of her *thoub* that it looked as though her breasts were distended well below her string-tied waist.

'You're back,' the woman said, as though it was not just a matter of fact, but an acknowledgment of an achievement. 'I have been waiting,' she continued. 'I'm the aunt of Raed and your student Taghreed. You need to come with me.'

Chapter 5

Something wild had taken over his arms, an energy that translated itself in his brain into a desire to spin his brother around and around right there where he sat. But as Rashid's hands pulled back on the wheelchair handles, he felt the resistance of its brakes (the radio was on: *The bomber has now been identified as coming from the Hajjar family . . .*), saw the cup in his brother's hand, realised the spill that would follow, heard Sabri's voice over the broadcast, 'Stop it! Stop it! What are you trying to do? What the hell?' and felt his brother's hands pushing his away from the chair. 'Did they say Hajjar?' Sabri wiped at the coffee on his desk with tissues, dabbed at the splatterings of it on his small lap. 'Was that Hajjar?'

'I think so. Yes. Sorry, *ya akhi*, brother, but Sabri—'

'Why did they choose a Hajjar? It was Hajjar they said, wasn't it?'

'Yes, I think so, Sabri—'

'What is it? You got the scholarship, did you?' Sabri tossed a sopping coffee-filled tissue across the room.

'The whole thing. Accommodation, fees—'

'And Professor Myres is retired or not?'

'Semi-retired, but he wants to do the thesis with me. I'll be living somewhere in North London.'

'He's still going then. Must be well into his seventies by now. I suppose I should give you some of his work.' Sabri started pulling out books from his shelves; not just books, *tomes* – one looked over a thousand pages long – slamming them on to his desk before ordering them by date of publication.

Rashid waited by the window. There was a better view of the town from there; the smoke from the hospital was strong, darker than the rest. Downstairs, their mother was haranguing Abu Omar again – in the man's own garden too. His mother wanted their neighbour's garden. She coveted it and regularly demanded it from its owner. She also asked for his apartment. She had been proposing that they exchange apartments ever since Sabri had lost his legs over fifteen years previously ('So that the boy can get out on his own, so we don't have to carry him down those stairs.'). She was now, in a protest gesture of sorts, kicking at the bare soil, which flew up around them. There was no need to actually hear it. Rashid knew what she would be saying. It would be along the lines of: 'You do nothing with your land, *nothing*, whereas I could grow tomatoes, I could plant thyme, potatoes . . .'

Abu Omar was not saying anything. He was feeling for the sunspots and moon craters on the back of his head. Rashid silently urged him on, *Come on, man, stand up to her, you tell her*, but Abu Omar's fingers continued to trace around the indentations on his head as though they were pads upon which he could transmit a message for outside intervention. With the edge of a sandal he tried to rub the kicked-up dust into the tiles that they stood on. He was saying something now, something worthless, no doubt. It would be along the lines of: 'You know I care for the boy as if he was my own, but how can I give up the apartment of my father?' To which she would reply, 'So he can wheel himself out, sit here, take his morning coffee in the sun; for shame, just a little fresh air for the boy . . .' (*He's nearly forty*, thought Rashid, *he's no boy.*) '. . . rotting up there, writing his books.' Abu Omar raised his head and Rashid willed for a retort – *Come on, this time you tell her. Go on! Where's the fight in you?* – but the man's grandson ran out to hug at his grandfather's waist and have his hair pulled at by the man's feeble hand. All Abu Omar could then do before he slunk off inside was to tenuously smile as though he had dribbled involuntarily.

Rashid's mother continued to stand in their neighbour's garden, her hands on her waist. Then she leant down and ran her fingers through the soil, weighing it carefully, as though touching the fabric of a dress she knew she would never be able to afford.

Rashid looked up at the smoke from the hospital generators, so black and so much of it, like an oil field ablaze. Endless.

'He bought a new car,' Sabri said.

Sabri was going bald; this was probably not a new thing but Rashid had not registered it before. If he had been asked to physically describe his brother, he would have said that he had large sideburns and hair like someone on the cover of a Motown album. But that was the old Sabri; the Sabri he was now looking at was a middle manager character with (specially ordered) frameless glasses halfway down his nose and a broad dome of a head that was becoming increasingly visible. The middle manager was making some loaded statement about a car.

'He bought a new car,' Sabri repeated.

'Who?'

'Abu Omar.'

'I know. Red. I was watching him cleaning it last night.'

'You don't find that strange? The man has no job, has been complaining about poverty for twenty years, the roads around his house have been bulldozed, but he chooses to buy a car. You don't find that somewhat bizarre?' Sabri asked.

'No, not really,' Rashid shrugged. *Give it a rest. Stop spying on the neighbours. Stop obsessing about minutiae. You can't let yourself become a middle-aged fart, whether you have legs or not. Who cares anyway? It's irrelevant. London! Lisa! London! Lisa! Lisa! Lisa!*

Sabri was watching him. Whatever it was, Rashid wasn't getting it.

'With a master's you should be able to get a teaching post when you get back, pass on what you've learnt,' Sabri continued.

'And then I can fulfil my national duty?' Rashid scratched at his neck. His T-shirt sleeve fell open over his armpit as he did so. Sabri read a lot from the exposed armpit hair that he didn't seem to like. Possibly there was too much of it.

'Then you can fulfil your national duty.' Sabri held open a book and looked up at Rashid through the edge of his glasses. 'If you think that's funny, then I really can see no reason for you to be taking up this scholarship. There are a number of very hardworking students who would give anything—'

'Oh, come on. I just . . . *Come on*, Sabri. I was . . . I'm *excited* that it worked out. Just pleased, really. That's OK, isn't it?'

Sabri moved the book pile towards the back of his desk and lined his forearms up so that the fingers of one hand drummed on the back of the other hand.

'And what reasoning would you attribute to them choosing a Hajjar girl for this suicide mission? They know the Hajjars are loyal to the Authority, to our great, wondrous leaders. Why do you think these religious groups did that?' Sabri asked with a purpose that made Rashid stop pacing the room, until he realised he didn't know the answer, which made him start pacing it again.

'Well, girls are less likely to be checked as thoroughly as boys, so they probably thought that would help, and if she was not veiled and religious-looking like most of the bombers are . . .' Rashid cupped his chin with his fingers as though his greatest point was yet to be delivered. It was a mockery of himself in an intellectual pose.

Sabri could not be bothered with either the pose or the point. 'I'll tell you what I think, because your assumption is no longer either relevant or accurate. Their security checks everyone: man, woman, girl, boy, stuffed bunny rabbit, veiled or in a bikini, everyone and anything. What I believe is that these religious groups are trying to show how powerful they are getting. What they are saying is, "Hey, look at what we can get one of the women from your most loyal families to do for us." That's what they're saying. It is an *internal* message, not an external one. You must learn to tell the difference.' Sabri gestured towards the window. 'And what we saw last night, that bombing, was a direct result of the pretext handed to the other side by that Hajjar girl's silly theatrics and the Islamic groups' divisive politicking.'

'I don't think her family will see it that way.'

'What? *Her family?* I am not concerned as to what her family think. They're no concern of mine. But, to be positive about all this, I think we should view these moves as signs of desperation on their part – the Islamic groups that is.' Sabri looked up at at Rashid as though he had little faith that Rashid could possibly be following what he was saying. 'Here.' He moved the books towards Rashid. 'You better start on these. You only have a couple of weeks before you go.'

Outside the room, the books were too awkward for Rashid to hold; his thoughts were too angry for his mind to articulate. And the door of his brother's room suddenly seemed sinister and horrible to him. The gunmen were still there, the fat one and the thin one, watching their building. Rashid had wanted to get Sabri's opinion on them, or better still, *tell* Sabri about them as he might not have even seen them, but now he didn't care. The hell with them.

He let a bit of light in for Gloria and snipped off some of her dead leaves with his nail scissors. Her soil was moist; her leaves were green. Everything about her was captivating, luscious, plentiful. She was divine. Gloria – the Finest Marijuana Plant in Gaza.

He looked around his room. A tape was stuck in the mouth of his video and the light was still on. He scraped out the tape with his nail scissors and placed them back into his open drawer of horror. On nights like the previous one when the ground shook, the sky was torn through and chemicals streaked through the air, he would go to this collection after coming down from the roof. He would lock himself into his darkened room with a screen of poltergeists, exorcists, zombies and vampires. He would listen to them scream out with the heightened sensual terror that only Gloria could engineer and would let them walk around his room taking over him and his reality to the exclusion of all else.

And then he could turn them off.

But *London!* Again he read the admissions secretary's email that he had printed off, tracing each line with his finger before hugging it to his chest.

There were still two messages from Lisa that he had not even opened yet. He'd been too blown away by the email. The first one was about work and the Centre as it was addressed both to him and to Khalil:

Dear Rashid and Khalil,

OK, I hope you guys are doing all right. It sounds a bit rough right now. Sorry that it's been a while, but we've been working late and really slogging at it here, to the extent that we hardly get to see TV and know even what we are working away *at!* Anyway, I always say that, don't I? I'm just working so hard – blah, blah, blah. But that's not what I was writing to tell you, what I am *really* writing to let you know is that we have managed to get the meeting with the Parliamentary Committee set up! I know, I know, I'm a star and all that. It did take a lot of lobbying and pulling strings but I hope it's going to be worth it. We agreed that it would be best to present on the following topics:

(1) impact of closure

(2) impact of bombing

(3) assassination policy

(4) situation on the ground in general

The meeting is taking place next week (Thursday at 6 p.m. in Westminster! In the Houses of Parliament!). I told them there was no way you guys could get here by then and they were a bit disappointed, you being the real thing and all that, but don't worry, they still want to hear from us. Can you get some data together by then? The more numbers the better – you know: declining nutritional rates, increased unemployment statistics etc.?

Have we missed some of the assassinations? I get the feeling only the high-profile ones are being reported over here. Let me know about any small fry, will you?

Anyway, send us what you can get. Look forward to hearing from you guys.

Take care,

Lisa

She had delivered. Khalil would not show it, but he would be pleased.

The second message from Lisa was just for him. Rashid read this more carefully.

Rashid,

It was a bad call, I know, and I realise that things aren't great for you right now, but you do have to think of alternatives to just *Getting Out*. What you are doing at the Centre with Khalil is really important, honourable work. I know you don't like voluntary work—

Nor, as he had spelt out to her on numerous occasions, did he like being dependent on hand-outs from his father when he was twenty-seven years old.

but we rely heavily on the data that the Centre provides, and I know that you are fed up and cynical but these things can make a difference. It is a war—

Rashid had tried to explain to her on the phone that it was not a *war*, that it was more of a *cage fight*, where the other side could throw these flying kicks but their side was limbless or heavily disadvantaged in some way and kept getting disqualified for spitting. The audience loved it. He could hear them rattling their cutlery, but Lisa had grown impatient at the cage fight analogy.

It's not really something that you can just escape from. It's part of you, part of your family. You have to remember that.

I just wanted you to know that I think of you and worry about you. I do hope that you get the scholarship if that is what you really want and of course I would love you to be here, but I do so respect what you are doing and think that you would be so much happier if you viewed your situation differently.
Miss you.
Love,
Lisa XXX

Miss you. Love. Three kisses.
Anyway, he had got it. Nothing else mattered. He would be there.
Miss you. Love. Three kisses.
London!
Lisa!

Iman's bed had not been slept in and she was not in the kitchen either. It was his mother in the kitchen. He didn't feel ready for his mother yet, but at least his sister was not in there trying to wash up or something. There was this state of mal-co-ordination that came over her after a night like the one before. Suds slipped out of basin on to the floor. She broke things. She walked into chairs that were where they were meant to be.

Rashid's mother stood firm in the kitchen, frying meat and onions in a vat. She was wearing her long, slopping-around-the-house *thoub*. Away from the house she was a flesh-coloured-tights and fitted-knee-length-skirt woman, a wearer of short-sleeved chemises and cardigans. For the outside world she blow-dried her hair into hard outward-turning curls. Unlike the rest of the family, her nose was trim and tiny, as straight as her eyebrows were curved, the latter being regularly threaded down to dark arches. With the *mandil* over her hair and her *thoub* she looked older, but fresher somehow. Her skin had an unblemished look about it that was unnaturally wax-like, as though an exploratory scalpel would find her flesh to be blood-free under its surface.

His mother mainly left the cooking to Sabri who could spend hours chopping parsley for *tabouleh*, stuffing vine leaves or trying out different seasonings on the Sultan Ibrahim, that prince of Gazan fishes. His mother just pickled.

'What are you preparing for, a siege?' he asked after the last batch, when every inch of counter space was taken up with fat, square-sided bottles stuffed with eggs, aubergines, olives and courgettes. To Rashid they seemed morbid: embryos in formalde-hyde, preserved body parts, mutated limbs bobbing around in tinctured jellies. She did not look up. 'We're already under siege, can't you tell?'

Rashid popped at the lids of the pickle jars with a wooden spoon. *Pickles. London. Pickles.* A sense of the previous night came over him. Part fear, part thrill. The leap under the helicopters, Gloria's stars under his skin. He stopped. A small pink-rimmed

31

mirror hanging on a hook over a dishcloth shot a look back at him, one that said he must've been truly stoned, no not just *truly* stoned but *royally* stoned; his eyes were amassed with stringy red veins. Rashid picked a pair of mirrored sunglasses from the top of the microwave and put them on.

'*The belligerent aerial attack, their military sources claimed, was in direct response to the bombing of a park yesterday afternoon for which the Islamic Justice Party has claimed responsibility . . .*' It was the local station who had chosen not to name the bomber.

'Did you hear she's a Hajjar?' his mother asked. 'Foolish girl gave those bastards the excuse to bomb the hospital.'

'I saw them do it.' Rashid moved so that she could get to the sink and lifted his sunglasses on to his head. They were scratched and covered with fingerprints and kitchen grease. His mother pulled her sleeves up from the elbow and banged again at the base of the pan with a wooden spoon. Steam hissed out from under a wodge of brain-like meat.

'They cut the power for over five hours this morning. Everything's partly defrosted; blood dripping out of the freezer when I opened it. All I can do is cook the lot, put it back and hope they leave the power alone. At least fifteen kilos I have still to do.' Arrayed on the floor on a waterproof sheet, shoulders of lamb and cubes of beef lay bagged up and oozy in see-through plastic bags.

She turned in his direction, as though there was something she remembered. Rashid pulled the sunglasses down. The sight of him appeared to confuse her. It was as though he were somehow misplaced, a lost man in her kitchen. His mother could do that. She could choose not to see things. She could choose, for example, not to see that Sabri was in a wheelchair with sores across his buttocks that she had to treat every night, a catheter bag that she had to empty several times a day, a body that she helped lift in and out of bed. Instead, she spoke as though he was still her strapping son, her noble warrior. Once Rashid had heard her say, 'Sabri could still have children, you know,' in a tone that challenged the world to contradict her.

And their father leaving? That, of course, hadn't happened either.

He would ask her about the split. He would sit her down, here in the kitchen and ask her why their father had suddenly shot out of the marriage like that, propelled himself out of it so rapidly, like a cockerel from a canon, only to find himself in the Gulf preening down his feathers and resuming a perfectly cordial relationship with them once he had landed, financial commitments intact, civility impeccable, marriage ruined.

He wouldn't ask her today though. Another day would be better for that. She was dealing with all that meat for a start.

Maybe it was not the time to tell her his news either, not with the bombing, the power cut and everything. His eyes focussed on her marked-up newspapers, piled up on top of a battalion of water bottles that spread out across the kitchen floor. She had done today's paper already. Blue pen circled items on British arms exports to Saudi, bread riots in Cairo and the death of a Marxist leader in Colombia. On the last evening of the month she would date the side of each article, cut them out and place them all into a large brown envelope. 'I can get you any article you want, whenever you want it. You can even find them by subject matter,' Rashid had tried to explain the Internet to her once, showing her a basic search function, but she had been distracted by Gloria's presence behind the screen. 'And when they cut our electricity, what will you do then?' was all that she had asked.

He could hear his mother saying something about his father from under the sink. She was moving detergent bottles and glass jars around so he was not sure exactly what it was.

'Is it his health?' Rashid asked.

'Health? Maybe. Who knows? But the last time he called he

started to say that maybe you and Iman should leave. He even suggested that you visit him.'

'Seriously?' Rashid made small crescents in the line of blackened putty around the sink with his fingernail.

'He'll probably change his mind tomorrow,' she said to the cabinet. 'Ah, here it is.' There was a clattering of glass as she sat back on to her knees, breathless.

'I got the scholarship, Mama,' he said, but her response was not clear; she had gone back into the cabinet. It sounded like, 'Probably drunk.'

'What?'

'Your father, he was probably drunk. Men, they get old. They get drunk. They get sentimental. They wonder what they've done to their lives, to their families.'

She handed a glass jar to Rashid and pulled herself up holding the sink edge with one hand, a yellow cloth in the other. The idea of a tipsy, maudlin father phoning late at night appealed to Rashid. Maybe he had misunderstood the man.

'I got the scholarship, Mama,' he repeated.

'Sabri helped you with the application, did he?' She looked up at him now. Rashid knew she had heard him the first time.

'He just checked it.'

'You should never cheat anyone or anything.'

'I didn't *cheat* anyone; he just gave me some advice.'

'You will get into such a mess if you start cheating and having things to hide,' she said. 'Such a mess.'

'I never cheated; he just checked through it and made some points. We talked about it.'

She stared at him, motionless. The cotton neckline of her *thoub* was frayed to a soft fluff. Some of the embroidered cross-stitch had come loose. It had been her mother's dress, the only thing of hers that she had, and she wore it out like a rag. She must be seeing herself in the blue curve of his lenses. Her face would be as distended as one of her aubergines, her pinched nose ballooning into something broad and squat, her eyes receding back into an endless forehead, her teeth bucked out, her mouth large.

'Stupid, that Hajjar girl. The harm she's done. Gone against her family's loyalties, playing into this factional outlook that is going to get us into so much trouble we won't know what's happened, and backing such a misguided mission. A park. To go and bomb a park? What's the point of that, I ask you? The sympathy our enemy will get for that one. Military targets only. We must stick to military targets. The only person she killed was herself.' Rashid's mother spat something nasty into the sink. 'Idiot.'

'She's dead, Mama.' Rashid watched Sabri's tray being prepared, the olive oil and *zaatar* laid out, fresh mint stirred into the tea, sugar added.

'Deserves to be dead. The twit. Look what they did last night, supposedly in *return* for that. The hospital! Bastards.' She looked up and flinched at the sight of Rashid without his glasses. 'I should give your brother his breakfast.' She gave Rashid a small squeeze to his upper arm before she picked up Sabri's tray and left the kitchen.

Chapter 6

Sabri's body was good at ghosts. It conjured up body parts that weren't there and made them itch. For example, his right ankle was prone to bites. These were normally, he surmised, two-day-old mosquito bites; there was still the pressure of the fresh bite but the skin had broken leaving a scab. There was often also a recurring itch behind his left knee, where phantom sweat had dribbled down and caught itself in a crease, forming a little mat of hair on the way down. The big toenail on that foot often felt ingrown. But that morning it had been a ghost of her body part that had come to him. It was her nose breathing out the prelude to a whisper in his ear, and when he woke up he stretched out his arm as he used to, to feel for her waist under the twisted wrap of nightdress but she had not been there and his knuckle had hit the wall instead.

During the night he had kept a record of the attack. He kept his notepad, binoculars and two sharpened pencils on the end of a shelf by the window in preparation for his eyewitness accounts. He timed strikes using a digital watch that he set against the *bip, bip, bips* of the BBC World Service. Last night was three pages of notes. The night before that had just been one.

Documenting destruction.

Chronicling chaos.

Point by strike by shot.

That was what he did and he liked to think he did it well.

His room had shelves all along the floor that went up higher than Sabri could reach. Each shelf was partly supported by the books underneath it. Many of the books lay horizontally, some diagonally. The sight of his books calmed him whenever he entered the room; they appeared to talk to each other like old men resting against cushions smoking *argeela*.

A photograph of Sabri's wife, Lana, and their son, Naji, leant back on its curled edge against the books; there was something nonchalant about its attitude as though it had been taken only the day before and that there were many more to come. Frequently it slipped on to the pile of loose papers and medical prescriptions that were washed up together into a heap by the slow movements of the room.

Sabri also had a signed photograph of their former leader. This had been ceremoniously gifted to him by a delegation that came to the hospital after he had lost his legs. He handled this picture with a greater sense of purpose; from time to time, he would drop it on to the floor and roll his wheels over it. As a result of this special treatment, the face of the Great Leader of the Resistance had lost patches of its gloss and gained the appearance of someone who had opened a letter bomb.

Sabri was tired. That was the problem. He had been up until the bombs had stopped, which was not until around dawn, and he could not stay in bed any more after that dream, or whatever it was. He needed a bit more sleep. That was all. Fatigue sat fat and greasy on his eyelids. A bad night. Too bright a morning.

He could smell her that morning too. He was sure of it. Not always, but it had happened once when he lifted his head up from the page. He had just managed to capture it when Rashid had walked in. And then it had gone. He had tried to save that smell of her before. It was unique: a French perfume which came in a white bottle with pastel roses painted on it, a touch of coffee and cigarettes and her own sweat. He had found that smell on the neck of a shirt after she had gone. It was the shirt she had worn for that first evening together in a Jerusalem café and he had wrapped it up tightly in a plastic bag to save it. He kept the bagged-up shirt in his cupboard.

He had broken the back of his work. He was sure of it.

Sabri wrote longhand, listing points for additional research on two strips of paper; these were usually in a mixture of Arabic and English, in pencil. One was for book research, the other for Internet research. A tidier ruled card system denoted those areas that awaited archival research, mainly in London's Public Records Office. He had written out the text longhand before typing it up, and now he was now doing rewrites. Not owning a printer, Iman had taken his work on a memory stick, a tiny thing no bigger than a finger, to an Internet café and printed it out for him in full.

His manuscript (the word still secretly thrilled him) had come back smelling of cigarettes and cockroach spray. It now sat on his table, bound up in treasury tags, fluttering with yellow reminder notes. He did not pay any particular attention to it when anyone else was in the room, but each night he squared its pages by bringing its bottom edge down against his desk. He enjoyed the satisfying *clunk* that it made against the wood, and the look of the strips of light and dark of the pages clustered together as seen from the side.

After he went to the bathroom with his mother to change his bag she came into his room and sat across the desk from him, smoking and sipping at her tea. They did not talk about the bombing, Rashid's scholarship or Abu Omar's car, and disregarded the silence that yawned and stretched around them.

'Where's Iman?' Sabri asked at one point.

'Committee meeting.'

'Until now? It's past nine.'

'They got the hospital, not the university.' She moved about the room, picking up the wet tissue that had landed next to the bin, wiping the top of the radio with the sleeve of her *thoub*. Sabri moved his papers away and brought out some clean writing paper. The door to Rashid's room opened and let out some music, that black female singer whose voice swept around aimlessly like a strip of lace on the end of a stick. The door to the bathroom opened and the pneumatic thump of the water heater banged against the wall. Sabri sharpened a pencil and his mother placed the glass cups back on the tray and stacked up the saucers. The bathroom door opened and closed again, then the door to Rashid's room did the same. Rashid turned his music off before he left his room so that his steps down the hallway and the slam of the front door behind him were clear. They were alone now. It was time to go back to what had once been.

'The Doctor,' Sabri's mother started, referring to her old leader, 'he was very upset by what they were saying.'

'This is 1971?'

'Nineteen seventy-two, June.'

Sabri's mother sat back on the chair in front of the desk. She pulled off her headscarf and folded it several times into a neat little square. Sabri had not intended to work on his mother's chapter that morning; he had wanted to get on with the section on the first Intifada but he could not depend on his mother to be in the mood whenever he was. She spoke for over an hour and ended with the phrase, 'Capitalist dogs'. He knew she had finished as she ran her fingernail between her front teeth and her hand went up to a loose curl to put it back in place.

Sabri pushed back his chair and massaged the lump on his middle finger that appeared when he wrote for a long time. The past had softened his mother. 'Rashid will be going to London,' he started.

'I know,' she replied.

He waited; he gathered his forces about him, poising himself to ask her.

'I'd like him to go down to the Public Records Office for me,' Sabri said. His mother lifted one hand up slightly in a gesture that he could not interpret, although he knew she understood what he was asking of her. 'The documents are going to be released at the beginning of next year,' he continued. 'It would really help the book to be able to include them.' His mother shrugged slightly. 'If I knew of anyone else, you know that I would ask them, but I don't know anyone in London.' He had hoped he would not have to ask so much.

She stood up and looked out of the window. 'He bought a car,' she said.

'I know.' Sabri waited before going back to his topic.

'It could be in the press. I'd like it to be in the book.' It was as close to a plea as he was prepared to get.

'Yes.' She was not convinced. One of her thumbs pushed up at the knuckle of the other thumb as though it was a bottle cap that she was trying to pop open. But there was little else he could say. In her upheld profile and her sucked-in nostrils he was sure he saw something close to a wave of nausea pass through her.

'*Biseer*,' she said. It happens.

Biseer. It amounted to the granting of permission, didn't it? But her eyes had been unusually skittish and he would not ask again. Ambiguity was preferable. Rashid's scholarship now took on a greater significance. *Bilaks*, on the contrary, it was great that Rashid was going. And the timing was perfect.

He put away the documents concerning his mother and arrayed the first Intifada material around him. This was history of an uprising that he had lived through. He *was* this history right from the beginning. His proximity to the subject matter was what made it unsettling. He had known many of the key figures whom he was now trying to write about. Some of them had been heroes to him; some he had despised. But how he had viewed them at the time was an easier question in terms of objectivity, compared to the other problem, which was how he viewed them *now*, in the light of what they had become.

But Lana was everywhere that morning. She would not leave him. His past with her kept coming back to him in these random flashes of memory where he could see himself, as an unwitting protagonist in an art-house movie of spliced film.

That morning just the sight of one of the Declarations by the Unified National Leadership of the Uprising had brought up a clip of memory, just one or two images of Ramallah at night during the first Intifada, right at the beginning in 1988 when, as he had described it, the battle for control of the shops between Occupied and Occupier had just begun. Repeatedly his memory showed them both bent over the clasps of the shutters fixed to the ground, where she was working on the lock of the shop next to his. He had had the tool bag with him and every clunk of its contents had chilled them to the spine. 'Goddamn it,' he had heard her mutter. 'They broke the clasp as well, the bastards. I'll need a drill to fix it.' *Not so pretty*, he had thought, glancing at her in the streetlight.

That was the entirety of it. It was just a snippet on the cutting-room floor in his brain. He tried to move the scene forwards logically, questioning whether they had managed to mend the lock and wondering what else she had said or done, and whether there were other shops that they had gone to that night. He had also tried moving it backwards – querying how they had arrived there and whether she walked in front of him or was there already when he arrived. But memory is mean and gave him no more than he already had. *They broke the clasp as well, the bastards*. Again and again. *I'll need a drill to fix it.*

He had started the paragraph on this era of history which he had contributed to making:

The Palestinian strikes and consumer boycott that started in 1988 aimed to jeopardise Israel's economy by the loss of its most important market, the Occupied Territories. In Ramallah, the battle over store closures raged for weeks. This was a battle for political control, between Occupier and Occupied. When the Unified National Leadership of the Palestinian Uprising (Intifada) ordered shops to stay open for three hours in the morning only and to close in the afternoon, the Israeli army would demand alternative times. Israeli soldiers would use crowbars to break locks in order to prevent stores and businesses from closing. In response, locksmiths and volunteers were organised to repair them at night.

He had not known who she was at the time. He was not allowed to, so that under questioning they could say they worked alone. *Not so pretty*, he had thought. He was wrong about that. She had been exquisite, but even the memory of that was going. The more he thought of her face, the more it faded; sometimes he had to rush up on a fragment of memory to catch it unawares and then he could see her face as it was. For a moment he'd catch it and then his chest would stop, his breathing would increase and he'd find himself wiping down the leather surface of his desk with his hand, examining the granules of coffee in the base of his cup and having to push himself out of where he'd gone to with a mental kick.

He did not remember a drill. How had they fixed it?

He had been at university in the West Bank at the time and the next time he had seen her had been in the student café. He had not recognised her at all. She had been wearing uncompromisingly red stilettos that had made his friends laugh. They all knew that she came from one of the notable Jerusalem families so they had had the standard bitch about the city's bourgeoisie. But her shoes had clicked out an irreverence that Sabri had found exciting.

It was not until he overheard her talking in a corridor and

caught her voice that he had made the connection with the girl curled over the shutter lock. He was so astonished that *she* was *her* and that they were the same woman. He had wanted to grab her arm and laugh about it. He had lunged towards her and she had looked up from her coterie of companions and without a single muscle in her face moving, she had conveyed to him that he must not, absolutely must not, do so. But he had known and she had known and they both knew that the other knew from then on.

He started letting the relationship he was in at the time slip after that, after the look, the *recognition* with Lana. The girl he had been going out with had not taken it well at all. There were tears and scenes and he had had to avoid certain places because she would be there remonstrating with him. It was all so silly. She should have been able to tell that he had already left. That he had moved on elsewhere.

But oh God, help him! What had happened to his body after that? Something forceful had ballooned in his chest. The more he saw Lana, the more it swelled. It was a skin stretched under his. He would awake in the morning so hard that it almost buckled him over. That was on the interior but his exterior: his face, his hair, his hands, and his voice, these could no longer be relied on either. He seemed to have discovered their true forms. They could horrify him. The break on the bridge in his nose from a fight in secondary school made his eyes squint. His hair was too coarse; his skin (however many times he washed it) had a murky pallor to it that could be confused for dirtiness and his voice around her had developed the panting undertone and the flurried laugh of a poof. His mind had been interfered with too; his sentences collided into each other, the sense of them piling up over each other into an incongruous mess.

He had found out the following about her: she studied history, her tutors thought very highly of her, her English was excellent, she was privately educated and she spoke German too. She was also Christian, but he did not see that as being much of a problem. He could see that she had a large group of friends, but there was not one specific *boyfriend* (the word alone made him sick) hanging around her as far as he could tell. Sabri came to notice other things about her too: that she was normally the one leading a debate, that however big the group sitting with her was, she would be the one to talk after everyone else and that they always urged her to speak. In her appliqué bag she carried flyers that she pinned neatly to the noticeboards in the hall, carefully moving aside those posters that they overlapped with. The notices were typed on a word processor and just said: 'NO. They are NOT the answer.'

One of Sabri's friends had told him that she was to run against him in the student elections. He mentioned it casually, in the same tone that they had commented on her shoes, after carefully discussing what the religious parties were saying and the other candidates put forward by the Leadership. 'But which party is she running for?' Sabri had asked.

'She's running as an *independent*,' his friend had replied and they found that hilarious too. 'Don't worry about her,' they had said to all his questions. 'She is not your worry.' But by then, she was.

He had been completely taken.

He was not able to get high enough to see most of Abu Omar's garden when he pushed himself up by the window. He could only make out the far corners of it. But in one of these, Abu Omar's middle grandson, Wael, had taken to playing at this time of day. He said he was playing, but Sabri recognised that you could not really say such a thing about a boy as old as Wael now was. Sabri was sure that the boy went to that corner just so that Sabri could see him. He seemed to be constructing a sort of rat trap out of fencing this morning, manipulating some old wiring he had found and placing strips

44

of fruit peel inside it. He had some kind of guillotine for a door. *Ingenious*, Sabri thought with satisfaction at the engineering of it. Sabri liked the boy's love of bedevilling everything and everyone; the kid exasperated his family. The boy looked up, gave Sabri a dismissive glance, then looked away. Sabri pretended to write in one of the notebooks that he had poised for the moment that the boy would do this and watched the boy bending the meshing a little more, before going back to his desk.

Sabri pulled out an original Intifada Declaration of the Unified National Leadership of the Uprising. The pronouncement started off grandly, calling on people of 'all sectors and classes' to adhere to the general strike. Sabri concluded the paragraph he had written about the merchants' strike in Ramallah and read through it with his editing pencil poised above it:

> As part of the Intifada's policy of non-violent resistance to the Israeli occupation, Palestinian shops would frequently be ordered by the Israeli army to stay open and shopkeepers were threatened with arrest if they left their shops unattended, but they continued to listen to the Unified Leadership and left their shops open against the orders of the Occupiers, their goods lying in plain view, none of which were stolen.
>
> It took several weeks but ultimately the Palestinians won the battle to control their own shops.

He could not decide whether it was objective enough. It should not read like propaganda. He read it again. To hell with it if it did. That was what had happened. He had been there. He had seen it. *Damn it.* All interpretations of history are propaganda for one idea or another. Sabri downed the pencil that hovered over the paragraph. He would leave it as it was.

Chapter 7

Khalil had been delighted by Sindibad's. This was mainly, Rashid thought, because the café was so far from the district where Khalil's parents lived, in an area where the town appeared to have collapsed into itself. Rashid had pretended that he could see the café's charm, but he had really found the place to be so mundane that it verged on the tragic. This did not stop him from encouraging Khalil to be amused by particular features of the place: the printed depiction of an alpine retreat framed in gilt, the row of faux silver vases sprouting leafless stems of plastic flowers on the counter at the back, the fairy lights strung around the air conditioning unit.

It was at Sindibad's where Rashid and Khalil usually congregated and it was there that Rashid was heading that morning, the two messages, Lisa's and the admissions secretary's, folded into his back pockets. He had refused to take Lisa to Sindibad's when she last came, the previous summer, even though that was before the situation got so bad. He had taken her to Pierre's instead, which she had hated. 'I might as well be in Vienna,' she had said, moving around on a satin seat covered in thick, transparent plastic. She had been so bad-tempered that Rashid had been forced to lie, telling her that the man spiking at black forest gâteau on the next table was a commando fighter from the seventies.

That had been Lisa's second visit to Gaza, only a couple of months previously, but it seemed like a lifetime ago. The first time she had come, when he met her, she had walked into the Centre wearing a crisp shirt and combat trousers and he had been over-whelmed. He had thought, possibly panic-struck, during her first visit to the Centre, that her interest was in Khalil, not him. He tried to put that down to Khalil's greater involvement in the Centre and when he had questioned her later (in between kisses when he had snuck her back to his roof), she had reassured him that that was all there was to it. *Lisa!*

A water pipe next to the road had been hit and there was water everywhere in the streets, a brown rush of it slopping around the potholes. The roads were narrow and the mass of people were so close together that they seemed to follow each other using their sense of smell, not sight. And then everyone stopped completely and the crowd became jammed up and stuck between the walls. The blockage was being caused by an old man and a donkey. The donkey had ground to a halt in a puddle in the centre of the road and the traffic, headed up by an old Nasser car, was wedged behind it. Someone was ramming at Rashid's ankles with a suitcase. 'Watch it!' Rashid called out, but the suitcase's owner was on a mission to get away and seemed determined to ignore the humili-ation that was involved in getting there.

The crowd took their frustration out on the donkey's owner ('Which one of you is the donkey? Take it around the edge, you fool. It thinks it's going to drown,' someone was shouting) but it did not help. They were still blocked in the road when a bullet-proofed Mercedes drove up. The crowd changed with the arrival of the car. They started spitting at the sight of their leaders. *Look at them! Negotiated us away in exchange for that car, did you? So you can move it up and down the one kilometre of Gaza you liberated, did you? Bravo! Bravo.* They turned on the anonymous figures behind the car's tinted windows and the donkey's owner became their brother. They gave him the reverence of a pilgrim (*Ya hajji! Ya hajji!*) and were working with him in trying to coax the donkey across the puddle when a scrap of a boy sprang from the crowd holding a carrot, which the animal went for, almost bolting straight out of the puddle.

The crowd held up the Mercedes for as long they could, trapping it behind them as they walked slowly, slapping at each other's backs before they allowed the car to push forward, leaving them with just the vision of its large, shiny bottom bouncing over the potholes ahead of them.

As the crowd thinned out, the people appeared from within it, the craned neck of the suitcase owner pushed into an opening, his arm pulling at the case behind him as though dragging an errant child. It was a flat suitcase with buckles hanging off its straps. Rashid recognised the back of a head in front of him, the dyed hair and pocked dome of Abu Omar. His neighbour was not in his usual tracksuit bottoms and vest but dressed in an ironed short-sleeved shirt and trousers with creases running up from the elbows and down from the knees. And it was into the backs of those knees that the suitcase collided, sending Abu Omar reeling forwards to the edge of a puddle, his hands catching at a wheelbarrow on his way down. Rashid, whose emails had enhanced his sense of goodwill to the rest of humanity, moved ahead to help. Abu Omar's hand had fallen on to a torn bag of cement in the wheelbarrow and a cloud had lifted up around him. His face was covered in a cloying film. He brushed down the dust covering him, and smoothed back his hair with two palms.

'Are you all right now, *Ammo?*' Rashid wanted to convey his empathy with the man's land squabbles with his mother, addressing him respectfully. He tried to do this with a look, but on seeing Rashid's face, his neighbour tore away from him and pushed through the crowd.

Chapter 8

The woman, Raed and Taghreed's aunt, had brought Iman to a house with two small rooms where the bodies were. The sun had moved up from the smoky horizon and pitched itself high in the sky by then, and the walk had been hot, the rooms they entered even hotter. They had gone through alleyways and areas where Iman had never been before, where camp and town became indecipherable from one another, where alleys became streets, streets became alleys. There were no other women like Iman walking bareheaded in the area where the house was.

There were two bodies in the house: Taghreed's and her cousin Raed's. The corpses were lined up next to each other in cotton sheets. Taghreed's sheet had been wrapped double and formed a bulbous shape around her. But on Raed, the sheet was not enough, his feet protruded at its end, as though he had hastily decided upon a siesta and not a death.

'She was visiting her cousin when they struck the hospital,' Raed's aunt had told Iman on the way to the house. 'Her mother said that Taghreed would want you to be here. She said she loved you more than her own mother.' She paused. 'Raed also spoke of you. He used to ask Taghreed about you,' she made it sound like a secret, 'in a special way, I felt, and it is for that that I came to find you.'

The room was overburdened with a sense of duty and disbelief. Iman cleared her throat against the antiseptic air. Outside the sun was bright, but distant and the sounds of children teasing and fighting each other along the alleyway made their way into the room as though transmitted down a pipe.

Taghreed's school bag had been left in the hallway. On the outside zip pocket a pink and blonde princess smiled two white bands of teeth into the room. Iman saw the bag bobbing through the schoolyard on Taghreed's back, under plaits that jumped.

Taghreed's mother was wading around in her grief trying to find her bearings with social niceties.

The bodies were burnt mostly; we had to hide those bits.

Last week I tried to tuck her shirt in for school but she was screaming and moving and the nail on my little finger caught her skin and scratched her back . . .

Would you like coffee?

God let them rest in peace.

The faces are not so bad.

May their lives live on in yours.

All day I felt that skin being scratched under my fingernail . . .

I knew, as soon as I heard the strike I knew it had taken them.

Your mother is well?

The room swelled out with women and Taghreed's bag in the corridor, and Raed's feet under the sheet, were lost from sight for a while and Iman found it a little easier to converse.

Something just under my navel went very tight, like a baby turning when it is too big and a sick, sharp feeling and I knew with the blast, I knew.

I keep thinking she will come in now, shouting, showing me one of the pictures she drew. Always drawing, Miss Iman, especially for you.

Your brothers are well?

We thought they might not find the bodies but they did. It was so hot, so much smoke . . .

Iman had never seen Raed's feet before, only felt them close to her. Now the foot that had pressed against hers was bare and hanging like a clodden thing off the side of the table. She had thought of him as *a body* and done so with an ache that was so alive that it was embarrassing to remember in this setting, in any setting. She could not bring herself to look at his feet.

She turned in the other direction and found herself focussing on the hem of a woman's skirt that had come unstitched. It is harder to cry with your mouth open. Somewhere in her inner ear she heard that laugh that came up out of him, so rich and fat that everyone around would turn to smile at it. It could lift the whole room.

She had even talked to him about poetry and he recited some back to her. *Ya mualima*, he called her. Oh teacher.

The loss went to her chest and her ribs felt yawned apart by it. The dark bodies of the women moved in and out of the room. Iman became focussed on where she was now, on the precise nature of the attack, on the details of the burns on the bodies, and the sense of loss made way for something greater, more directed, that forced her to breathe more and faster.

Manar was waiting for Iman in the alley outside the house. Iman felt no surprise. It was right that she should be there. Manar looked exactly as she always did, just a little prouder this time. She had been expecting Iman to be there and greeted her as though she was escorting her to a groom. Her hands reached forwards to take Iman's.

"You know your role now Iman, don't you?" Manar asked.

'Yes,' said Iman. 'Yes.' Because it had to stop. Immediately. It had to end.

'You will know him. The contact. He knows you already.'

Manar left by way of a small alley between the houses, leaving Iman who did not know where she was. The road Iman was left on was

51

sloped, sandy and populated only by children. She walked towards something pale and fluttering on the ground ahead of her. It was the head of a pink carnation. The road was scattered with them: heads, stems and small clusters of flowers in the colours of toilet paper.

There was a farmer with some boys and the farmer had bunches of flowers in his hand, a gathering of people around him and he was shouting. About the closure. About the flowers rotting. About the flowers being a high security risk. About it being an end to him. He would feed the flowers to his cows. He would shoot them (the crowd like this). No, he would give them to the women. Then the boys were running around with the flowers and Iman found herself cradling a wet bouquet in her arm as though it was a baby. She could see all this, but distantly as though it was all going on on the other side of a thick wall of dirty Perspex of the type that their guards sat behind and she stood in the street motionless waiting for nothing more than for the wall to lift.

Chapter 9

Sindibad's appeared packed, although once inside Rashid could see that it was only one table that was occupied. A long banqueting set-up had been assembled through the café's centre. At it a group of fighters, half in half out of fatigues, hunched over plastic bowls spread across a newspaper surface.

The two armed men, the thin one and the fat one, who had been in the garage across from Rashid's house that morning, sat at the heads of the table. The fat man had a thick Stalin moustache and welted skin whereas the other man in green fatigues was gaunt and bony. He sat completely still and struck Rashid as having a sympathetic air about him.

The café took on silence on hastily when Rashid came in, like a child putting on a makeshift disguise. The men stopped wiping bread on the edges of plates, made it pause on the way to mouths, or held it mid-mastication. Rashid, awkward at the shut-down his arrival seemed to have caused, found a table and stared up at the TV. It was prayer time and the screen displayed a low-angle shot of a crenulated mosque with clouds behind it. He watched the streaming clouds and the static mosque with feigned curiosity until the fighters accepted he was going to do nothing else and turned back to their food.

Khalil was not there yet. The metal shutters were only pulled up halfway and Rashid had had to stoop as he came in. The café was dark. The strip lighting plasticised the food under the counter and a small fly kept settling on Rashid's face. Sindibad's was poised to destroy his good mood; he could feel it. He hoped that if it had been Khalil's father in the Mercedes he would not have recognised him, or heard him shouting with the rest of them against the Leadership. But then again, who cared? Khalil's father didn't speak to Rashid's father any more and no one spoke to Khalil's father, not even Khalil unless he absolutely had to. What could the repercussions be? He was leaving anyway. Could Khalil's father stop him from getting an exit permit somehow? Could he? Would he? It was far-fetched, paranoid. He was smoking too much.

Lisa. London. Rashid sang to himself, trying to imagine Lisa in Sindibad's, but the image was confused. He saw her legs first, the way they protruded from her light floral skirts. Her knees were square like her face. He would have to cover her up completely to get her into Sindibad's, if he could get her in at all. He had explained that to her a million times; there were no women in Sindibad's. None. Rashid tried to put an imaginary *abaya* on her imagined body, but all he kept seeing were her bare knees and the curved shadowy triangle between them.

The fighters filled the place with a smell of exertion like a changing room and the clanking of their guns gave the café a spiky, industrial feel. Rashid realised that he'd got the group's pecking order wrong when he had assumed that the fat one with the moustache was in charge. Now, upon examination, he realised that it was not the fat one but the thin one in the green jacket who was their leader. With just a look, the gentle closing of his eyelids, he could get the whole table to fall silent. This realisation was followed by a glow of an unfamiliar sensation in Rashid, something positive, strong but yet so intangible in its nature that he found himself clutching his fists together, as though that gesture would help him to grasp the feeling, to name it. It didn't.

Rashid got up and went to stand at the entrance to the café. It was midday and bright now but the outside world viewed from the doorway of Sindibad's seemed like a parade of the walking wounded: stooped moving figures of adults run through with flurries of schoolchildren. At the corner of the road, the carrot boy was peddling mobile phone chips, and next to the boy a woman in jeans with a bare head stood staring down the road in the opposite direction with several bouquets of flowers in her arms. Her hair was vast and magnificent, but she had to be deranged to be walking around with it on display like that. Some passers-by stopped to look at her. A man approached her, but then carried on when he realised that he had achieved nothing from trying to talk to her. Rashid wondered if her face looked as good as her hair. He didn't have to wait long. The woman soon turned towards him and Rashid found himself staring at the face of his sister.

Walking into Sindibad's with Iman and her bare head was not easy. It was as though she had mistakenly tucked her skirt into her knickers. Her entrance was met with jubilance by the fighters, one of whom began tapping out the rhythm for a *dabka* with his fingertips on the table. They only stopped when they picked up their leader's disdain, the flick of his index finger made them shut up completely.

The leader looked from his men to Iman, nodding at her and she seemed to almost balk at the sight of him and moved closer to her brother. Iman's face flushed and her eyes watered as if stung.

'How do you know him?' Rashid asked when they sat down and the fighters had gone back to their own business again. The café owner had brought out a large napkin for Iman and was indicating that she should tie it around her head.

'I don't,' Iman said. 'I don't know him at all.'

'It looked like . . .' Rashid left his observation hanging. Now wasn't the time to second-guess Iman. If she said she didn't know him, she didn't know him. There was no point in pushing it. 'What are they for?' Rashid asked gesturing at the flowers. It was about as close to the question of *What the hell were you doing walking around like a mad woman in this part of town after being out all night?* as he could get away with.

'Demonstration.' Iman put the flowers on the table and cupped her hands in front of her as though not quite sure what the purpose of them was. Her palms were greenish and crinkled from holding the stems.

'He wants you to put it on your head,' Rashid said, nodding at the napkin that the café owner was still holding.

Loose, her hair was too big for the napkin so the owner returned with an elastic band apologising that it was a little dirty. He waited for Iman to use it and once he was able to assure her that every wisp was hidden from sight, he tapped Rashid on the shoulder: *You owe me one, brother.*

'Here.' Iman held out the flowers to the café owner. 'For you.'

'Oh no, miss. I can't. They take so much water.'

'Please take them.' She pushed them towards him. 'I can't have them. *Please.*'

The owner looked at them suspiciously before spreading them out on the counter.

The fighters murmured and straightened up as a small eager-looking man entered. The room fell still again as he sat down on the table next to Rashid and Iman. With not a small degree of theatre, the café owner poured him a glass of water from a great height.

Rashid tried to swat a fly with the menu as it sat rubbing its forelegs together in drips of water that had come off the flowers, but it nipped up to the wall before flying to the back of Rashid's head.

'What were you doing in this area?' Rashid asked.

'Attending a wake,' Iman replied, watching the man who had taken the table next to them. He was sinewy and bearded and was staring at his table as though an invisible chess game was being played out on it.

Iman appeared to have forgotten that Rashid was there. She was lost somewhere behind her face. The fighters' interest in her had gone, except for their leader who had moved his chair to an angle so that he could see her more clearly. His nose was like Rashid's; it went straight from the hairline to the tip, Greek like the Mesopotamian priests of Ur. He had the same body type as well; his long limbs hung off the back the chair.

The fighters were also watching the bearded man on the table next to them. He had spent some time flipping the menu back and forth before demanding plain tea. Did the owner understand? Just plain tea: no sugar, no mint.

'Do you know him too?' Rashid asked as the bearded man looked towards Iman.

'His daughter's in my school. He's from the Seif El Din family.' She was studying the man's shoes; they were slip-ons and he was shuffling them around slowly on the linoleum tiles. 'This woman in the Committee, Manar, is related to him – I heard he lost two brothers in three months.' She was barely audible. The leader of the fighters was still staring at her and did not look away when she turned towards him. Iman confronted him with a glare. *Drop it*, Rashid thought. *Stop it, Iman. Enough.*

'Where were you last night?' Rashid asked sharply. She was his sister. He could ask.

'Women's Committee.'

'All night?'

'All night.'

'He looks religious,' Rashid observed, looking back at their bearded neighbour, Seif El Din.

'Who isn't?'

'Err, well, I'm not; those guys aren't; you aren't; Khalil isn't; Mama isn't; Baba isn't; Sabri isn't. Stop being like this, Iman. What's happened to you?' He put his hand down on the table so that he could reach across and try to connect with her but she wanted none of it. She pulled her arms away behind the table.

He wanted to tell Iman about the scholarship, to squeeze her very tight and to tell her that absolutely everything was going to be all right, not just because of the scholarship but for other reasons as well. He was sure of it.

The individual coils of smoke that had curled like strips of chiffon over the men's heads now spread out into a beige cloud absorbing them all. One of the fighters had got hold of the remote and was flicking through the satellite channels. *Flick*. To a Lebanese dance competition. *Flick*. To a Gulf Arab in a white *dishdasha* singing in a meadow to a woman in black lace with heavily outlined lips. *Flick*. To the picture of the scene of the suicide attack by the Hajjar girl, of a ripped-up park bench, of an overturned pushchair. *Flick*. Lebanese dancers again. *Flick*. Back to the pushchair. The fighter had turned up the volume so that Rashid could no longer eavesdrop on their conversation. He was not able to catch the end of a long-winded joke told by the one with the Stalin moustache, except for the word for arse, *teez*, upon which the joke centred, and then the name Hajjar, spoken in seriousness by a fighter with a husky voice whose hand would throw itself out into a bulb in the centre of the table before it opened up in explanation. *That Hajjar girl. What she's done.*

Khalil entered the café looking like he had walked through the wrong door. He was hot and frowning, but coming in next to the metal and grime of the fighters he looked out of place, too clean-shaven, too slight. Seeing him enter Sindibad's, Rashid saw for the first time quite how silly Khalil's ponytail was and understood why Khalil had once been described as pretty.

'What's going on here? What's with the flowers?' Khalil asked, avoiding commenting on the more obvious anomaly of Iman being in there. The owner had arranged the carnations in jugs and placed two of them on the fighters' table and one on Rashid's and

Seif El Din's. Rashid started to answer but as soon as Khalil sat down Iman started to talk.

'Your friend Raed got killed in the bombing of the hospital last night.'

'Raed Abu Warde? The communist?' Khalil and Rashid asked at the same time.

'Yes. Dead. And his cousin Taghreed who was in my class. You remember her, Rashid? You called her Tagweed because she couldn't pronounce her "r"s. The one who drew those pictures of tanks and cows? Cows eating tanks, that sort of thing. Remember?'

Rashid did remember a girl, a springy little thing presenting Iman with pictures, 'And this one, Miss. Is this one better than the other one? Shall I do another one, Miss?'

'Raed Abu Warde. He was seriously impressive. I always thought that one day he might . . .' Khalil's head fell, almost involuntarily, until his hand caught his forehead. The gesture held the café, held everyone in the room, tore them away from the TV and froze them, froze them all because by doing so he was breaking an unwritten rule, the one against spreading despair. 'That's such a terrible loss. I'm sorry about his cousin, Iman. Are you OK?' Khalil tried to get Iman to look up so that he could see for himself, but she refused to do so.

'I'm OK. What's new? A student of mine got killed. It's hardly the first time is it? It's not going to be the last. Does it matter any more?'

'Of course it matters. It has to. Otherwise they've won.' Khalil spoke with more urgency now. 'Listen, the only way to get through this is to retain humanity and compassion, not to abandon it. You know that, don't you?'

Iman glanced up for a moment. Khalil raised his hand as though there was so much more to be said in a far grander way, but nothing else accompanied the gesture. Rashid waved the fly away from Iman's face.

'I don't mean to lecture. But the family? He's the oldest son, isn't he? Are they OK?' Khalil's hands were unable to reach out to Iman in the café.

'No. They're not OK. I don't know about the father, as obviously he was not there this morning. He's probably out and about pulling his party into the funeral arrangements. You know he's with the religious parties.'

'Of course, he's . . . Yes, I'd forgotten.'

'The mother looks like someone has sucked the bones out of her. She kept giving these practical, hospitality, yes-of-course-it's-for-the-good-of-the-nation speeches, but she is all collapsed inside. It was awful. It's just . . .' Her arm jerked out as if hitting something away. 'It's *intolerable*. It has to stop.' She looked up and her eyes latched on to those of the man on the neighbouring table, who did not look away. No one spoke for a while.

Khalil stood up to readjust himself. His flannel shirt was buttoned up and tucked in at the front but it had come loose from the back of his trousers. There were streaks of dust down the side of one of his arms and a slight tear close to his collarbone. He removed his bag from his shoulder showing the sweat under his armpits, tucked the tail of his shirt back into his jeans and started brushing himself down. It didn't make much difference.

'I thought maybe this place wouldn't be open,' Khalil said as he sat down. 'Most of the restaurants are closed. There are queues at the bakeries everywhere. They were waiting for an excuse to close us in again and attack and this Hajjar girl handed them one on a plate. Every border is absolutely sealed. Nothing's going in. Nothing's going out. Strawberries, flowers, and vegetables – everything's rotting at the borders, north and south.'

'You were in the south?' Rashid asked.

'I tried to get down there as early as possible because I knew they were going to close the roads. I wanted to see how bad things were,' Khalil said.

'I would have thought it would be impossible.'

'It was almost impossible.' Khalil brought out a map. Some of the fighters turned around to watch. 'They closed the main road and all the arteries off it.' Khalil traced his finger along the stretch of road. His fingernails were always perfectly trimmed, cut square across the top, but today they were blackened and, noticing them against the map, Khalil tried to clean them with a corner of paper, but it didn't work. 'You can't get to any of the southern camps; they are totally isolated. You can't even get as far as that village.' Khalil stabbed at the map.

'Shit.' Rashid's hands drummed against the table. 'Shit.'

'They have totally sealed us in. And they are bulldozing houses on the outskirts of the camp.'

'Why?' Rashid asked.

'Who knows? They don't indulge us with *reasons* any more.' Khalil folded up his map. It was made out of four printed sheets of A4 taped together and he smoothed it flat along its joins. He turned back to Iman. 'Why did the family want you there? You didn't need to see the bodies. I don't get it. Why did they ask you to go?'

'I did need to see them like that. It's important. It will help me . . . I need to know what to do. It will help me decide.'

Iman was looking up now, past Khalil at their neighbour. Khalil looked as though he had so much more that he wanted to say. He cleared some ash off the table with the side of his hand.

'What is it?' Khalil asked Rashid, who was looking agitated.

'Nothing. Well, actually, this doesn't seem like the right time but you should both know that I got it. I got an email this morning.'

'Got what?' Khalil asked.

'The scholarship.' Rashid's hands opened up, *what else?* 'For London.'

'Well done,' Khalil said. 'Congratulations. *Mubrook.*'

'*Mubrook*,' Iman said, looking up at Rashid. 'Is that the proposal you were working on with Sabri?'

'That's what Mama said.'

'What does that mean?' Iman asked.

'It doesn't matter. Forget it. It just means I'm out of here. A couple more weeks then I'm gone for a year, at least a year. Hopefully longer if I can get to stay there for a while.' He would ignore them. It was just the wrong time. He could still fly. He was still going. It would still work out.

'Stay there? No chance,' Iman said. 'They'll kick you straight out of there once you finish your studies. You would need a visa to stay, which no one would give someone like you or me. The only way you could stay would be to find an English wife.' She cleared out her nose by blowing it hard, so hard that her jaw moved as she did so. No one spoke for some time.

'I expect you'll be more interested in this then.' Rashid spread out Lisa's message flat in front of Khalil. Khalil would not have had the chance to get to the Centre yet, but at the thought of it Rashid jerked as though someone had just kicked the seat of his chair. Rashid forced Khalil to look up by covering his hand over the message that Khalil was trying to read. 'Is the Centre OK?'

'I really don't know. I presume it is, because I spoke to Jamal last night and he told me that their army had not entered the camp, that they were all on the outside, but I haven't spoken to him since around midnight. His phone is disconnected again. I am going up there after this. I just needed to go south first before it all got closed up.'

Iman looked at Khalil. 'It's got more doors than a CIA safe house, your Centre. I'm sure it will be fine.'

'Yes, it's got to be,' Rashid agreed.

Khalil lifted Rashid's hand up and read Lisa's message carefully. 'Ouch. *"Small fry"*?' And then he read it again. 'I think we can get what she wants. We'll need to mention Raed, of course. I think he had a fairly senior position with the Party, didn't he? That's worth mentioning.'

'Do we have casualty figures for last night?' Rashid asked.

'We can get them. I sent some fieldworkers out.' Khalil's hands were moving again; his voice had lifted. He looked up at Rashid and paused. 'What's this?' He brushed a bit of sand away from the edge of Rashid's scalp.

'Who? Which fieldworkers?' Rashid was finding it difficult to stay focussed. Their neighbour, Seif El Din, seemed interested in everything that they were saying. The fighters were making no bones about staring at their table. The conversation was not going as Rashid had expected at all. Iman was in and out of it and the man on the table next to them, this supposedly religious man, could not stop checking Iman out. Neither could the fighter in green.

'Jamal would have tried to collect those figures without even being asked,' Khalil said.

'Of course, Jamal,' Rashid said. Iman and Khalil's admiration of Jamal bugged Rashid. *What does Jamal think?* Iman would always ask following a political development and Khalil would always know, because the camp viewpoint that Jamal represented was the one that would always give them the authenticity that they needed.

Iman was smoking. She seemed to be completely unaware that she was in public. Saying something about it would make her worse. He should take her home.

'I expect Jamal's doing eyewitness statements around the hospital. I left one of the newer volunteers over at the camps in the south. It's a nightmare down there. They demolished this house – well, a row of houses – but in this one house a gas canister in the kitchen had blown up. I went inside to get a bike for this kid who was standing outside screaming for it. *My bike! My bike!* on and on. Anyway, the smell?' Khalil closed his eyes and shook his head, 'Smoke, sulphur, sewage, rot, the lot. I can't even describe it.' He shuddered.

'You don't have to. It's still on you,' Rashid said.

'There were these chickens running everywhere and once I got inside the family started shouting for blankets and fridges and I don't know what, and I started telling them that I was not a removal man for God's sake. It was pathetic. We are pathetic. They brought a donkey with a bucket of water to put out the fire. A *donkey*.'

'Maybe a fire engine wouldn't have made it in there,' Rashid suggested.

'Still, come on, a donkey?' Khalil seemed beaten down and then rose up again. 'But from our point of view, it's good.'

'It is?'

'For the talk. It backs our argument about the applicability of human rights law in areas under siege. We can use it to evidence the complete sealing-off of an area. It backs up what we are trying to say about the breaches of the Conventions.'

'Ha!' said their bearded neighbour, and with it finally acknowledged that he had been listening to everything that they had said. 'You think that will make a difference?' Khalil's eyes widened, the applicability of international human rights and humanitarian law to areas under siege was Khalil's passion. 'I have been listening to you two,' Seif El Din said, 'and it's all well and good this work, but all you are doing is just playing their game. You create some interesting little jobs for some friendly Europeans and you ease their consciences a bit, but if you want change, if you *really* want change, this is not the way.'

Iman and Khalil were now completely alert. The whole café was. Rashid could tell that Khalil liked the 'interesting little job creation' angle; Rashid had heard him say similar things himself.

'We don't have enough of the world supporting us. Nor do we have the time,' their neighbour continued.

Although the man's words were addressed to Khalil, Seif El Din appeared to speak only to Iman, who had stubbed out her cigarette and now sat up as though she was about to take notes.

'You,' their neighbour said, deliberately poking a finger towards Khalil, 'are taking the legal route which is, of course, virtuous. But what are we waiting for? The conversion of the Jews? The Conventions? It does you as much good to consider the laws of Hammurabi. These Conventions will turn to dust without our situation improving. Little girls and brave men will continue to die before your international laws are enforced. We're not trying to discipline children from some private school here. And then you say "international", but is that right? Was your grandfather's village leader consulted, or any representative of his? No, my friend, these are the justifying laws of conflict and empire. They are the Occupier's laws; they create them and they benefit from them, as and when it suits them.'

The man stared hard at a transfixed Iman.

'It is essential,' Khalil started after swallowing, moving his head slightly to emphasise each word, 'that we believe in the Western governments' ability to change. It is crucial that we communicate our situation. It is imperative that we document the Occupier's abuses. It is . . .' but Seif El Din seemed to know these arguments already.

'If you want them to change, let me ask you this: what would alter your behaviour if you were benefiting from a situation? Feeling guilty about something? The loss of money? Or the

65

prospect of someone you love getting hurt or killed? I would say only the last two, and those are the only things we can use to get this situation to change, to get them to stop.'

He stared at the group, bowed his head to Iman and left. He seemed to leave a vacuum in the room behind him.

Outside, the carrot boy had made a sale.

'I'm going,' Iman said, pulling the napkin off her head. Rashid had not thought that it would be possible, but she looked even worse now than she had when she first came in.

'Where? Where are you going?' Rashid asked.

'I have to do something. I need to do something.'

Iman pushed herself out of the door as the carrot boy pushed his way in. The boy went up to the counter and ordered as much food as the fighters had had all together.

'Where are your shoes?' the café owner asked.

'Are you bourgeois or something?' the boy replied. 'Food comes before shoes.'

The fighters liked this and repeated it. They rallied to the boy's support until the owner capitulated. Once his mouth had been thoroughly stuffed at least a couple of times, the boy turned to the audience that had been held spellbound by his eating and spoke, his mouth still full of bread.

'They're using that gas again.'

'What gas?' asked the fighter with the Stalin moustache.

'That gas, the one without a name or an antidote but with a nice sweet minty smell, the gas that makes you do this.' The boy started kicking his legs and throwing his forearms about in convulsions. His head lolled to one side, the bread fell from his mouth. He replaced it and went back to eating.

'Where?' Khalil was ready to burst now. 'How do you know? When? Where? How much?'

'Last night, on the edges of the Shore Camp. They say some

canisters were also dropped by the Sultan's Well. And I know these things. I get around.'

He had hummus smeared around his mouth now. Rashid's fly had adopted the boy and buzzed twice around his bread before the boy reached out and squashed it between the fingertips and the palm of his left hand. He continued to eat with his right hand.

'Gas. Do you believe that?' Khalil asked.

Rashid shrugged. 'They've done it before.'

'That's all we need. That and some zealot making me feel like a neurotic housewife who only focusses on the things she can control: she can't stop her husband screwing around so she puts her energies into keeping the lid tight on the toothpaste tube. It's that kind of behaviour. So what kinds of bullets were used? How many metres of barbed wire? What kind of gas? What the hell? Is he right? Is there no goddamn point in any of this anymore? Maybe the donkey with half a bucket of water is of greater use.' Khalil could feel the weight of his fall on Rashid and checked himself, straightening up. 'We should go and check on the Centre.'

'Sure. Sure. But it sounds like we'll need to take the beach route if all the roads are closed.'

'Not closed,' said the boy relishing his expertise, 'dug up. Dug the whole lot up. Bulldozers all over the place. Back to the beach.' He started singing a song to the sea, spitting grainy particles of green *zaatar* across the room.

The owner presented Rashid with the bill that included the cost of their neighbour's tea. 'No way. He was not with us!' Rashid protested.

'But he's a religious man.'

'That doesn't mean I have to pay for his tea now, does it?' Rashid tried to argue. He didn't mind paying, but he didn't want to be seen to be paying, people might think all types of things, 'Look, I'll pay for him but I'll pay for the boy too, OK? No special favours or anything, all right?'

'*Bon abeteeh*,' the boy said, one of his feet propped up on the seat in front of him as he munched at his bread.

Rashid was watching the boy, wondering how anyone of his size could eat so much so fast, when he noticed Abu Omar for the third time that morning walking quite fast outside the window. Surprisingly fast for such a lazy-arsed man. Rashid was following his neighbour's movements when the fighters all stood up at the same time and blocked out his view. It was only when they crammed their way out of the door that Rashid realised that their green-jacketed leader had gone before them.

Hope. Rashid recognised it as soon as the men had gone. That was what he had felt. Hope. That was the feeling that the leader had evoked in him when he first saw him. Rashid felt ashamed for having experienced it; so often it felt like the thing that could devastate them all.

Chapter 10

In the café it had been as though a jeep had her in its headlights at the end of an alleyway. She had realised who the Seif El Din man was and what it meant that he was there. It was when he had started staring that the noise in her ears had begun. The approach had come, as Manar had said it would.

It was too much in there, Seif El Din and that fighter in the same place at the same time. Twice in one day she had seen that fighter in green. He had to be after something. When Khalil had cleared his throat to respond to the man's arguments, she had almost wanted to touch his leg under the table and tell him not to, not to say anything, but she could not move. The fighter in the green jacket had seemed too interested in decoding her actions for her to make a move like that.

The noise in her head did not stop when she left the café. It followed her; it was not constant but as though a vacuum was pulling all sound away only for it to return with an intense rush. Maybe it was just too crowded in there: the stares, the sound of the chairs scraping, the echo, the muttering of the fighters, the fear in Khalil's voice, his leg juddering on the ball of his foot under the table, scratching sand into the flooring as it moved around, the smoke, Rashid's eyes with the irises strung up by crazed red veins. And then there was her heart and the clenching, clenching, clenching of it. She had thought she was panicking deliberately which was why it was racing so fast and she had tried to calm it and it had not, it would not, and so it had started panicking her more because she could not believe that it could continue to go that fast without breaking. Her lungs had gone, too. It was like gum inhaled backwards into her throat so that there was nothing to breathe with any more.

Being outside made no difference this time. The noise in her ears had not been left behind in the café. It didn't help that the air was stale and that the crowd was thick, human, and full of close smells of bad nights and sick children. She could not feel the air above her because those around her were breathing it in faster than she could get at it. It was hard to keep sight of Seif El Din, her contact. She plunged into the crowd; angles of elbows were between her and where she wanted to be, wheelbarrows pushing up against her shins, carts bruising her legs. The roads were down, blocked and dug up. You could tell. The alleys were packed.

'What do they want with us now?' some woman was screaming up at the sky where others were pointing at a surveillance drone. 'Didn't they get their fill last night?'

'They're never satisfied,' said another. 'Never.'

Parts of the crowd seemed to be reconsidering their direction, watching the drone move ahead of them; they were heading back in the direction they had come from and by doing so they made space for Iman to move forwards and catch sight of Seif El Din ahead of her. His head held up against the other heads that were bare and bent.

They worked fast that group. Manar had said they would contact her and it was just hours later that the man was there, addressing her, persuading her. The contact had come. She had said she was ready. Well, she was. Maybe that morning, after the meeting, she had not been, but that was a long time ago, before Taghreed, before Raed. She needed to contact him, tell him that she was ready. That was all.

Khalil had to rethink. They could do it his way but it was not for her, not any more. She needed to act. She had been there. They had not seen Taghreed and Raed all burnt like that, all charred and

70

twisted. It changed things. Deaths of children changed everything. Resistance movements started with dead children. And there she was, for it did not matter *who* it was that she followed really, all this hair-splitting about what party you backed, which leader and what position that had been taken on the agreements of 1973, '78, '94. Who cared? To hell with it. The thing was to *act* and that was what she was doing. Peoples Fronts, Popular Wings, United Leaderships – the hell with them, too. It was all about *action*; there were no alternatives.

She was not about to stay at home making pickles like her mother. For all her talk, what had her mother actually done? Marry her father? And her father, for all his former days of glory, where had he ended up but out of it? Fobbing them off with a money transfer every couple of months, away from this place, from family, from politics. Living in the Gulf. The Gulf? And Rashid just prostrated himself before anything Western. Sabri tried, but fussing over his book was not going to solve anything. It was not as though the world did not know what they had done. Rashid's assumption that gathering evidence of these violations mattered was flawed.

It went back to what Seif El Din said. They were relying on conscience, on a sense of guilt, but these people did not have one towards them. Violence was justified if the other side viewed you as less than human (Mandela, right? Or was it Brecht?). And that was how it was. They would not expect it of her. No one would expect it of her, Iman, to act in this way. She spent her time reading poetry in her room. Maybe they would say that it was being unmarried at her age that drove her to it? They would need to find some kind of justification for a non-religious girl like her doing such a thing.

The solid mass of human traffic pushed out into the square and fanned out around its sides. Seif El Din was just ahead of her. His step was far younger than his age. Now out of the alleyway, Iman became aware that there was someone following her, someone trying to match her pace through the crowd. Maybe it was one of

Seif El Din's men. She could not look. She needed to keep moving. He was in front of the statue of a phoenix that the Leaders had built, now scrawled with graffiti. *Return to the Egg! Embrace the Ashes!* demanded the red spray paint.

She was about to catch up with him (there *was* someone behind her; he was almost running now), and then he would just have to look and he would know that she was ready (why was somebody following her?). She just needed to establish contact. They would talk elsewhere. The drones had now gone but a helicopter was coming in close, the palms were bending down low, low, deferential, bent like reeds, to clear a path for this machine cutting through the sky. Water was being sprayed out of the dirty fountain in the square. It was like those Vietnam films with a cloud of dust blowing back at the sky, rushing into her face, and the helicopter was low, low so that, with its open sides, she could almost make out through the window a real face, a human one next to the profile with feathers painted on the side, *Apache*. Are we to be killed off in reservations by helicopters named after others killed off in reservations? The marketplace was emptying fast, back into the alleys and side roads, but Seif El Din moved ahead, not looking up, weaving between parked cars.

And then it came. So instant and heavy that the ground seemed to bounce up beneath her and the air was alive with light and dust, screams filled her eyes, her mouth, her ears. *They killed him! Mustafa Seif El Din! Abu Mohammed! They killed him!* Hands on her arms, around her waist, pulled her back, had pulled her back, before the strike, and the heat was so angry that she was red in the face from it, and there was a burnt hair smell like that morning with the cigarette, and something sweet-smelling and fleshy. But the noise had stopped, the whirring engine noise that had been coming and going since she was in the café. It had gone and she was left with something trivial, almost domestic, a ringing sound in her ears as though somewhere, far off, a fridge door had been left open.

Chapter 11

'Damn it,' Khalil swore at the packed beach that had absorbed his key. 'We'll never find it. We'll have to go back to my place and get the spare.' He scraped the lumps of wet sand off his shoes on to the kerbstone. 'And I think my mother's there.'

They were taking the beach route to get to the Centre and it seemed as though the whole coastline was on the move. The over-riding current was heading north but there were streams of people that were going against it, pushed to the limits, on one side paddling through the edges of waves with children on their shoulders and plastic bags in their hands. Arms were being pulled from their sockets and baby fingers were slipping over eyes from foreheads, blocking visions of makeshift paths. The centre of the beach bore the heavy traffic of carts and donkeys while bicycles were carried and dragged across the sand.

Iman had been in a state in the café. Rashid couldn't remember when he had last seen her like that. He had wanted to follow her, had meant to take her home, but by the time the bill had been sorted out there was no sign of her and she didn't seem to want him around. He resolved to spend more time with her before he left. Maybe this evening he could get her to come and sit on the roof with him for a while. Khalil could talk to her and there was always Sabri. Iman went to Sabri for guidance and Sabri went to their mother, and his mother never needed guidance from anyone. She had probably come out of the womb that way.

The smell of the sea, the expanse of water, the salt of the air, the seagulls shouldering each other in the sky, the sense of being part of a purposeful mass lifted Rashid. He had run into two friends that he had not seen for years and they had laughed about what a lucky, lucky bastard Rashid was for getting the scholarship.

'It's sort of romantic,' Rashid had said when they first joined up with the rest of the human traffic.

'There is nothing romantic about being bombed and starved back into the Middle Ages,' Khalil had replied, unwilling to risk looking up from his feet for a minute.

It did not take long for Rashid to stop seeing the charm of the beach. He grazed himself on an upturned fishing boat; his trouser legs had become plastered to his calves; his cuts stung with salt and splinters; his shoes were heavy with water, his toes gritty with sand. Khalil had stumbled when his toe caught in a half-buried plastic bag, but it was not until they got to the pavement that he realised that the key for the Centre must have dropped out with the fall.

'You won't find it in there,' Rashid said looking back at the lumbering crowd of people walking down the beach. 'Impossible.'

The only spare was in Khalil's flat. He had no choice but to go there with Rashid and risk Rashid meeting his mother. Since moving to Gaza, Khalil had only once asked Rashid back to his family's flat and he had made sure that his mother was in Paris and his father in DC, when he had done so. Khalil could not bear anyone talking about his parents, let alone meeting them. Khalil tried to put as much physical distance between his family and himself as he put political distance.

'Sure,' said Rashid, trying to ease Khalil's anxiety, 'no problem.'

The Sea View development where Khalil's family lived was a row of eggshell-coloured apartment blocks along the beachfront. Khalil knew a lot about the financing structure for the construction of Sea View and he had once, when stoned, divulged what he

74

knew to Rashid and then regretted having done so as most of it had implicated his father.

The pale Sea View buildings hovered on the shore as though they were contemplating slipping away into the sea and dissolving palidly into its watery mass. They were calm, clean buildings with elevators that worked and doormats that were guarded by plant pots that shone with the spit and polish of imported labour.

If he had allowed himself to be, Rashid would have been insulted by Khalil's determination to keep him away from his family. It wasn't as though Rashid didn't know them. The two families had been close in Beirut, in Tunis, and briefly in Scandinavia, but as the Outside Leadership made peace with their enemy, they had made enemies of each other. The families had split apart at the same time that Rashid's parents had.

As Khalil's mother ran to kiss Rashid, her mercurial, silky outfit billowed around her. Her orange-streaked hair was noodle-like, her eyebrows accentuated by a bluish pencil and her front teeth had caught on a lipstick, as though she had taken a quick snap at it.

It was after greeting Rashid that she noticed the state of Khalil. 'Look at you! What happened to your shirt? You are filthy. You smell terrible. What is this smell?'

'It's gas. I went to the south, Mama.'

'You went to the south? Are you mad? One of these days you'll get yourself killed. You go right now and take a shower. But wait, before you go, stay here. Stand here. You two boys, I haven't seen you together for so long . . .'

She brought both boys into the sitting room and got them to stand next to each other and appraised them, compared them, while blowing smoke into the air above her face with the manner-isms of a twitchy dressmaker.

There was something so brittle about her. It was as though she had snapped and was jangling around inside. Here was a woman who had been brought up according to the best of French educational systems, who had been groomed assiduously to find a husband from the best of families, to cook, entertain, and to pack suitcases in ways that emulated the preferences of the European aristocracy. All this she had done to perfection. She had hosted and preened, spent and saved, complimented and listened while furthering the path of her husband's career. But no one had taught her how to deal with her husband's infidelities, to cope with the humiliation of their multiplicity, their diversity, and the publicity that surrounded them. For everyone knew about them, from the Spanish waitress in the restaurant bathroom, to the Indonesian maid molested in the kitchen in front of her. She never got used to them; each one had floored her, each one had struck her down afresh.

'Just so high, up to here!' She had started upon seeing Rashid, as they feared that she would. Rashid had not seen her for possibly as much as a decade and Khalil had not been able to stop her grabbing at his friend.

A little devil you were as a boy, we used to say to your mother. No more boys for you Jehan, this one is more work than five!

And so handsome. How did you get so handsome? Better-looking than both your parents.

A scholarship! You're getting out! Khalil, you didn't tell me! Why didn't you tell me? This is wonderful. Wonderful. Here, we shall drink to it!

She propped Rashid up on a cane bar stool against Khalil's protestations. 'Mama, we're going to the Centre. He can't go into a refugee camp smelling of alcohol.'

The bar was backed with mirrors and adorned with whisky bottles, china windmills and miniature crystal pigs. A clay model of a man smoking a pipe sat in the centre of this display.

'No. I insist. This is a great day for Rashid, a great day. Go

Khalil. You go have your shower. Change your clothes. We'll have a drink. Catch up on old times.' She was busy mixing two multi-layered cocktails, calling to the maid for ice, for lemon slices. 'See how pretty!' she said. 'A cause for celebration, Rashid. *Mubrook.* Congratulations. What are you studying? Such a clever boy and so good-looking.'

Two drinks for the two of them and then another two.

Your father! The stories I have about that man. There was the one time that we were all together in Paris . . .

No, that was after the assassinations in Rome before we left Beirut—

Your mother is not really one for – how shall I say? – relaxing, enjoying herself . . .

The years in Stockholm were the best for us.

Tell me, your uncle – is he still with that woman?

All of this was merely a warm-up for what she really wanted to say, which she did as soon as Rashid had drunk the first drink, urgently, holding Rashid's arm.

'You must help me with Khalil. You must persuade him to do what you do, to get out of this place, get a scholarship like you. He's a bright boy. I don't know what he's thinking. This Centre? In a camp? Things are not like they were; he could get into such trouble and for nothing. For *nothing.*'

'The Centre's doing very important work. A lot of people – my girlfriend, her organisation in London – they use our data to lobby the British Government. For them it's vital.'

'Yes, yes, but you saw what happened last night and I heard another strike just now. What is the point, really? Do you think these people care? No. You tell Khalil. You tell him that it is time to get out. You tell him to come to London with you. You have a girlfriend there? That's lovely. See? He can get a girlfriend too. You can go out. Have some fun. I don't know what he wants with staying here. I really don't.'

'Shall we go?' Khalil picked up his bag from the table by the window where the maid had placed it. But the drinks had hardened his mother's resolve and she held on tight to her son's arm.

'You should follow your friend. Get out of here.' Through the open veranda doors the view down the coast was clear to where the smoke streamed upwards and then dissipated over the sea.

'Yes, Mama.'

Her face peered up at him. The sea breeze caught in the light damask curtains and they inflated into air pockets behind them.

'I don't know what you want. This *politics*,' her face contorted, 'it will make you like your *father*.'

Khalil stood very still, the curtain pushing up around his back like a satin pillow for a jewel. His mother had sunk low and she knew it.

Rashid chose to leave them for a while. He waited in the bathroom for some time, his fingers tracing along the labels of the sedatives, tranquilisers and mood stabilisers lined up inside the bathroom cabinet until he felt it was safe to come out.

Chapter 12

Sabri and Lana had run against each other for the Student Council in the year that they had met. Lana's platform, as an Independent, was one of opposition. She opposed Sabri's party, the Outside Leadership, on the basis of its corruption and condemned the Islamic alternative on the basis of its social conservatism. No one had anticipated her success. She had attained over five per cent more votes than Sabri and all other Outside Leadership representatives, fifteen per cent more than the Islamic alternative. Sabri's friends had stopped laughing at her shoes and started examining her flyers instead.

When Sabri had tried to persuade her to join his party, she responded with a diatribe, an unnerving diatribe against the abuse of power by the Outside Leadership, against his party's receipt of funding from conservative regimes, their undermining of 'true' revolutionaries, their failure to enforce discipline for a 'true' guerrilla fighting force, and their nepotism, cronyism and errors of judgement. *The corruption! The corruption! The corruption!*

Sabri did not ask her again. He had instead channelled his energies into a more primitive form of wooing, an attempt to seduce her body by pleasing her mind. His strategy was developed around her obsession with history and love of folklore. In those days it had not been so hard to travel across the boundaries from one enemy-controlled area to another and into the land that was once theirs. So he took her to Greek fountains in the Occupied Syrian lands of the north, to Roman ruins lying under destroyed villages, to Canaanite temples and Solomon's wells. Wherever he could, he found cafés to take her where *qassaseen*, storytellers, recounted tales passed down from generation to generation.

The strategy had worked.

Lana agreed to marry Sabri after a night spent huddled at the back of a Jerusalem café listening to three hours of recitation of the story of the one-eyed ghoul. The audience had been rapt. Each line had been followed up by commentary from the coffee-drinking, *argeela*-smoking gathering. He had watched her looking towards the crowd in the soft light with her hair the way he liked it, fluffed into curls at the front, hanging down long at the back over the chain of red cross-stitches running around the collar of her shirt. He had surprised himself by the thought that maybe this in itself could be enough: just to see her like that sometimes, to give her pleasure that way. Maybe he did not need to try to have her, or even to touch her. But she must have felt his gaze because she had turned and, with a gesture that was both manufactured and aimless at the same time, popped a piece of sticky, honeyed *baklava* into his mouth with her fingers, as though it was something she had done many, many times before, and then he knew that he had never thought anything quite so *stupid* in his whole life.

Her family had opposed the marriage. They objected to Sabri's place of origin, to his religion and to the party he was affiliated with. They did not dare to voice their objection to his peasant lineage as they knew that if they did, she would have only become even more determined to stay with him. But their objections did not stop Lana.

Sabri and Lana had married in a small Jerusalem hotel where their faces were beamed by a video camera into hearts dancing on a wall and Lana's head had been scraped with combs, rose stems and metal pins; her face had been whitened to that of a Geisha.

'Like a death mask,' she whispered to Sabri as they placed her next to him on a raised velvet throne. He had lost her in this pile of tacky lace. This was not what they had wanted. The Intifada was going on. Celebrations were banned. They had asked for something simple, old-fashioned: a dress with embroidery, hennaed hands, and a troop of men dancing the *dabke*, at most. They didn't want the hall. Or the mealy-mouthed waiters. Or the Lebanese and Egyptian pop music about lost love and dying hearts. But both families had vetoed their modest plans absolutely, far more effectively than they had vetoed the marriage itself.

'I want you to take it off. Now,' he had whispered back to her.

'What, this?' she said, pointing up to her face. 'Or this?' and she had plucked at the neckline of her dress revealing just enough cleavage to drive him wild.

Afterwards, his extended family commented on how inappropriate it was that she looked so relaxed. She had not appeared to be intimidated by the prospect of the night that was to follow. But she had neither cared about upsetting everyone then, nor had she cared later when she had screamed at a delegation of women from Sabri's family who came to ululate outside their window.

'But I thought you liked tradition, custom, hmm?' Sabri had asked after the women had obediently got lost, his nose nuzzled against her cheek, his bent knee resting against the side of her newly waxed one, the agitated voices of the dismissed women dying away outside.

'All traditions and customs except for those that subjugate women and deprive them of sleep.' She turned to him so that their noses touched. 'And other pleasures.'

Naji had been born nine months later, disappointed by his surroundings. The baby's colicky objection to the universe rarely subsided. From being dedicated to the pursuit of national liberation, his parents' lives were transformed into a perpetual quest to find something, anything, that would quell their son's grief. There was no pattern as to what pleased him. On some days it was after-noon sunlight fluttering between the leaves of a tree; on others touching the shorn hair of boys' heads would make him gurgle and coo, his toes curled into each other with excitement. He was, according to all who met him, a cranky baby and his parents some-times said that he was only saved from being given up on altogether by the look of absolute trust that he gave them when he fed. With his mouth around the bottle's teat, he would make an eye-to-eye plea for understanding of quite how difficult it was, how hard it was for him to accept his disappointment. His eyes would widen, one hand holding on to the bottle, the other seeking out tender-ness of any kind: a hand to hold and play with, a forearm to stroke.

Like everyone else in Gaza they were living the Intifada and it was still going strong. Sabri had had to go underground on more than one occasion, hiding in the camps for long periods. It was a time of smuggling messages across the border in swallowed sealed capsules, of army raids to remove fax machines, of banned flags, songs and school books, classes being held at home with the curtains drawn, of food being grown in back gardens to encourage self-sufficiency, boycotted produce being smashed against the walls in front of cheering crowds. Those were the heady days of resistance. Heady days indeed!

It was in that first year of their marriage when, buoyed up with international support, the Outside Leadership had made a Declaration of Independence. Sabri, like many, was sure that it would work. Legally and morally (as he kept stressing to his audi-ences), their position could not be disputed. And even Lana, Sabri assured himself, almost confessed to being in accordance with the Leadership's position.

The Occupier's response to the Declaration was predictable, but harsh: a curfew had been imposed and all lines of communica-tion with the outside world were severed.

Sabri needed to speak to his leaders, to let them know what the situation was on the inside. He needed to find a phone line that had not been cut.

'We could try the hospitals?' Lana had suggested.

'I wouldn't get through the roadblocks. The army's everywhere.'

'We could come with you. If they stop us we can say Naji's ill. I'm sure the doctors will let you make a call,' she replied.

'That's not what I'm worried about. No, I'd rather you didn't come.'

'What is it? You want us to stay at home? Do you want me to take up crochet too?' Naji wailed at his mother's raised voice.

'The army's very jumpy at the moment. I don't think we should take unnecessary risks.' Sabri said, putting a bent finger into Naji's mouth for him to chew on.

'You do want us to stay at home, don't you?'

'That's not it,' Sabri said. One year into marriage, he was already getting sloppy about hiding his petulance from his wife.

'How else are you going to talk to them? There's no other way. Stop arguing about it. We'll go tonight.'

The night before, Naji had slept and they had managed to be together in a way that had they had not been for such a long time, and well into the next day he could feel himself inside her. The night had wound itself around them throughout the day, tying them back to each other. He had not wanted it to break. He had not wanted to argue with her.

Sabri's car had been parked outside the gate for so long that he was not sure it would start. They had spent a long time deciding what outfit Naji should wear, trying to imagine what would appeal to the soldiers at the checkpoints and had settled on a sailor suit that had been a present when he was born. They were still fussing as they started loading themselves into the car, about whether made-up powdered milk bottles could be reheated and where the

83

spare nappies were. They kept asking each other whether Naji was going to be warm enough and going backwards and forwards on the question as to whether it was better for Naji to be in a car seat in the back or on Lana's lap in the front. They had been hissing at each other as Naji had been asleep. Lana said it was more convincing for the baby to be with her. And so Sabri had tucked Naji in on his mother's lap and had put the spare nappies by her feet, the water bottle by her side and the dummy (wrapped in plastic cling film) into the glove compartment. He had walked around in front of the car, irritated, until he looked up and saw his wife through the windscreen, her head bent down to their son, her hair falling forwards and had felt the old pride that they were his. His family.

They had just exchanged a final 'All right?' as he had put the key in the ignition when Naji, predisposed to diarrhoea, produced something of such vast and gaseous proportions that it woke him up into a state of bawling indignation. Sabri had looked at his watch.

'I'll do it upstairs, it's easier,' Lana said, opening the car door, leaning backwards to get out, making her way to the porch, jogging the bundle of baby and blanket with one arm as she searched in her back pocket for the door key with the other.

They had been a while. Seven minutes. Sabri had waited. The moon had been full that night, an orange disk strung between the buildings at the end of the road shining like a Ramadan *fanoos*. Sabri had seen the bedroom light go on. He had heard Naji's wails from the window and had been able to make out the murmur of Lana's comforting. The crying continued as the light went off and Naji had only stopped as they entered the stairwell. Sabri had seen them come back out on to the porch.

He must have turned the key in the ignition when they reached the gate. He was not sure. It was a guess. He did not know what had happened. He could not remember. Something white and definitive had blasted reality from him and then they were gone. The psychiatrist who visited Sabri in hospital afterwards said that it was surprising he remembered so much. But it was all untrustworthy. If asked what his last memories were before the explosion he would have said that they were of being with Lana and Naji on the staircase (he could clearly see them walking down the stairs: Naji in a beige blanket with a satin rabbit in a bow tie on the corner, his hair tufty with patches of baldness at the back where its softness had been rubbed off by sleep, a face blotchy from tears, his eyes trying to focus on the thick blue ceramic tiles outside the neighbour's door. There was Lana too, her blow-dried hair stuck behind her ears, lipstick remaining only on the edges of her lips, her hand on Naji's back). But for all its clarity, it was a scam, that memory. A fabrication. He could not have seen them on the stairs. He had never been on the stairs with them. He had been in the car.

To hell with memory. It was like feeling around in basket of apples only to be confronted by a snake.

Chapter 13

The fighter had pulled Iman backwards just before the strike and she had landed in a slump on her bottom, like a girl in a mood. Then he had pulled her forwards and lifted her up on to her knees, off the ground and away from the crowd that had surged into where the strike had been. Once he had her on her feet, he led her, his forearm around her waist, to the entrance of a derelict building where they could be out of sight. She realised dimly that they were in the entrance to the old Andalus Hotel, the one with the roof terrace, but was not sure what the hell the building was doing there. He was wearing the same green jacket that he had worn that morning and the gun was still across his back, but he had gained a new intensity, a focus that seemed to be her. All pleasantness had gone. There was anger in the way he grabbed her arm and dragged her there, and the way he looked at her was filled with unblinking contempt. It was a reflex, and she hated herself minutes after experiencing it, but she had found herself smiling at him in an attempt to dispel his derision. Her smile angered him more. He hated her.

'Who told you to follow him?' he asked. 'Who was it? Where did they find you?'

Her heart was still pounding up in her eyes, in her fingertips and the palms of her hands. There was dust and gravel in her mouth and grazed into her hands and knees. The gentlemanly courtesy of that morning had gone. She had smiled at him like a fool, asking him to forgive her. *Look*, her smile tried to say, *I'm only a girl*, but he had refused that absolutely. He hated her like an equal.

'You have to tell me who it was.' It was an attempt at a shout but his voice faltered. 'Who contacted you?' He had a sickly look about him and his lips were dry. He appeared to have forgotten that his hand was still clasped on to her upper arm.

'Let go of me.'

He was not up to it. She could tell that, even with her burnt eyelashes and the blast of caked dust over her face, she was in a better state than he was. He was breathing hard, his chest lifting and falling in an exaggerated way like an asthmatic and his hands weren't steady. She pulled herself away but he grabbed her back into the porch. Her feet crunched on broken glass. They were in the entrance to the hotel. Circles were punched out of the sides of the concrete porch, while the aluminium swing doors, their handles all wrapped up with chains, were criss-crossed with triangles, where only shards of the coloured glass remained.

'I know what you were trying to do.' His tongue was sticking to the top of his mouth and filling out into the space he needed for it to function. 'I know that you were trying to make contact with that man, Mustafa Seif El Din.' He was barely audible above the panic outside.

'I was not trying to do anything.' Her voice took its strength from the weakness in his. 'And anyway, it's none of your business what I do.'

'But it is my business.' He coughed at the dust.

She dropped her voice. 'Let go of my arm. Let go of me. I'm not going to run off, but you can't hold me like this. Stop it. *Bikafee*. Enough.'

She pulled herself back from him and he let go, but she didn't step back. She had no desire to be seen from the road, standing there with a man she did not know and was not related to.

It was not possible that he knew about that girl, Manar, and about the conversation. Even if he had been in the café it was impossible that he could know anything – Manar had gone in the opposite direction to her when they had parted that morning.

His breathing was becoming more regular although his eyes were still bleary. He moved back into the corner of the porch stepping on a drink can. The strong smell of urine overrode all others, even the burnt-rubber air, the rush of dust and bodies outside. Six men carrying an orange stretcher lumbered down the street in a running march like a pantomime animal. Iman tried to salivate, to spit out the grit from her mouth.

'They want you . . .' he was calmer now, and trying to be clear and to be loud enough, '. . . because of the family that you come from, that's all. It's got nothing to do with you as a person. It's got nothing to do with whether they think you can do anything that will make any difference at all.'

'What are you talking about?' Iman pulled her shoulders back. Her bag was still there, a strap ripped off by the fall or by his pull. She picked up the body of it and held it against her stomach.

'Listen.' He reached towards her forearm, not harsh as before but to get her to look up at him. The tenderness in the gesture made her more afraid of him. 'Listen, I know these people, I know how they operate, and I know that they approached you. I've been watching that man you were following, Seif El Din, and the others that are with him.'

Iman tried mentally to grab at something she could say that would push him away. She felt that he was forcing her backwards.

'Who are you, anyway? I've never seen you before. But today you're everywhere, following me, spying on our house, in that café with my brother, chasing me down the street.' Iman worked herself up with the absurdity of it. As she spoke she convinced herself that she was entirely innocent, a girl going about her business, someone to be liked, not reprimanded. He refused to see her in that way.

88

'It was not you that we were watching by your house.' He waved his hand in front of his face, *no matter*. 'It will become clear later what I was doing, but I am from the Authority, from the Patriotic Guard and I can tell you that these people, Seif El Din's people, are only trying to recruit you so that they can undermine us. They are trying to attack us so, yes, what you are trying to do for them is very much my business.' He spoke slowly weighing up each word, pausing to find exactly the right way to communicate his message. 'It's internal. They want to get people like you, people from families like yours, who are historically associated with *our* party, not because they think you can really *do* anything worthwhile, but as a show of strength on their part. It's divisive. Internally divisive.' His shoulders dropped; he kept double-checking; he needed to be reassured that she had got to the point where she understood. 'Haven't you seen that the enemy – and you mustn't forget who that is – that the enemy is justifying last night on the basis of that Hajjar girl's attempted attack? Do you want to be like her? The spittle that allows them to unleash this hell on us?'

'What Hajjar girl?'

'You haven't heard?'

'No. I haven't heard anything. I was up all night at a meeting. I've lost a girl, a sweet girl in my class and her cousin who was . . .' she wanted it out too: *You want suffering? I'll give you suffering*, '. . . a good friend of mine. And I saw their bodies. That's what I have been seeing and hearing all day. Not the news. Just dead bodies and crying relatives.'

She needed to punch this man. There was something in the way he pulled her around and stood there with his legs apart, as though she was not a woman at all, or as though he had had enough women not to care whether she was one or not.

She trusted no one from the Authority.

She trusted no one.

And yet she had trusted Manar.

'Who told you to follow Seif El Din?' His eyes were hostile. She disgusted him.

'They weren't trying to recruit me,' she lied, and flipped her head back in his direction to try to dislodge the growing sense of having been duped that was taking possession of her and making her feel ill.

He shrugged, *whatever you say, however you want it to be*. His disappointment in her was palpable. It was also deeply personal. He leant forwards. 'Sometimes, Miss Iman, you will find that saying nothing when you know something is as damaging as doing the wrong thing.'

She didn't want to look at him, but she had; she didn't want him to think that she was afraid. He was now holding her arm as a friend or a companion would and it scared her. His T-shirt was pulled down from his neck by the strap of his gun and his collarbones stuck out like bars.

'This could've been the end for you,' he continued. 'It did not end as they would have wanted, but they won't see this as being the end of their plans for you.' He did not expect her to respond or, if he did, whatever she had to say was of little interest to him. 'You will have to get out of here.' He nodded as though it was a conclusion that they had reached together.

'Get out of where? What are you talking about?'

'You need to get out of Gaza. To leave, at least for a couple of months.' Now that he had regained himself, he could talk more easily. His eyes appeared less sickly, but they were remote. He was still restless for her to understand. '*Get out*. Do you see? It will become a matter of pride for them to get you involved in whatever plans they have for you and you can't do that. It's a pointless sacrifice. Nothing you do for them will harm the enemy, the real enemy, it will only draw in more support for them as a party.'

A small ambulance drove past, forcing Iman to give up on the effort of responding. Raised voices ordering the crowd to stand back echoed in the porch. She could not remember her reasons for chasing Seif El Din any more. She had lost them. She wanted to cry because the reasons had gone and for a moment there had been a purpose to it all, a purpose to it and to her. She *couldn't* cry and she *wouldn't* because of him. Iman focussed on the poster on the wall behind the fighter, an advertisement in a metal frame that depicted a big-nosed man smoking an *argeela* in front of cluster of *mezza* bowls. Hummingbirds with flowers in their mouths chased each other around the edge of a menu.

'Why should I trust you anyway? You are nothing to me. I don't even know who you are. Patriotic Guard or not.'

'I'm Ziyyad.' The man's arms hung down straight at his sides, his voice seemed a little saddened by its own identity. 'Ziyyad Ayyoubi.'

'Iman Mujahed,' she replied automatically as though he had challenged her to spar by announcing his name.

'Miss Iman, I know. I know who you are and I am asking you, explaining to you now, why you must leave. But if you don't listen to me, and I fear that you won't, I will get you out of here, whether you like it or not.'

'Get me out of here? You can't do that. Who do you think you are? You can't.' He was treating her as though she was *dispensable*, or worse, simply *exportable*.

'Your father used to work with us. It is easy for us to contact him and to tell him to get you out.'

'You wouldn't. How could you? Interfering in my life like I'm a child. I have a job, you understand? I have my family here, my mother, my brothers.' But he was now back into his official role and she suddenly realised just how far she had witnessed him slip out of it.

'Go with your brother to England, or join your father in the

Gulf. I don't care. I'd rather you did it of your own accord; I don't *want* to have to make contact with your father, but you look like you are going to force me to do so.' Iman's glare had no effect on him. The decision had been made and her feelings about it were immaterial. He had no choice. Neither did she.

'I am coming with you.' He held her arm as she started to leave and the words said in a neutral voice, even from him, conveyed a protection that she wanted to hold on to. His arm alone, it felt, could carry her out of the mass of mangled life outside.

'No, you're not.' She had to say it. She didn't want to be left to choose where to go, but she didn't want him to think he could tell her what to do either.

'I am, but it's nothing to do with you. You will follow me back to your house. I have business there and I am late for it, so you will follow me, understand?'

He breathed twice before stepping back into the street. As he did so, the body of a live woman with drowning eyes carried by three men jogged past them. The woman was screaming at her blood-stained hand. Her head and legs were bare, sandals hung off her toes, pale hair fell over an arm. Ziyyad stepped back so quickly that he knocked Iman against the door handles. He tripped awkwardly. His neck was next to her face and some of his sweat dropped on to her.

'What the hell are you doing?' she screamed. His skin was runny with perspiration as he turned to check on her, breathing hard from the bottom to the top of his chest, before he moved off into a smaller alley away from the crowds, walking with huge paces ahead of her. He looked back every minute or so to ensure that she was still with him, but he never let on that he might care whether she was or not.

Chapter 14

It did not look good to Rashid. In fact, to Rashid, the road to the refugee camp where the Centre was based was littered with portents that Khalil was refusing to see.

Khalil kept trying Jamal's phone and Jamal's phone kept telling him that it was unobtainable. Barbed wire in spangled loops lolled around the outskirts of the camp. A man sat on his haunches by the entrance, cleaning out his front teeth with a thumbnail. A truck loaded with valuables (either cement or flour, it was not clear) was attracting a small gathering by the side of the road. Most of the destruction was new. Two buildings, their sides punctured but the concave half bubbles of bullet holes, were still smoking. The alley was empty of people. Unnaturally empty. No rugs hung on the walls waiting to be beaten and no clothes were pegged on to the lines that fanned out from single hooks, slicing the sky up into long triangles. It was just cement, graffiti and the sandy earth.

Rashid walked behind Khalil, close to the wall, avoiding the slow run of liquid through the middle of the street. Wild grasses sprouted around the edges of the puddles. The chemical smell of burnt rubbish came and went. The houses were all the same on this stretch: two rooms, a bathroom and a kitchen. Boxy squares of concrete with roofs of corrugated iron held down with breezeblocks and bricks. Occasionally one had a tiled floor, otherwise it was just sand on the ground and cables and wires strung across the ceiling.

A metal door to a house stood open. The inside walls were

painted in the patterns of the mosques of Granada. Beige rugs, their corners folded with precision, covered mattresses on the floor. The floor tiles had just been mopped. A large engraved copper plate was propped up on foldable wooden legs, Bedouin-style. A girl sitting on a mattress drawing stuck out her tongue at Rashid as he passed.

Rashid started formulating a question about place, belonging and his role in all this as he walked, contemplating whether it was worth asking Khalil and if he would know the answer. He wondered whether he owed it to Khalil's mother to talk to Khalil about leaving, but there would be significant fallout if he did. It would be no less than treacherous, no more than self-interest, as on some levels the idea of having Khalil with him in London was an amazing possibility, on other levels it was the carting of all of *this* over there with him, when London was the opportunity to reinvent himself. Would that be such a bad thing for him to do, to have a break from this for a while, to come back revived? He wondered what Khalil thought. He thought he should drink cocktails before visiting the Centre more often. It took the edge off things.

'Khalil,' Rashid started, but Khalil was calling out to a man walking towards them. The man was not looking up. Khalil called out his name again.

'Ah!' The man finally stopped and smoothed his beard down several times. 'Khalil Helou. Greetings. What brings you here?'

'We're just going to check on the Centre.'

'You don't know?' The man looked awestruck at the ignorance before him.

'Know what?' Khalil asked, hiding the irritation and anxiety that Rashid could nonetheless see. The man's hands expanded outwards from his thumbs. 'Nothing. Nothing. God be with you.'

'And with you,' Khalil replied, although the man had already gone.

'Who's that?' Rashid asked, hoping to find something to discredit the man as a source of alarmist statements.

'You know that boy who comes to the Centre who's a computer whizz? The one who can hack? That's his father.'

'Religious?'

'Who isn't?'

'That's what Iman says.'

They stopped and said nothing more because by then they had seen the Centre and there was nothing else to say.

The destruction ran right up to its doors: graffiti, bullet holes and gutted buildings. The door to the Centre had been blown out into a rubble-filled cavity. A tetchy-looking cat sprinted down the stairs and out of the entrance.

It was worse inside than they could have imagined. The smell was overwhelming. The afternoon heat was invigorating every stinking molecule in the room. It was hard to breathe. A pinboard covered with children's paintings had been removed from the wall and shat upon. Computer screens were smashed; wires had been cut; the drawers of the filing cabinet had been emptied and thrown to the floor. Everything left in the room was sprayed with paint, pissed on, scribbled over. All the documents had gone and the computer disks removed. Khalil examined the backs of the computers.

'They took the hard drives.'

'And Jamal? *Shit*. They must've taken him.' Khalil walked around. 'We have to find out where. That's what I have to do first.'

'We don't know that for sure.' Rashid's chest felt as though it had a thin plastic sheet wrapped around it that was being tightened twist by twist with a tourniquet. 'Why would they take him? He's just a volunteer.'

Khalil kicked against the wall leaving a newer, fainter mark than the others. 'It's my fault. I should've taken the risks more seriously. I know they've taken him. I can feel it. It's my fault.

95

Fuck. And he's getting married.' Khalil crouched down with his back against the wall, his head on his knees. *Fuck.*

Rashid tried to move into his friend's space. Khalil's ponytail was not silly. There was nothing silly about Khalil.

'Come back to our place, Khalil. Talk to Sabri. He'll know what we can do to find out where he is. Don't stay here.'

Khalil looked up from his hands. 'Raed and Jamal in the same day. One killed, the other taken. And the Centre? Three years' work and look at it.'

Something had attracted Khalil's attention; he got up and walked over to the other side of the room where a small line of army graffiti, *'Feeling fucked now?'* was scrawled in red marker pen across the newly painted wall.

Khalil laughed out loud at the communication from the departed forces of destruction that had trashed his Centre. 'See that? *Feeling fucked now?* That's excellent. Ha!'

'How is it excellent?' Rashid's skin was telling him that the army could be waiting to come back and get them too. The skin on his face felt really tight.

'It's excellent. It's *excellent.*' When excited, Khalil's voice had a tendency to squeak slightly. 'If this poxy little Centre really disturbs them that much, it has to be good. It must be worthwhile. It means that what we are doing is annoying them, even if it is just an irritation factor. It's important. It's something. Just to bug them. Get under their skin. This,' he said, tapping at the writing on the wall, 'is a victory.' He stood back and smiled at it again. 'I will put a frame around it.' He glanced up at Rashid. 'You think Sabri can help us to find out where Jamal is?'

He walked around the room as he spoke, moving whiteboards against the walls, straightening chairs. He went into the kitchen and emerged with a broom.

'You want to start clearing up now?' Rashid asked. 'Right now? I thought you were going to find out about Jamal? Don't you think we should leave?' The stink of the place seemed to be coating itself around the sides of Rashid's mouth.

'Sure. Yes. I just wanted to show you that this is all very super-ficial. We can clear it up in no time. See? We did a full backup only last month. Of course it'll be a bit harder getting that data for Lisa, but not a total disaster. And the computers are just money. We'll get the funding, see? Nothing to worry about, minor setback, that's all.'

Khalil was brushing splintered glass into a small heap in the corner of the room, making the broom stop along the edges of a tile so that the lines of grouting delineated the pile of glass. Rashid put his hand around Khalil's back.

'Let's go now. Let's leave it for now. We'll clear this up tomorrow. Iman will come and we'll organise some volunteers. And gloves. We need gloves. You're right, a lot of it is superficial. A bit of paint and it'll be fine. But right now it really stinks.' Rashid coughed.

'I know. I know.' Khalil kicked at a broken CD case on the floor.

'Just leave it for now, OK? Let's go and see Sabri and find out how we can sort things out for Jamal at least.'

Half of Khalil's face was covered with the bent palm of his hand, in a gesture that was partly down to stress, partly to block the smell. The eyes that looked up at Rashid from over the hand expressed more affection than Rashid had felt in a very long time.

Chapter 15

Two pairs of feet stuck out of one of the larger tents in the waste-land around the Mujahed home. The man's feet still had shoes on, shoes that had been transformed into morose moulds of over-stretched leather, and the woman's feet were knubbly and wide. The woman was wearing men's socks with panels of pale leg flesh visible above them. The two pairs of feet were locked around each other's ankles.

Lisa! Rashid ached at the tenderness of the connected feet. *Lisa! Lisa!*

'Watch it.' Khalil pulled Rashid back as he nearly walked into one of the zigzag metal joists that had been left sticking up out of the ground.

The group of fighters were by the gate of Rashid's house. The tall man from the café who Rashid liked to think looked like him, their apparent leader, had managed to overtake the fat fighter with the pocked face and thick moustache who had told most of the jokes. They were approaching the Mujahed building purpose-fully as though they were about to claim ownership of it. *They should take it*, Rashid thought wildly. *I'm leaving. They can have the house, and Mama, and Sabri.*

Rashid was trying to decide whether they should have Iman as well (he could never quite decide whose camp she was in) when Khalil said, 'They've got Iman too.' Rashid looked behind the group and saw her straggling along, following the path of the fight-ers. She was hanging back, trailing a fair way behind them. As they came closer to her, Rashid noticed that she looked abject and spooked. She did not seem to see Khalil and Rashid when they arrived, or at least if she saw them, she did not appear to recognise them at all.

Two fighters moved around the back of the building, another banged on their neighbour Abu Omar's door. On seeing Khalil and Rashid, the leader threw back his arm, *Stay next to the wall!* Rashid did so, briefly, before stepping forwards to see Abu Omar open the door with the look of a man watching his life belongings being washed away in a flood. His shoulders and back fell a little. He didn't ask anything. The large fighter with the moustache pulled Abu Omar out of the doorway. It was completely unnecessary; he would have come out anyway.

Abu Omar turned his head towards the inside of his apartment where a tricycle stood in the corridor and members of his family were visible at the door's edge. He took in his breath and blinked at this group of visitors. On seeing Rashid, he opened his hands to the sky as if to let fly some explanation that he had held captive between them.

'You, Khaled Mustafa Hiya,' the leader read out Abu Omar's full name from the document that had been handed to him, 'are found to have collaborated with the enemy.'

Iman had moved around to stand closer to Khalil and Rashid, and Rashid suddenly felt her clutch at him. He dropped one of the torn bags of vegetables he had picked up for his mother and courgettes rolled on to the ground by his feet. Abu Omar opened his mouth and spoke to the air like a fish out of water. He still wore that morning's pressed trousers but his shirt had gone and his vest was stringy; it could not make the distance over the mound of belly. A sad lip of fat pouted over his belt.

There was a raising of guns and the sound of metal being guided into place. Iman's nails broke through Rashid's skin. The fighter with the heavy moustache was up against Abu Omar, so close that they must have smelt each other's breath. Their leader stepped forwards. 'Not here. Bring him with us.' The other fighter pushed hard into Abu Omar before pulling away so that their captive's hands could be tied up with rope as the indictment was nailed to the doorframe.

The leader turned to his audience. 'Ziyyad Ayyoubi, from the Patriotic Guard,' he was saying, holding out his hand, when the door to Abu Omar's apartment opened and the smallest boy rushed out towards his grandfather. He was met with a row of guns lined up at his head.

'Jiddo!' the boy cried out at the back of the figure who was not turning to face him. 'Jiddo!' Grandpa.

Rashid shoved past Abu Omar and pushed the boy back into his family – they had formed a wall of cheap cloth and soft flesh at the doorway of the apartment – and closed the door on them.

'What has he done?' Rashid asked the leader. 'Mr Ayyoubi, what has he done?'

'More than enough. I am not entitled to say more than that at this stage but we have evidence—'

'Evidence!' Iman spat.

'Evidence that he has played a significant role in attacks on our resistance.' Ziyyad glanced superciliously at Iman. 'Attacks on our resistance and on us.' He looked away now at the tents and up at their apartment above.

'And his family?' Rashid continued. 'What will happen to them?'

'If he was *senior* enough,' Ziyyad said, 'which we believe that he was, then the chances are that they will take the family in.' He nodded in the direction of the border.

'They? You don't mean the Is—' Rashid looked at Ziyyad again and towards the fence. 'Seriously?'

'Again, we would like to stress that we are sorry for the distur-
bance. *Tsharafna*. It was an honour to have met.'

'*Tsharafna*. An honour,' Rashid and Khalil murmured, caught
out by the man's formality.

'And now you must excuse me.' Ziyyad gestured to his men.
He waited for Iman to raise her face so that he could nod in her
direction before he bowed his head and lead his men and their
captive away.

There was no sound behind the door to Abu Omar's flat. Rashid
imagined them still standing behind it in a row as though waiting
to either be photographed or shot, and then behind them, on their
coffee table, he saw the tissues rustling in the breeze from the
overhead fan next to the crystal bowls that held the multi-coloured
sugar almonds for guests.

Chapter 16

It had made up for the rest of Sabri's day to see the fighters finally arrive across the wasteland. Every afternoon for several days now, Sabri had wheeled himself into the living room hoping to witness their approach. *Bureaucracy! Bureaucracy!* Even in these matters of internal security, the Authority was slow. 'Do not underestimate the appearance of the leader, Ziyyad Ayyoubi,' they had told Sabri when he had called the day before to ask why the hell it was taking them so long. 'He's more than he seems.' And there he was, Ziyyad Ayyoubi, son of the martyred intellectuals of the revolution, the hope of the people, tramping over the wasteland behind his men, with what looked like Iman in tow for some reason. *Iman?* The leader did not look up to much. And then from the other direction came Rashid and that Khalil Helou friend of his, as if this was a spectacle they had all paid to come and watch. *Roll up!* thought Sabri, *Roll up for the de-ratting that is about to take place!*

Infuriatingly, they had all disappeared just below him. If he were able to stand he would have been able to see them. He sat and waited for a while, not entirely sure what for, as it was unlikely that the punishment would be meted out right there and then, but he stayed there all the same, by the window. Alert, hearing the murmur of voices, a shout was it? The scream of a boy. Not the boy he hoped, not Wael, not the middle grandson. He stayed waiting, listening, hoping for a gunshot.

Got you! Ha!

The day had gone bad that morning an hour or so after his mother had left his room. The smell of Lana had come back to him again, teasing his nostrils with nostalgia. He had a shirt of hers that he had bundled into a plastic bag at the back of one of his cupboards and he had made a mess searching for it that afternoon. Piles of ironed shirts had cascaded down on him before he found it. The bag was dated now, *Toys for Fun* was advertised on it and that place had shut down years ago. The bag was not closed as tightly as he had remembered. Sabri had wheeled himself a little closer to the wall before he took out the shirt to sniff at it. It smelt of woven cotton and dust. A moth had eaten out two spots on the shirt's front. He had put it back where it had been and looked out at the wispy smoke. He couldn't find her in it. She had gone.

He had felt it happen. It happened often.

The ballast would slide across his decks causing him to list dangerously before he capsized completely and was down.

Goddamn the ghost smell that had been sent to tease him.

Afterwards, the lump of papers sat in the centre of his desk, pathetic. There was no point in it. No point at all. Now he could see that the thesis was flawed. The focus was wrong. All wrong. What he really needed to write about was *us*, not them. Not how *they* screwed *us*, but how *we* let ourselves be screwed by *them*. About how *we* were now about to screw *ourselves*. It was all contemptible and disgusting. No one had the guts, the balls, to admit it, to confess to it, except him. He, Sabri Mujahed, knew the truth. *Our neighbours collaborated with them when they took our country in 1948. Our stinking feudal system allowed for that. Then our Arab brothers assisted (although they say that they countered, no, worse, that they fought against) in the takeover of our lands in 1967 and since then we have missed opportunity after opportunity. Pusillanimous diplomacy. Corrupt leadership. Can't even fight. No discipline. A bunch of men wanting their own piece of the pie, yearning for cheap suits and desks with name plaques. No ability to work together, to fight together, to assist each other. It was one long history of betrayal. They screw us; we betray ourselves.*

Sabri's thoughts had continued along the same murderous trammels until the arrest of Abu Omar, and he was in a considerably better mood when Khalil and Rashid came into the living room than he had been in all day.

Khalil and Rashid hesitated at the door as Sabri was sitting with his amputated leg ends thrust out at them. The younger men wavered as though they had caught him naked. Sabri liked people (even his own family) to see him behind a desk or on the other side of the kitchen table, where he would slide down the sides of the wheelchair so that only his arms were visible and everyone could pretend that the chair was not there and that his legs were. He was getting a bit fat too, this last year, and tables and desks hid the rope of soft flesh around his midriff. Sabri gestured for them to sit down.

Khalil had never been in that room before and Sabri watched him take it in as he hovered around the pea-coloured velvet chairs. None of the large objects in the house held memories for their family. Fragments of personal recollection were attached only to the small things, the ones that could be thrown into suitcases and scurried away with as the family had, like escaping thieves or decamping gypsies, run from invasions, wars, upheavals, the cranking up of political heat, or the increased activities of professional assassins.

The small objects in the room were mainly souvenirs: an engraved wooden plate with the leaning tower of Pisa on it, the cuckoo clock that Iman had spent a summer saving up to buy in Geneva and which was still functioning to a rhythm of its own, and a tin replica of Big Ben together with its own static red bus that had been Rashid's. There were also the embroidered cushions his mother had made, with the pictures of eighteenth-century white-bosomed French women in crinolines. The other furnishings had all belonged to Sabri's aunt, anonymous furniture made in the Far East out of mashed wood and strong glue.

Sabri feigned disinterest as they told him about Abu Omar's arrest and then appeared to only half-listen to the pink-skinned Khalil (*Naaim! Naaim!* Such a soft, soft boy!) who explained, so plaintively, so touchingly about the feared fate of their comrade in arms, Jamal Baseet. Had it been another day, there would have been nothing Sabri would have liked better than to discuss prison with men who had not known it. He had some fond memories of his internment, of the camaraderie of the committees they formed, the lectures they gave. He even liked explaining torture methods to men who cringed. But it was not a day for reminiscing.

'Try what you like,' Sabri said. 'Go get a lawyer if you wish, but they will have put him in preventive detention which means that a lawyer can do nothing.'

'Nothing?' Khalil said, laughing slightly, as though discovering that maybe at the heart of it all Sabri was just another fool.

'Yes, a lawyer can do nothing, because they don't have to show that your friend's done anything. So what can a lawyer do except say, "He did nothing," and maybe the judge will agree and say, "You are right. He did nothing," and then how much further along would anyone be?'

Sabri rolled himself back to the television screen under the framed photographs of the grandfathers, their mother's father smiling triumphantly as he sat outside the family house in Jaffa, their father's father staring furiously at the camera. The television continued to broadcast the image of the overturned pushchair in the Israeli park.

'Still not mentioning the hospital,' Sabri said. 'Shocking.'

'I know,' Khalil replied, unable to keep the impatience completely

105

out of his voice. This offhand way that Sabri addressed him was all because of who his father was, because his father was a sell-out, a profiteer, a Class A prick. Khalil was sure of it. They never let you free of your parents. Even the leftists. No, *especially* the goddamn leftists, with their emphasis on equality of birth – disregarding poverty was one thing, but was one allowed to surmount having a political wanker for a father? No chance. These guys believed political wankery passed from generation to generation unaltered like an extra chromosome. 'Could Jamal have been arrested because of his involvement with the Centre?' Khalil asked with not a little pride.

'That's not the point. It's of little relevance whether or not he's done anything. It's *preventive* detention so they just need to show that he could *one day* do something.' Sabri, it appeared, was bored.

'What about challenging the order on a technicality?'

'The order is valid no matter how low-level the issuing authority. The burden of proof is on your friend Baseet to show that he is innocent.'

'Innocent of what?' asked Khalil.

'Who knows?' Sabri lifted his palms to the ceiling. 'There is the rub. As he doesn't have to be charged with anything, it is very difficult to show that he is innocent because no one knows what it is that he has to be innocent of.' With that Sabri gave a smile that was particularly disagreeable. *Idiot,* Sabri thought looking at Khalil, *setting up a Centre with glossy brochures and business cards and he doesn't even know how preventive detention works. Twit.*

No one spoke for a while as Sabri smirked and Khalil smouldered.

'How is the book going today?' Rashid tried to avoid looking at Sabri, as he didn't want to see the stumps any more than he had to. The way they ended like the knots on sausage meat was disconcerting. He closed the window with a slam as the air was blowing in dust and the smell of manure from a nearby farm.

'Not bad but I was sidetracked. I came across something different.' He looked at Khalil. 'It may be of interest to you, perhaps. Maybe not, but it was a transcript of the conversation between the soldiers when they shot that girl last week by the checkpoint. The one that was leaked to their press somehow.'

'Oh yes?' Khalil said, still trying to digest the concept of preventive detention (he would get a second opinion; he found it hard to believe it was quite that arbitrary) and the loss of Jamal. It annoyed him that his inner desire to ingratiate himself to Sabri had not been dislodged.

'Soldier on guard says that they've identified "someone *on two legs* a hundred metres from the outpost". The other soldier, in the lookout, says, "A girl about ten," but by then they are already shooting. Girl's dead, etcetera, etcetera.' Sabri wheeled around to Rashid who was still standing by the window and looked him up and down.

'I remember that incident,' Rashid said. 'I'm sure I heard about it on the TV or something.'

'The point is this use of code, *on two legs*, denoting human. It reminded me of that speech by their Prime Minister saying that we were beasts *walking on two legs*. I thought I could make something of this. The idea that having legs makes you human. I thought of adding a Primo Levi-ish dimension to it. Merging this two-legged idea with a sort of general question about what is a man, you know, linking in to "if this is a man who labours in the mud/ who knows no peace/ who fights for a crust of bread?" That kind of thing.' He stopped and twisted around to face Rashid before going back to Khalil. 'My thesis being that the Occupation, the closures, the siege have made amputees of all of us, crawling around in the mud. Legless in Gaza. The lot of us.' He forced Rashid to look at him. 'Do you know what I'm talking about?' The boys nodded although Rashid didn't do so with much vigour. 'What do you think?' he asked Khalil after sneering slightly at Rashid.

'Well, it's an interesting idea, *Ammo*. It's an interesting idea.' Khalil's eyes were not focussing on Sabri. He was struggling. 'I mean Levi is—'

'You can pass me the blanket,' Sabri gestured towards a tartan rug on a chair, 'if it makes you feel better.'

The clock whirred and cuckooed twice although it was well past five. No one spoke.

'Oh, could you do something for me?' Sabri said. 'Could you possibly bring up the notice that they pinned on Abu Omar's door? They did pin a notice, didn't they?'

'Of course.'

Khalil and Rashid jumped up as though in front of them a door was sliding shut leaving them only enough space through which to fit their fingers before it closed.

PART II

LONDON VIEWS

Two months later

Chapter 17

From Rashid's window he had a bit of everything: vast poplars bouncing light off their leaves, stained wooden telephone poles, smutty-faced Victorian town houses, grey drainpipes, a squat spire, the tower of a council estate and the rail tracks that spread out over the foreground like entrails.

Rashid turned the toast over in his mouth, giving the jam direct contact with his taste buds. His tongue sought out the sugar lodged in the bread's perforations. He gulped to wash it down.

Lisa's tea was bad. Lisa's tea was gully water.

He had woken some time before her. His sober sleep rarely carried him through until morning as it was, but here the morning came early slicing a chunk out of the night. Lisa had slept pyjama-ed hugging at her boobs sulkily, as though trying to reclaim them from his grasp.

As soon as she had woken, she was up and out, down to the shower room, back to get dressed, then out to the shared kitchen in the corridor and bringing him tea and toast. Englishy things for old ladies with blanket-covered knees. Lisa had been bent on coddling him since the visit to her parents' house and the dream incident that he was trying to forget.

He had tried to pull Lisa back on to the bed for a final fondle before she left but something sharp on her head scratched at the side of his eye, the under-wiring of her bra trapped the tips of his fingers and one of his toenails had snagged the leg of her tights. She had pushed him off, redone her hair (brushed it straight, down, down, down, as though it was part of a military drill, then pulled it through a hair band twice, her fingers straining pink and unsteady as they stretched it wide to pull the hair through, up high and bouncy into a girly ponytail) and she was off. Off in her puffy hip-length coat with the diamond shapes stitched over it. Gone. All strapped up and padded and off to do big things with her little laptop all packed up into its own miniature flak jacket.

Lisa's family's house had been cushioned and soft, with clocks that had tocked, clucked and whirred into buffered surfaces. Her parents' movements were synchronised around the clocks' under-stated commands and seemed to be conducted in complete isolation from the outside world. The heavy wooden front door automatically locked (*click!*) and was then manually latched after Rashid and Lisa had arrived and stayed that way until they left. The doorbell never rang, nor did the phone.

Close to her parents, Lisa had seemed drunk or at least very highly caffeinated. Her conversation was jittery and full of show-offy statements and brash confrontation, which was never followed through but caved into simpering cuddles (with her father) and a chummy snuggling up of shoulders (with her mother in the kitchen).

'Will you be getting changed for lunch?' her mother had asked, as they stood in the corridor seemingly unsure how, or whether, to greet each other. Lisa had chosen to wear one of Rashid's oldest sweatshirts, climbing boots, jeans and a checked black-and-white *keffiyeh* that they had bought together in Gaza.

'No, should I?'

'Of course not, dear. Not if you don't want to. I was just wondering.'

Lisa's mother went back to the kitchen, leaving them with her father, who kept leaning his weight forwards on to his toes as though the pressure could cause him to emit something of impor-tance each time.

'Would you care for a little something? Say a G & T or a sherry, perhaps? Lisa didn't say whether you are, you know . . . unless of course you would like something soft, if you're *observant*, that is?' And at this proposition Lisa's father had braced his hands together at the knuckles and set his mouth in preparation for something truly horrible.

'Oh, no. He drinks anything,' Lisa put in, 'anything.'

Rashid had not spoken and was silently wishing that he was wearing something else, but he only had one pair of smart trousers which were far too light and Lisa had laughed off a jumper Khalil's mother had given him for London ('You can't wear patterns, Rashid, *really*! You look like a computer technician or something') so he had ended up dressed identically to Lisa, but uncomfortable with it. Lisa, however, seemed to be very pleased with how he looked in her parents' house. It was as though she had brought home a particularly gaudy piece of jewellery from a junk shop and could now, against a plain background, appreciate its particular panache. When her parents left the room she leant over him and kissed his mouth with hers in a pout, her eyes open, and with an air of hungry sexiness that he felt she must have copied from a celebrity.

The G & Ts and wine went to Rashid's head. Lisa's father had grunted with satisfaction each time Rashid accepted another glass but the food, which interested Rashid far more than the alcohol, was guarded jealously with a foot-long knife sharpened repeatedly at the table, and a fork shaped like a witch's claw. These implements stood between Rashid and the meat and vegetables in the centre of the table. It was not that the meal had made any effort to entice him; it tasted to Rashid as though it had all been rinsed under the cold tap, but he was hungry and his allocated portion was insufficient. The drink had only stirred up his hunger; it came very far from sating it.

'And what effect will the recent attacks have on your situation?' Lisa's father asked, as though the question had followed on from a detailed debate when it had actually come from nowhere. When Lisa's father spoke, he focussed on a willow tree at the end of the garden and when he listened, he tipped his head to the side like a security guard receiving commands over an earpiece.

'It's a disaster,' Rashid said. 'We were gaining sympathy for what was happening to us. But now no one is interested. They are trying to make out we are the same as those extremists who have nothing to do with us. No one wants to know about what we are going through any more. It's a disaster.'

Lisa's father had carefully removed a line of fat that curled around the pale meat and moved it to the side of his plate with the tip of his knife to where a twin sliver curled around it causing Rashid to think of the word 'spooning' that Lisa had taught him.

'Yes,' her father said, focussing on the rain moving in the hanging branches of the willow outside the French windows. 'I can see that. I can see how that would happen,' and with that Rashid and Lisa's father's contribution to conversation was fulfilled. Talk turned to the regatta, Lisa's sister's habit of driving with the clutch down, the unreliability of the men repairing the central heating, the mouse in the garage and the office affair of the next-door neighbour but one.

'Daddy's changed.' Lisa hugged at Rashid's arm as they crossed the wet lawn after lunch. 'Mummy thinks it's losing the house. It belongs to the estate, you see. When he retires it goes on to the next doctor for the village. It's tragic.' She stopped at a damp bench that stood in front of a row of pruned laurels that had been cut into the shape of a giant sponge. 'You can smoke now,' she said, waiting next to Rashid as though he was a toddler needing to pee.

'I didn't bring cigarettes with me.' Rashid looked back at the house, which seemed to be watching them with every glinting window.

Lisa frowned. 'I was even born here, you know. Daddy delivered us.'

He looked with her across the lawn that was panelled with muted green and whitish shade as the sunlight pushed through the clouds and the trees to hit it in shafts. There was something of the cross-dresser about the house, the sloppy thatch flopped like a lady's hat and the climbing roses were like rouge on its builder's jaw of brick structure.

'I want to show you something,' Lisa said, leading him further down the garden past the weeping willow that trailed over the wet grass and dripped fingers down Rashid's neck.

Behind the willow, propped up on bricks at the back, stood a painted gypsy caravan backed by a row of conifers. The caravan was more spacious inside than he expected, with the cosy feel of an underground bunker. The secrets of teenaged girls were tucked everywhere: under the cushions and in doll-sized drawers. The smell of damp wood took him back to a time when his family had been in Scandinavia and he had been happy. A stove sat rotund and blackened on the floor.

'Are you sure it's safe?' Rashid asked more than once as Lisa leant forwards to light it, poking around with a skewer, her straight hair wrapped with the *keffiyeh* so that it bulged about her head into a round-bottomed 'W' shape. She passed him a packet of cigarettes, her sister's, and they watched the crackles coming off the fire while he smoked. He tried to do better things with her, but found himself snuggled into the warmth of his own sweatshirt, now filled with Lisa and, once there, he was pushed into a deep sleep by the alcohol, a boot nudged him into a trench backwards and he was gone.

But even there, in the peeling wooden caravan in Lisa's garden, it had found him. It had winged its way across land and sea, stretched wide, bat-like, its nose conical and tipped, its approach low and precise. It had found its way up into him, up the leg of his jeans, over the skin of his chest and had made its strike in the centre of his brain. After the thud, the windows had burst in first and had shattered into frisbees of glass that shot through the room. He could see Iman and his mother fall to the floor, Sabri trying to throw himself from his wheelchair as the glass crashed at the walls, and the room was overwhelmed by a raid of flames.

His body jolted, calling for his sister, 'Iman!' and his arm hit Lisa in the face. He woke streaming, coughing and crying on the edge of the seat, Lisa holding him tight, as though that would prevent him from falling off the bench too.

It had taken him a while to remember what the caravan was.

How dried-up English toast was. How calcified. It was like sliding a slab of compressed insect carcasses into his mouth. Rashid opened the window and dropped the crusts down to the ledge below.

Ian knocked lightly on Rashid's door and ignoring the half-hearted nature of Rashid's encouragement for him to enter, slid in anyway, his hoodie slopping around his collarbones, his jeans threatening to give up on his hips and make their descent to the floor alone.

'Got a skin, Rash?' Ian spread himself – a long jumble of elbows, knees, legs and trunk of dirtied fabrics – on to the tussle of Rashid's sheets. The band of his greying underpants (always the same pair, the writing on the wide elastic around the top never changed) rested against the part of the bed where Lisa had lain the night before; Rashid could still see the white of Lisa's inner thigh where he had held it, just *there* where Ian now sat.

Ian had first cornered Rashid after a development policy lecture and given him the full lowdown. The lowdown as to where it was at and how it was not going to matter, Palestine that was, because you had to get it into *context*, and the starting point was the dysfunctionality of British politics. Ian told Rashid about the erosion of national morality, the corruption of the West, the number of right-wing Labour MPs masquerading as left-wingers, the demise of the Communist Party, the integrity of the Revolutionary Workers Party, the short-sightedness of the environmental agenda, the limitations of the current select committees and the number of Labour ministers with children in private schools. Rashid had been given a whole load of it and there was a lot more where it came from.

'She's gone then, your Lisa? Yeah?' Ian had already burnt the nail of his forefinger orange with his lighter in the process of trying to soften the miniscule amounts of hash he carried around with him. 'Quite a job she's got.' Rashid peered down at a couple of sparrows wrangling over a crust on a lower ledge as Ian continued. 'I mean, I am not sure that I would work for them. There are some real bureaucrat types in that organisation and they're really never going to rock the boat on anything, but it's still got great exposure, contacts, you know.'

Rashid wondered how Ian's ankles (a corpse's ankles, the pallor of them with their dark hairs was just unnatural) coped with the heftiness of his shoes that badly attached swung on them like weights. He also did not understand how it was that Ian's tiny bits of hash did not disappear under one of his orangey fingernails and just get lost down there, with the rest of the decade's debris, for ever.

In an adept one-handed movement Ian sprung up and covered the smoke detector with a piece of cling film and wrenched forward the aluminium frame of the window with the other so that it cut through the room on a horizontal plane. Only then did he light up.

'Quite fit though.' His grin was approving. 'Your Lisa. She's quite fit, isn't she?' Rashid did not understand what Lisa's health had to do with Ian. 'Want some?' Ian squeaked at Rashid, keeping his lungs full and going slightly pink, as though he was being gassed. The more difficult the process was, the more Ian enjoyed it. He loved to show off his prowess at surmounting the legal,

117

practical and physical obstacles standing between him and the art of dope smoking.

'No, it's all right, thanks. I need to check a couple of things before I go.' Rashid nodded at his computer.

'Go for it. No worries.' Ian exhaled greyness into the bright air outside and the outside air buzzed traffic back into the room in return.

Sabri. Sabri. Rashid clicked on the message and scrolled down. It was the longest message he had ever received from his brother.

Ian was still talking. 'So what you were saying last night about Tripoli? During the war in Lebanon, you were saying that you think that, had the other faction won, that Palestinian leadership would have been different? Do you really believe that? Because I think you can't just consider bad leadership in a vacuum,' Ian said, fluent now he had been fuelled.

No time to read the message now. Rashid printed it out, folded it over and stuck it in his jacket pocket. He sifted through the papers on his desk, creating a small pile, the proposed thesis at the bottom, a couple of books on top.

'No?'

'Of course you can't.' Ian's eyes glistened with bloodshot pleasure. He was exactly where he wanted to be, pontificating with a joint. 'You can't just say, "This micromanaging dictator came up and wrecked everything for us, destroyed our struggle." You have to say, "Right, so how did this guy do it? How did we let him?" Take responsibility, brother. There must have been some kind of . . . of culture (in the non-static sense of the term, you understand), that promoted him. He didn't come from Mars or Blackpool, say. He was one of yours, man.'

The stoned grin was something that Rashid greatly enjoyed having himself but hated intensely in others. He particularly disliked Ian's version of it. When faced with political questions of the type Ian particularly liked to concoct, Rashid never knew where to start. Did he start with revolutionary movements in general or the assassination policy aimed at their moderate politicians, writers and thinkers more specifically? He could also, he supposed, defend the Outside Leadership's successes and its democratic nature during its heyday. Victim or propagandist, take your pick; Ian always forced him into one role or the other.

'Anyway, I thought your brother and your dad were in the mainstream party, the Leader's party. So what did they see in the guy?'

Rashid started, stopped, and then threw his hand in the air as though signalling to an invisible attendant to take it (whatever it was) away. The day was heating up; a low urban glaze had overtaken the dawn's harsh side lighting. No. Fuck it. He was not going to do it now. He was off duty.

'I've got to go, Ian. Got an appointment with my supervisor.'

'Oh, OK, sure. Love the way you said my name just then, IYUN. Like a Rasta.' Ian urged the glowing cherry to fall off the end of the joint before putting out the edges against the side of the bin and placing its bent, stunted body back into his matchbox. 'Any chance you could pick up an eighth for me later? Your guy's stuff is much better than mine.'

Rashid's bag was ready, but he was trying to remember what he had forgotten. He had not really planned to go back there. He had made a deal with himself. No Moroccan snooker bar. No dope. There was no Gaza any more. He was out and therefore there was no need now, was there?

'Yes, OK, but not tonight, I'm going out. But when I next go there, yes, OK. Tomorrow or something.'

'Cheers. Catch you later, all right?' Ian almost sung out at Rashid as he ambled down the corridor on his gangling big-footed legs.

Chapter 18

Rashid found two empty spaces next to each other at the end of the tube carriage. Opposite him, a hunched woman in flip-flops sat alone. Her pink T-shirt stopped well above her knees. Her legs were strange, knotted together like ropes of rind. Rashid took out Sabri's email. The woman tested the air twice with her nose as though trying to detect prey and looked up and down the carriage.

Rashid looked at what she was looking at. It had to be the otherness of the passengers that was disturbing her. Their darkness, for they all were, without exception, washed up there like him. *I could be from here*, he thought, *in the same way that they are not from here*. But what of their national duties? What of his? Pulling him out of any comfort zone presented to him, pushing him out into a conflicted world where he had no place. And here was Sabri's message to remind him that he could never relax, never be part of anything or anywhere unless it was part of a push for change, for resolution. But such a long message from Sabri, even on that subject was rare and curious.

Brother Rashid,

It was good to hear your news. I trust you are studying hard and doing well and that you found my comments on the 1948 expulsion policy to be of benefit to your essay. You are indeed honoured to be able to conduct your research under Professor Myres. I would have greatly enjoyed having the pleasure of meeting him myself, having perused so many of his books and articles, and I am confident that he would be interested in the findings of my own research.

I appreciate receiving the articles and the links for the information on the village evacuations and massacres of 1948 that Prof Myres passed on to you. As you are aware, these will enhance my research on the subject. I think it is only a matter of time before more of these violations come to the fore and our cousins across the border will be forced to acknowledge their history and relations with us and we will be able to move ahead. They cannot continue to pretend that we were nomads from outside who rushed in to feed off the growing Jewish state. It is preposterous and has no basis in fact. This should become clearer with time and accurate research, making the future of our two peoples possible.

With the arrival of the New Year and the opening of old records, there is some additional research I shall want you to conduct on my behalf. You will find this research to be of great interest and importance, not just to my book but also in terms of adding to your understanding of our history as a people as well *as our own particular history as a family.* Your Mama and I are in agreement that the time has come for there to be greater knowledge of our own circumstances and the roots of the divide.

Rashid read this paragraph several times over. Italics and underlining were used sparsely by Sabri, who had once described them as vulgar. They now screamed out of the page as though they were in capitals. These lines were about as clear to him as some of the political communiqués his brother put before him to test him with ('Can you see why the authors of this one here say *People's Committees* not *Popular Committees*, Rashid? Can you get that at least?'). When Rashid looked up he realised that he had missed his stop and had to wait for another train to take him back in the opposite direction.

121

We have been very busy and have not had the opportunity to explain the situation at home. Mama and I are well, but things in the house have changed.

Abu Omar's family left only a few days after you and Iman. It became apparent that Abu Omar was fairly high up in the ranks, if collaborators can be considered to have ranks, and must have provided some extremely useful information to the enemy about very important resistance leaders on our side . . .

Why had Sabri underlined this? Was Sabri hinting that these were leaders that they knew? He didn't know any leaders. The man who looked like him, Ziyyad Ayyoubi, the man who had arrested Abu Omar, was a leader; could he have been targeted by Abu Omar in the past? Was Abu Omar's arrest connected to that, was it a revenge arrest? The obliqueness was annoying as hell and just so typical of Sabri.

. . . because his family were taken out of Gaza to a camp in Israel for the families of people of his 'stature'. We have been given to understand (his wife, Umm Omar, told Mama) that he has been working in the service of our enemies for over fifteen years. You know how these things start. First they asked him for petty information about student elections in exchange for a permit that was required for him to take his mother to a Jerusalem hospital. Apparently, or so the man claims, Abu Omar's brother in the States urged him to provide the information to our enemies for the sake of his mother. Of course, once he had provided this information there was no way back. The man chose his family over his people and for that he is now paying the price.

Before she left, Umm Omar paid us a visit and gave Mama the key for their apartment (they have no other relatives in Gaza, you understand), asking her to look after it and saying that we should

122

live in it while they were away. I always thought Umm Omar had a good heart, God only knows what life lies ahead of her and her family. They should not be cursed for the sins of Abu Omar, but of course it seems unlikely that they will ever be able to escape them. Needless to say, Umm Omar's family have benefitted considerably and materially for years, which should be a factor we bear in mind before we displace too much pity in their direction.

Mama and I decided that it would be best to move downstairs and have brought all of our belongings with us. Mama is, of course, far more excited than she will allow anyone to see. She has dug up half that ring of soil around the tiles already and planted tomatoes, thyme, potatoes and mint.

I say that Abu Omar's family left, but one of them chose not to. The middle grandson, Wael, apparently refused to leave and says that this is his place and he will not set foot on enemy territory. We have therefore decided to take the boy under our wing and to treat him as one of the family.

Wasn't Wael that lanky teenager with the large nostrils and the bum fluff for a moustache, the one with the greenish skin around his mouth? Was Sabri telling him that they had decided to adopt that devious little shit? No, worse, that that devious little shit was so noble as to choose country over both self and family?

In the circumstances, we couldn't just leave our flat empty upstairs. Mama and I decided it best to arrange a rota for our neighbours who are still in tents to get a roof over their heads. We can't house all of them so we have arranged for stays in two-week shifts per family per room and have formed a small residents' committee to supervise this. It's working fine at the moment. I just hope that as the weather gets colder, tempers don't rise when we have to ask people to leave at the end of their two-week sojourn.

Politically, you will have seen the news, it's not as bad as it has been, but the signs are not good.

Wishing you the best, Rashid. I trust that this year will help you in your quest to find your own role in our struggle for justice and understanding in the world.

Your brother,

Sabri Jibril Mujahed

Chapter 19

When Professor Myres opened a book he would automatically open his mouth at the same time. His tongue would widen across the base of his mouth, loll out, and then the tip would touch his upper lip as he found the point he was looking for.

'Yes, yes that's it. That's the one.'

Myres soothed the book, verbally patting it for its loyal delivery of information. The apartment smelt of wet dog. The coffee was wet dog. Rashid's essays came back after supervision as though they had been rolled upon by wet dog. Rashid drew himself closer to the geraniums. Their dried-out odour reminded him of a relative's courtyard he'd been in as a child – Amman or Damascus, perhaps? Or that aunt in Alexandria?

'Yes, yes, these accounts, you see, show how some of these early Jewish immigrants to Palestine were absolutely shocked. There they were, just escaped from the jaws of hell in Nazi Germany or elsewhere in Europe. They've arrived in Palestine, this Holy Sacred Land, this place of new beginnings, where they soon find themselves witnessing the same tactics being used by their people against the Arabs – the Palestinians – as had been used against them. Just three years. It's nothing in an adult's life. Some of them left Germany as late as 1945 and by 1948 they are being asked to join people – their fellow Jews – who are blindfolding men, bundling them into trucks and dumping them across borders. These accounts are important. There aren't many of them, but they are the ones that interest me, not the ones where the Jews complain about their own treatment by the British, but the ones where they consider how they are treating the 'Other' the Arabs. Many of them chose not to see them at all. They still don't.'

Professor Myres' mouth widened again, the tongue drawn back waiting for its next find. Unsuccessful, it fell back into place on the floor of his mouth. Eyebrows raised, Myres looked over at Rashid. 'Not pretty, discrimination, bad treatment. Always makes people rather vicious, doesn't it? Vicious and ugly. That old adage about the repressed of yesterday and what not.'

Rashid thought of the accounts of their Authority using Israeli torture methods against their own people. 'It's made us ugly, too.' Rashid conceded national flaws easily to Professor Myres. He would not have done so with Ian.

'Ah, yes. Ah, yes, but everything can be changed, everything. Nothing ugly about you, at any rate. Fine-looking young man. Shall I make us some coffee?' Myres marked the book with a strip of paper covered in intricate pencilled script. The book joined the others on the pile prepared for Rashid, forming a rustling cascade of scrawly paper tongues.

'You've always worked on Palestine?' Rashid asked. He wondered what he would have done if Palestine had played no part in his life. Film, he thought, or music. The only time he had heard the word 'talent' being used in connection with him was when he had had piano lessons. He had been about twelve. That was in Beirut and then they had moved to Paris, and couldn't start them again because Paris was only 'temporary' (everywhere was temporary but Paris, for some reason, had been known to be temporary from the day they arrived; for the next two years, they had only unpacked two boxes to show quite how fleeting it all was). They had just decided to unpack the rest of them when one of their representatives was shot and Baba was asked to replace him. This, of course, led to another move and the piano lessons had not been as important as anything else that was going on, and by then he hadn't had any for at least two years so what was the urgency?

'Always Palestine,' Myres said with a sigh. 'I do often think, though, that I could have done it differently.' He was speaking from the kitchen and Rashid stood by the narrow door to hear him.

'Oh really?' Rashid said, as Myres seemed to have lost the thread of his speech together with the coffee lid that had slipped off the sideboard and on to the floor. Myres looked down at it, bereft, as though it was stranded at the bottom of a deep pool. Rashid dipped down to pick it up and pass it back to Myres. The professor did not acknowledge the gesture and went back to stooping over the kettle, concentrating on getting the tremulous fairtrade coffee granules to make it into the two half-clean mugs with brown oval motifs.

Myres' tongue touched base on his lip. 'Take the Kurds,' he said to his raised teaspoon.

'The Kurds?' asked Rashid, who had by now also lost where Myres had been going.

'As an example. I do ask myself, why did I choose one group of destitute and abandoned people rather than another?' Rashid did not feel like being thought of as either destitute or abandoned but did not say so. 'It would have been quite different had I chosen the Kurds.'

'Why did you choose us, then?'

'Well, that's just it, you see. I have gone through this with myself again and again and I feel that, well, at the end of the day, when all is said and done, I just *did not have a choice*. It's a funny thing this idea of decisions being made for you, of how one becomes involved in an intractable dilemma you can't find a way out of. It doesn't happen often. I know people say they met this or that woman and they knew she was their destiny. Not that that happened to me, mind. Fine woman that I married, but it was not that feeling. No, no. Not at all, but with Palestine it was like that.'

Rashid wondered whether Lisa was his destiny. When he had first seen her come into the Centre in Gaza he had felt so desperate for her he could hardly stand up. Then there had been her response to him. All that bright-eyed enthusiasm that flooded back at him despite the errors in his speech, the gaps in his knowledge (both of which could sometimes feel overwhelming around her). It was as though she saw a place and a purpose in him that no one else did. But it was not quite the same thing as Destiny. ('Don't say *ass*,' she had said to him the night before – right in the middle of everything, 'It's so *American*.')

Myres passed him a cup; it was not particularly hot and the milk had formed small oil bubbles on the top of the brown liquid.

'My brother told me that you were in Palestine during the war,' Rashid started.

'Oh yes, I was there. As a terribly young man, posted there as a junior police officer. Not much choice about things like that then. Came from a big family. Too many boys. The first went to university; the second to the clergy; the third to teach; the fourth to the services, and then it was me and I was packed off to the colonies. Just missed the war, you see. Too young. Lost two of my brothers, though. I was still in my teens when I got to Palestine. Seventeen. Apish, foolish kind of a boy. I spent most of my time moping around wishing I had a girlfriend.'

Again, Rashid thought of Lisa. He could never call her his girlfriend in front of her, or to anyone who might know her, in case it got back to her. But what was she other than his girlfriend? They slept together, didn't they? But when he had said that he loved her, she had looked two things neither of which were good: one had been *indulgent* and the other had been *put off*. She had looked put off. It was the only way that he could explain it.

'But, you know, it got to the point where even I, clueless as I was, could not help noticing that things were getting really rather nasty. It just was not fair play.' Myres appeared to be addressing an invisible commission of enquiry. 'The sugar's over here if that's what you are looking for.'

'What kind of things?' Rashid asked. He tried to find in Myres' face the features of the past, tried to make out whether Myres' nose would have been distinguished or goofy, but it can be as hard with some old people, as it is with some babies, to tell what or where a face has come from, and where it will be going. Clearly, the man had always been stupendously tall, even now with his stooped stature he was a head taller than Rashid.

'In my capacity as a member of the Mandate Police, we were required to go round the Arab villages on weapons searches. This was 1947 and tensions were high. Our orders were to go into the villages and search these *fellahin* peasants in their houses, often at dawn, waking the women, slashing through the mattresses, pouring the olive oil on to the floor, sifting through flour. For what? Occasionally we would find a bullet. Once in a blue moon we might turn out a pistol of some sort, even then it was often Ottoman and antiquated. And when we did find something – well then, it was out with the men, marched down to the police station, handcuffed and the rest of it. Women crying, usually.'

Professor Myres had not sat down since Rashid arrived. He did now, on a high three-legged stool.

'We hung a man once. I was there. We found a rusty German revolver under a ledge in his well and a round of bullets. He told us that he'd sold half his livestock to purchase it. Hung him for that. All justified under the Emergency Laws of His Majesty's Government in Palestine, the same laws that are now being used for closures, house-sealings, curfews, demolitions and the rest of it. All British, those laws.'

Myres raised his hands in a gesture of what? Rashid wondered, admission? Responsibility? Guilt?

'Strung him up in the village like a sheep. Big, portly man. He was not the *mukhtar*, the leader, but he was not far off. Huge moustache and a cigarette filter. Could not get that out of my mind for some reason, that filter. Very dignified chap. The whole way through he was an absolute gentleman. Shameful. I think it was that cigarette filter that sealed my fate. But it would not have mattered so much,' Myres continued, 'I think it would not have changed everything for me – I am sure I would have found a way to justify it to myself, as the necessities of Empire etcetera – if it weren't for this disparity of treatment, which annoyed me even then, wet boy that I was. You see, the Jewish immigrants were being trained by us, armed by us, when we were shooting Arabs for hiding a couple of rusty bullets. And then the Jews decided that we weren't doing enough so they started attacking us, too. Well, of course, you know the rest of the story. By 1948 it was a total walkover for them. The Jewish settlers were – what did one observer say? – cock-a-hoop? No fight needed at all.'

Myres pushed the window open. A small pocket of autumn air challenged wet dog until it was absorbed by it too.

'Disgraceful conduct on our part. A disgrace, really and truly.'

'And the Kurds?' Rashid asked.

'Oh, I don't know anything much about the Kurds. It just would have been a lot easier. Could have been the Armenians. Why not, indeed? Damn shoddy history all of them. I just know it would have all been different: the ability to get published, to get and keep university tenure, to get heard, not to have this hate mail, not to . . .' Myres looked around his somewhat mouldy-looking purpose-built property, gestured vaguely. 'Well, they would have given me my own office at the university, for example. Instead I am *persona non grata*, relegated to the backwaters of the Thames. All would have been different I can tell you, if I had not chosen the Palestinians or Palestine had not chosen me.'

Myres seemed glad it was out. It steadied his resolve. He wandered back into the sitting room, stately, expecting to be followed even in his humble premises, *especially* to be followed in his humble premises.

'Now, young man, what do you have for me on this fine morning? What have we here?' His pencil ran smoothly down the edge of the page of Rashid's draft thesis, his tongue curled up at the ready. 'Ah, yes, good. Good. I am glad you picked up on that point, I thought you would.'

Sabri, Sabri, Rashid was starting to think again, *You so should be here instead of me*, when he noticed some markings at the side of his essay. Next to the paragraph Rashid had taken straight from an email from Sabri on the topic were two question marks and a large cross and below, clearly marked, next to the paragraph he, Rashid, had typed out without looking at any other source, as an articulation of ideas that rippled away at the back of his mind, was a large tick and a word before an exclamation mark. Rashid leant closer to this man with his smell of old waxy things and cloth left in damp drawers for too long, he leant through the mist of wet dog to make out the word. A solitary, magnificent word scribbled out by an accomplished hand:

'*Excellent!*'

It was unmistakable.

Chapter 20

Rashid had been driven through the area the restaurant was in on the first night he arrived in London. It had been a similar evening, post-rain clear, the gleaming black pavements pattering with feet. There had been hurry in the air as the street dressed itself up for the evening. And he liked the way that each building on the High Street had a different height, face, origin, but they sat alongside each other amicably, like members of a Cuban jazz band. The lights had been on already, many neon but others were strung from trees to the buildings across the road. Some of the windows were slatted with white wood and jutted out from the bottoms of the buildings like birdcages. Chairs and tables had been arranged in squares and rectangles under striped canopies.

On that first night, the street had been rich with promises for his future in London. These were bars and cafés that were waiting for him. They were places where Rashid would be known. There would be a cheer from the tables as he entered. His friends would pull him into discussions, jokes would be told, and they might even cajole him into playing instruments that he would discover an untapped talent for. He would be known. He would be loved. He would be free.

Lisa did not understand what he saw in these places. She had pointed out the number of chains, laughed at the prospect of going to a couple of restaurants he had named ('I don't think you can afford that place, Rashid'), and described the rest as 'passé', 'singles joint', 'gay'. With a little time he had learnt to view the street and ultimately the rest of London in the same way that she did.

The sign for the restaurant Lisa had chosen was lit by bulbs in copper cups. In the window a carpet hung like a curtain and a clay pot sprouted gnarled twigs. Lisa was already there by the door, twisting her tube pass in her teeth. 'You look beautiful,' Rashid said, leaning over to kiss her. She winced. He wondered whether he had let the street Arab inside him (a horny vagabond hiding right there under his skin) slip out again. This beastly doppelgänger seemed to be making his appearance more and more frequently around Lisa. He was unable to get him under control. Rashid wanted to pull her towards him or to say something to lift her agitation, but he didn't trust himself to speak. He didn't know how it might sound. Perhaps there was a way of kissing her that would soften her, or maybe she would hate that, too. He felt taken over with *Hey, pretty girl, come look at my carpets. I give you nice price* and it made him unable to act.

'My sister's coming,' she said, the rim of her plastic tube pass still in her bite. Rashid resolved not to say anything. Whatever he said on the subject of Lisa's family was invariably wrong. When in doubt, Sabri had taught him, one should gather information. Sabri had been referring to guerrilla warfare at the time, but Rashid chose to adopt this tactic now.

'Why's she coming? I thought you didn't get along that well?' He couldn't help it, it come out despite his promise to himself.

'We don't. She's only coming because Charlie's coming, and Charlie and Anna were at university together. I asked her to introduce me to him. But she won't fit in with everyone else. At all. She just won't fit and I told her that and she got all arsey.'

'Who's Charlie?'

'Rashid, for God's sake. I told you: Charles Denham, the contact at the Foreign Office. That's what this whole thing's for. He's just been moved to the Middle East desk. I told you all about him. It's really important that you get through to him about what's going on. He needs to know about Gaza. About the Centre.'

'Sure, sure, Charlie, fine.' Rashid did remember discussing the man. He had a clear image of him already – Charles Denham wore a bowler hat and had a pipe that he tapped on with his little finger. Rashid had not made the connection with a university-going Charlie.

The concert tickets in Rashid's pocket were tickling him. He shuffled around. A couple in suits stopped to examine the menu in the brass box close to Lisa's head. The woman rubbed her hand against the man's hip, as though she was trying to ignite it. They were black (*Afro-Caribbean, Rashid,* he could hearing Lisa stressing, *not black*). Lisa smiled at them consolingly. Rashid stubbed his cigarette out in a pot holding a tree modelled on a lollypop. The couple walked on. Rashid, deciding that an appropriate length of silence had passed, pulled the concert tickets out and flashed them in front of Lisa.

'What's that?'

'Saturday, the Albert Hall, the man himself: Eric Clapton. Two tickets.'

'Rashid! They must have been so expensive. How can you afford them? You should have told me. Or asked. I can't even do Saturday. I've got this charity dinner I might have to go to.'

He had not thought that she wouldn't be able to make it. He had anticipated the scene of handing over the tickets as being one of delight (there would be a hug, a long kiss), that she would only question him about how he had managed to get them as that was a tale in itself. It hadn't been easy and now she didn't even seem sure as to why she couldn't make it.

'No, I'm certain that I can't,' she said, handing the tickets back. 'You should've asked before you bought them. All that money,

Rashid. You probably can't even get a refund.' Her voice was cross but when she looked up at him she made herself look sweet, her brows frowning up above her nose. 'Sorry,' she said, moving a bit closer.

A significant presence was approaching from around the corner, clattering towards them in high heels. Lisa stepped back from Rashid and dropped his hand at the appearance of her sister's tightly suited body.

'It's Anna. Look, I think it's best if no one knows about *us*, that we're, you know, together. OK, just for this dinner?'

He was not going to take Ian to the concert; he would rather go on his own and waste the money. Khalil would have loved it, but he was not coming over for ages. There was no one else.

'Anna, Rashid,' Rashid shook hands with a neater, slimmer version of Lisa: plucked brows, tiny static pearl earrings, a cleanly cut fringe. She had the kind of look that would be used to advertise a telephone company or a law firm.

'Ya, hi! Rashid? *Rasheed*? Is that right? Great. You're umm . . . a *friend* of Lisa's, right? You went down to see the parents, didn't you? I heard all about that. *All about it*. I can't remember, where is it that you're from?'

That question again; a box requiring a simple tick when he really needed to write an essay.

'Gaza?' Rashid raised his eyebrows at the anticipated incomprehensibility of his answer.

'Sure, sure. God! The places Lisa gets to! Hey, sis, you all right?' The two women bobbed their heads a bit at each other, but did not in any way touch.

'You like it over here then, Rashid? I got it right, didn't I? *Rasheed*, ya? Who else is coming, Lisa? Apart from Charlie, that is?'

'Just us and Charlie. Then Ali. He's Kurdish. And Steffi who's just started an internship with us,' Lisa said.

'Steffi?'

'Short for Stefanie, Anna.'

'O-K. Well, why don't we go in, sit down, get a drink? I've had such a day. The tube! I just . . . the City sometimes – it's just *too much* and my boss . . . you know, Lisa, I told you about my old boss?'

They were moving towards the door. Rashid heard bits and pieces of the conversation: '. . . boob job that got infected, anyway so she's gone, so now I have this complete neat freak anal guy. Gay, I'm sure of it. Won't get off my back. It's just a nightmare. *Nightmare.*'

'He's anal because he's gay?'

Lisa was pointing at the chairs, Rashid next to Anna, Lisa down at the other end.

'Of course not. Oh, Lisa give it a break, will you? *Yuhooo!* Charlie, we're over here.'

A man in a casual shirt moved towards them. Rashid found himself looking beyond this youngish orangey-faced man for the man in the bowler hat he had anticipated. Expensive schooling seemed to have set the man's face in a way that had prepared for any eventuality. Breeding had also genetically disposed him to being able to rise above his freckles. He gave Rashid a solid hand-shake and awaited Lisa's directions before taking the seat opposite Rashid, placing the napkin to the side of his plate and moving the cutlery slightly to make a space for his hands.

'Did you find the place OK?' Lisa asked with such concern and politeness, with such *propriety*, that Rashid's mind steamed up with images of her pink nipples and her pubic hair spread out before him.

Ali was the kind who looked to Rashid like a common pick-pocket. When he arrived he went straight to Lisa and rested his hand on her waist when he kissed her cheeks. Three times.

Kurdish or not, at the end of the day the man was a Turk and everyone knew those Turks would sleep with the devil to get a bit of international acceptability. You just had to look at the way he held Charles' hand between two of his, as though he had just been reunited with his long lost exiled leader, to know that. And the way he had nodded at Rashid, as though Rashid had just made an adequate job of cleaning his car. Ali moved towards the chair next to Lisa.

'I can sit somewhere else if you two would like to sit next to each other,' Anna offered to Ali and Rashid. 'I don't mind.'

'No!' Ali, Lisa and Rashid all spoke at the same time. 'It's fine as it is,' Lisa added.

'Of course, boy-girl-boy-girl and all that,' Anna said smiling over at Charles with the complicity of parents at a children's birthday party.

Rashid had finished off his second beer by the time Steffi arrived. She had run to the restaurant and as a result smelt neglected. Sweat formed small blisters on her nose and moistened the hair of her upper lip.

Hardly anyone spoke. It was as though they all stood on a muddy field in their best clothes with a ball before them. No one was willing to take the first kick. Then Ali started describing his escape from Turkey. 'All my documents were in a plastic bag in my mouth, like this,' his lips straightened out, his nostrils flared, 'and I swim and I swim.'

'Swam,' said Lisa.

'I swim, swam. I nearly died. I cannot swam so well. Then this ship found me and take me to Italy.'

He had Lisa's attention and she kept looking over at Charles to make sure that he had some of his too, but Anna remained restless next to Rashid and seemed keen to knock some self-interest into the gathering.

'*Ghastly*,' Anna offered to Ali when he ended his account (which included several appearances before the Immigration Appeals Board, the last of which, held the day before, had been successful). '*Ghastly*,' she said in the same tone as she pronounced, '*Fabulous*,' to the waiter when he read back the order to them.

Charles took the opportunity to examine Rashid. He was not how Charles had expected him to be, he was more like a type he was familiar with from school that Charles was wary of, those bike-shed-smoker types. The more they had, the more disdain they possessed for everything and they always took the effect they had on women for granted. He could see now the flutter this man was having on Anna and obviously on Lisa, too. It was not just the man's height; it was also the straight nose, perfectly Greek, thick eyebrows, and that air of boredom. Charles never had and never would have anything like it. He had known that since prep school. It had become easier since university when women became a bit more discerning. They seemed to want to be treated better for one thing. But men like Rashid could still make him feel as though there was a stage of life that he had completely missed out on, a stage Charles, for some reason, always associated with the idea of Moon Parties in Goa.

Charles decided however that Rashid's manner of dealing with food was not really to type. Rashid had arranged hummus, taramasalata and all the various other bits and pieces in neat blobs around the edge of his plate. He had then diced a raw chilli (he had sent the red pepper back to the kitchen and offered to speak to the chef before they managed to bring out the right chilli, one of those scrawny little red ones) into very, very fine cubes before squeezing lemon (also requested from the kitchen to be cut into quarters) onto the meat. Each piece of meat had been wrapped in bread and dipped into the chilli and the pastes. He had also, and Charles was not sure whether he had meant well by doing so or not, mixed diced chilli and lemon juice in a saucer that he had placed in the centre of the table for everyone else to use. Charles had tried some but the stuff had been inhaled into his windpipe; his eyes had stung, and he had had to blow his nose several times before he was able to speak again.

'So how is the situation in Gaza nowadays?' Charles had, what Rashid thought was a doctor's tone, a sort of *How many cigarettes are you smoking a day then?* concern. Lisa flashed Rashid a look that made him straighten himself up and push his beer away. It didn't really agree with him. The table seemed to be waiting now as though the question was a whistle blowing on the field. Rashid responded, drawing on Khalil and Sabri's most recent emails, some blogs he had been following from the south, and the latest news broadcast that he had seen. Charles nodded gravely, as though it was all as he thought it should be.

Charles dropped in the name of a person in Gaza that he wanted Rashid's opinion on, someone that the Foreign Office had identified as a possible partner in a new peace-building initiative. Rashid laughed. He could not help it.

'Him? Well yes, I mean, he speaks good English but I guess you could say that he's not very highly regarded.'

'And why would that be?'

'Well, as an example, I went to one of his parties. It was right in the middle of this phase when they were pounding the hell out of the south. There were tens of thousands of people living in make-shift tents because of the number of houses that had been bulldozed. And he holds this party. And it was not just any party. People were calling us and telling us we just had to go and see to believe it. I went with my friend, Khalil.'

'Khalil Helou?'

'Yes, that's right. You know Khalil?' Rashid's eyes became bright at the prospect that Charles might through some far-fetched possibility know his friend.

'No, just the name,' Charles said.

'So, the party . . . there was even a belly dancer, and there were quite a lot of *muhajabat*, you know, veiled women?' Rashid drew his fingers around his face. Charles and Steffi nodded, Steffi with particular vigour.

'A lot of people were drunk and there were these cups on the table, with err . . . well, with joints in them.'

'Marijuana?' The doctor tone again. Rashid could feel Lisa looking agitated. Somewhere in his thoughts he recognised that he was probably going off script, but he was enjoying holding the table's attention. It was fun to remember the party, too. It had been nuts.

'No, nice guy and all that, but it was a seriously bad move to have that party then. I don't mean that you can't have parties; you have to do something. You can go crazy in that place. But the timing, and considering his position? No, I mean, that's just not on. But sure, he says some really good things sometimes. He's all right, but I can't say he's got much, shall I say, *credibility* right now. It's not a one-off that party, there were other things—'

'Khalil Helou and Rashid work together at the Human Rights Documentation Centre in Gaza,' Lisa interjected, also cutting off Ali, who had started an account of his years in prison.

'Now tell me about that.' Charles folded his napkin across his lap and leant back slightly in his chair. Rashid obeyed. He gave the full rundown of the Centre's activities, the summary pages of every project proposal he and Khalil had ever drafted. Talking about Khalil made Rashid miss him a lot, made him even miss the Centre, although he never thought he would. They had put so much work into it, particularly Khalil.

'Well, that's what it was, but you know, we are not able to do much at the moment.'

'Why?'

'It was trashed. Destroyed. During the August incursion, the one where they bombed the hospital. Do you remember that one?'

'Yes, yes I do, just after the municipal elections?'

'That's the one. Well, their soldiers blew open the door, broke in. They took all of our disks and smashed the computers, burnt the books and, to top it all, they shat on the floor. Well, they put some children's paintings on the floor then shat on them.'

A circle of blank faces gasped at Rashid as he kicked the muddy ball of social interchange into Charles' stomach, into all his finery.

'Right,' said Charles, refusing to be winded.

'*Euch,*' said Anna.

Lisa was looking more than a little disconcerted. Ali's monologue was on hold. The waiter started clearing up. Rashid squashed what was left of his bread into the small mush of hummus debris. He placed his hands wide apart, open on either side of his place mat, *What else? What more do you want?* Beer did not agree with him. He took against the room with its burnt pots and old brooms hanging on the wall, against the tinniness of its echo, against the blank white faces fed on stodge. Anger had built up in Rashid, talking about the situation, trying to give these people Gaza like it was chilli on a saucer. Goddamn it. He wanted to forget it. His anger was at the top of his skin running down his arms. By the time it got to his fingers he could barely control it.

Charles adjusted himself in his seat. Anna took one of Rashid's cigarettes without asking and pushed her chair back to go out. Rashid held the pack and was about to get up as well although the mood around the table stopped him from moving. Lisa's chest rose and fell stroppily, but it was Steffi who broke the silence.

'Tell me,' she said, her hands crossed at the fingers, her thumbs stroking each other with approval, 'do you then have female genital mutilation in Palestine?'

Chapter 21

'What the hell do you mean, you're taking my sister?' Lisa was more furious than Rashid had ever seen her. It lifted his mood completely.

'Well, why not? You can't make it. Who else am I going to go with? Ian? Steffi? Who do I know here? She really wanted to see him. She bought the ticket from me, insisted that she paid for it. I don't see what the big deal is.'

Lisa had left Ali at the corner of the road, his stooped form bent against a wall. His physique had not changed, he seemed acclimatised to rejection, bad treatment and hanging around on street corners.

'Well, you just wouldn't understand, would you,' Lisa started.

'What do you mean by that?'

'Oh, nothing. It's just – what the hell have you got in common with my sister?'

'Eric Clapton?' He was moved by her fury, her apparent jealousy. 'You?' He slid his hand behind her hair and moved it along her shoulder.

'She knows nothing about me, and I am not sure that you do either.' Lisa looked like she was about to slap him. It was great. She cared. The straps of Rashid's bag were cutting into his shoulders. He placed it on the pavement.

'Look, Lisa . . .' he started, about to say that he would not go.

'And what the hell do you think you were doing in there? Going on about druggy parties in Gaza? I take you out to meet someone very important and you act like some drunken clown, bitching about his . . . his future partner in some valued initiative . . .'

'Partner for Peace?'

'Yes, Partner for Peace and you make it sound like you are all just a bunch of jokers, sell-outs, hypocrites, potheads,' she spat out at him.

'"You" being who?'

'The Palestinians. That was the best you could do, was it? Forget the suffering, the bombing, the arrests, the targeted assassinations, the whole damn Occupation and its economic devastation. Not to mention the destitution or the enforced malnutrition. No, no. You just sit there drunk in front of a senior government official telling him about some party where they served joints in cocktail glasses.'

'That was not the point I was making, I was just saying it was bad timing for that party.' Ali had not moved and Rashid could feel his attention on them. Someone else was watching too, a man in the Internet café, smirking through the window.

'Yeah, well, maybe you would have been better off keeping your mouth shut and just letting him carry on thinking that there were people out there he can believe in.' Lisa's finger was pointed, as though she wanted to squash Rashid into the ground with it.

'Of course there are people there that he can believe in.'

'Well, you should have said so. Listed them. Like who, anyway? I thought you were *way too cynical* to believe in anyone?'

'Well, like Khalil.'

'Oh great. Yeah, your best friend. And that gets us where exactly? That's just typical, isn't it? So tribal, just stick up for your own little group. You just don't *get it*, do you? You can't just go around showing your dirty laundry in public – dope, corruption, hypocrisy, all that *crap* that you're so good at. Keep it to yourself. You can't afford the luxury of showing that off.'

'We can't just present ourselves as graciously suffering all the time either. The stress of that place: people feel suicidal. When they get just a whiff of what freedom feels like they do strange things. That's understandable, isn't it? It's not like anywhere else.' He tried to hold her arm but she moved away from him. 'Come on, Lisa, I was out for the evening having a meal, I thought, with you and your friends. I didn't know that I was expected to sound like some zealot standing outside a mosque shouting propaganda.'

'OK, Rashid. Listen, enough, all right. Look, I need to help Ali out with something and so I am going to go. I am just going to leave it here.'

'Lisa, come on, don't just go off in a mood. It's all right. No harm is done. I think the guy liked me in the end. He gave me his card, see?' Rashid pulled it out of his pocket, but it slipped out of his fingers on to the pavement. When he stood up again, Lisa was standing with her arms folded in front of her. 'Look, I really appreciate you introducing us, OK? We're going to meet again. Don't start trying to make some excuse about Ali. What can you help him out with now? It's nearly eleven o'clock. Come on, come back to my place.'

'No, Rashid. I agreed this with Ali earlier. It's got nothing to do with you asking Anna or what you said to Charles. I just need to go with him right now, OK?' Her hand touched his jacket. 'Let's try to get together later in the week,' she said.

He tried to kiss her but only caught her forehead before she found Ali, who was scuffing around the postbox. He watched her purposeful bottom move off. Attractive as it was, it was quite a bit heavier than her sister's.

Chapter 22

'We're closing in five minutes,' the man in the Internet café blocked Rashid at the door, 'and you've got to pay for fifteen. It's the minimum charge.'

'It doesn't matter. I only need two.' Rashid pushed the door. 'You're still open, aren't you?'

Outside, with Lisa going off like that, the road looked hostile and sad. There were police cars moaning in front of one of the bars and he'd nearly tripped over a homeless person (*Watch it, wog!*) when he had turned the corner. It was cold and there was too much rain and petrol in the air. The trees were black shapes and the clouds were scudding fat and fast behind them. It had all become very rocky. The expelled pub crowds were angry too, angry at the road and with each other. They wanted to eek out more from the evening, to stop their sense of being ripped off by it. Rashid was fretted at by absence; the people that he thought of weren't there, the place he thought of was not there. He craved email. To each of the questions that ricocheted in his head about his family, about Khalil, there was an open window of an answer somewhere. He was sure they were waiting to be downloaded on to any computer he could find.

Force had got him in. He had made the guy feel it against his toes.

There was only one message, but it was long and it was from Khalil. He printed it off. He didn't feel like going back to his room yet. He was not in the mood for Ian, hanging around trying to cadge a bit of black, lecturing him on Palestine. The employee, a bit watery-eyed now from the cold, was pulling down the metal

145

shutters and, with thoughts of Ian, Rashid decided he liked this sad, lost stranger with his dead-end job. He even tipped the grumpy bastard, for now with his jacket bulked out and warm with Khalil's message, London had become a bit of an adventure again.

All the pubs and bars on that street were closed or closing. He walked through the side streets, smoking with a song in his head, a song with *fat chords* by the man himself. The term *fat chords* and the tickets in his pocket lightened his pace into something casual and *London*. The globes of streetlights expanded diagonally and then shrank as he passed them. Above, the sky was still churning itself up, but holding itself back for the time being. He headed east with his bag hung between his shoulders to spread the weight, through rows of squat Georgian terraces with slanted roofs, weaving in and out of parked cars, slapping his feet into puddles.

Some boys hung around in front of graffitied walls and garages and the canal shone black between the buildings. Rashid walked through warehouses and buildings squeezed into awkward triangular plots. Still quiet. A brightly lit bar, like a glass cube dropped on to a square, shone out at him and he moved towards it, but everything inside it was stiff, noisy, self-aware. He walked past posters of bad-tempered-looking people, brick walls babbling with spray paint, underground bridges, an empty library building guarded by a woman with muscular breasts and a spear, Ethiopian restaurants, boxing clubs, rows of estate agents, kebab vans. There was nowhere for him to go at all. He was about to go back to the glass cube bar with its high-heeled women, when ahead of him the door to a pub opened and a man in a suit ushered him in.

It was filled wall to wall with men holding pints, clustered into groups of three or four. The barmaid wore thick-rimmed black glasses. She was barely tall enough to reach over the bar and moved fast, alone, ringed in by the thick wooden pen, her feet restless, her face immobile. Perched on stools by the bar two old men in tweed caps explained their indignation about something to a woman whose nipples under a thin white T-shirt pointed to the ground like fairy lights.

The dancer came on as Rashid was buying his drink. She threw her open mouth out at the audience, her sweaty-looking hair swinging around her, then removed her dress and thrust forward her other orifices. Her body was smooth and alien in its hairlessness, rubbery in texture, and she bent and wound it around a vertical pole, hopping with a masculine strength on to the higher poles so that she could suspend herself upside down. Her breasts remained focussed, static, liquid-filled mounds. The men talked quietly among themselves, watching respectfully, diligent in their role as spectators. The barmaid's head stayed down.

Rashid found a deserted table by the entrance to the bathroom, covered with peeled lager mats and crisp packets. Relieved of his bag, he sat with his back to the bar, to the dancers, and took out the message from Khalil.

Rashid *ya zalame*, comrade, how are you? I hope London is treating you well. How are your family? How is Iman getting on in the Gulf? And Lisa? Have you been to any meetings with her? Were the statistics we provided what she was looking for?

Mishta' habibi, I am missing you here. I haven't been down to Sindibad's since you left. What the Mustafa Seif El Din's killing has done for expanding the number of supporters of his party, I can't tell you. They are signing up in droves. Even my father has picked up on the strength of the Islamic movements and has told me that if I don't cut my hair I am going to get attacked for being a devil worshipper. It is the only subject he talks about. Also, do you remember the computer genius who used to come down to the Centre? Two weeks ago, his father pulled him out of all the programmes I was trying to line up for him and has sent him to a religious *madrasa* instead. When I tried to persuade him to leave the boy in the classes, the father replied, 'What value is success in this life compared to eternity in the next?' I was not sure whether I could even try to answer that one in the circumstances.

The good news is that we have managed to get the Centre up and running again with the newly donated computers working. It took a lot of scrubbing and painting. Our biggest cost was mending the doorway. Next time we should just leave it open to save the cost.

I am spending most of my time trying to get Jamal released. As Sabri anticipated, he's in administrative detention on a 'preventive' basis. I found him in Shohar IV – in one of those centres where the detainees are in canvas tents, four of them per two-man tent. In the summer they bake in the sun with all the desert dust blowing in at them, in the winter the tents fill up with mud.

A song blared out in the background, a burst of an introduction from something very eighties, either Flashdance or Prince. The lights started rolling around. Rashid found a bright cotton-covered crotch pushed up near his face, a paper cup rattling in front of him.

'All right, love?'

Familiar with the homeless, he plopped some coins into the cup.

'You all right here, darling? Can't see an effing thing down here. You'll miss the show.'

'It's all right. I'm fine. Don't worry,' Rashid had to shout for the girl to hear him.

'Suit yourself, love.'

Rashid caught the barmaid watching him as he twisted back around into his seat.

Jamal seems to be doing OK though from what I've heard from his family he's sharing a tent with some Gazan fishermen so he has learnt one hundred different ways to bone and cook a fish. He seems to be very impressed by the leaders from the religious

148

parties that he's met in there. Why does this depress me so much?

To be honest, Rashid, I have no idea how I am going to be able to get him out. We are trying to get an appeal, but even if we manage, it just means that he comes up in front of a kangaroo court for ten minutes and the success rate is so low. His family are wretched because he was meant to be getting married in March and they've already paid for it with their life savings. Can you see if there is anything to be done from there? Could Lisa's group help?

Anyway, *habibi*, missing you a lot. Go see a Bertolucci for me, will you? I may still come to that dodgy funder's workshop in Leeds in April if I can get an exit visa. Regards to Lisa and wish Iman the very best.
Your friend,
Khalil

In the middle distance, somewhere close to where the heels of one of the old men in the flat caps were perched on to the rung of a bar stool, Rashid could see Jamal crouching in a prison camp. The heels moved. A stripper stood next to Rashid and waited. 'Got a light I can borrow?' She leant over him with her all of her excitable bulbousness. Her body's desire for attention was exhausting. The pub had almost completely emptied. The barmaid put two large scooped glasses filled with a beige drink and ice on to the counter. The stripper took one and strutted back to Rashid, who was stuffing Khalil's message back into his jacket pocket.

'Mind if I . . . ?' She indicated the chair. Rashid nodded, although he found her knickerlessness somewhat perturbing.

'Not your kind of thing, then?'

'No, not really. I just needed somewhere to go.'

'Aww. All alone are we?'

'I just had a letter I wanted to read. I didn't feel like going home.'

'Trouble with the wife?'

'I'm not married.'

149

'So, where are you from, anyway?'

'Palestine.' Was there even any point in saying that?

'Oh, right. My mate. Her man's from there. Always joking about how he needs to walk around with see-through plastic bags and a couple of cans of lager to stop himself getting arrested.'

'Are you sure he's not from Pakistan?'

'Pakistan. Yeah, that's it. Would not carry around a bag like yours anyway. What you got in there?'

'Books.'

'You a student then?' Rashid nodded. 'Like her behind the bar. She's a student. Studies women's issues. Not even a dyke or anything.' Dyke? Some words still threw Rashid.

A second lurid-coloured-cotton-clad woman came over to them. She stroked down the other dancer's hair and kissed her mouth. Dyke? OK, he got it. The other woman turned to face him, 'Who's this then?'

'Show's not his kind of thing. We were just having a chat.' Rashid was holding the canvas straps of his bag. They were still watching him.

The bouncer moved in from the front door. 'Ladies,' the bouncer said. 'All right?'

'I need to be going.' Rashid got up. The bouncer was standing behind him, blocking his way out.

'All right, ladies?' he asked.

'All right. All right, love, see you,' the ladies replied, one of them stirring the ice around her glass with her finger. Rashid wondered whether it was a trap, whether the door, like in the films, although appearing close, was actually going to be impossible to reach. Whether he would be grabbed back into the bar. He tried to walk close to the wall, away from the bar to where the bouncer stood, but found himself banging into chairs ('All right?'). It could be a trap and if it was a trap then the barmaid in the glasses would save him, but, when he looked around one more time ('All right?'), he realised that she had already gone.

PART III

GULF INTERIORS

The same week

Chapter 23

Iman flew over the Gulf in the dark and below her the tankers bobbed around in its water like fireflies in oil. The coast was elaborate; it had been dredged into loops, pearl drops and crowns, pinpricked a million times over with electricity, but Iman could think of nothing except the state that she was in.

They had questioned her for over ten hours at the Gaza border. Rotating the young soldiers with the old, the men with the women, the clean-shaven with the bearded, the plain-clothed with the uniformed, the hugely muscular with the puny and bespectacled, until the only thing they had in common with each other was their guns: hand guns, dinky pocket revolvers for the women, Uzis for the men.

'Why were you in Switzerland?'

'For school.'

'You went to school in Switzerland?'

'For a while.'

'How many others, like you, in Switzerland?'

'You mean Palestinians?'

'Yes. Like you.'

'I don't know, say, three or maybe five?' Iman was not sure what answer they wanted.

'What are their names?'

'I don't know.'

'How do you not know?'

'I did not know them.'

'I don't believe you.' The good-looking one had gone off to talk about her with a small man in plain clothes with metal-framed glasses.

'Do you belong to a political party?' It was a woman with cropped hair now.

'No.'

'Do you belong to a political party?'

'No.' Look them in the eye.

'Why are you leaving?'

'To see my father.'

'Who is your father?'

'Jibril Ali Mujahed.'

'We know your father.' Then why ask? 'He's in the Organisation.'

'He left.'

'When? Why?'

'He wanted to get out of politics.'

'I said, when?'

'About eight years ago.'

'Do you belong to a political party?'

'No.'

They went through everything: every seam, every tube of anti-septic, face cream and toothpaste, every scrap of paper. Then they stuffed it all in see-through plastic bags and threw them back in her case. The charade of personalities and questioning techniques seemed unrelenting, the questions being asked from behind her and in front, from the side, from ones, twos and threes, while she watched the others who were trying to enter or leave having their belongings thrown across the long white tables and on to the floor in the fluorescently lit room. Old women in embroidered *thoubs* being screamed at by girls a third of their age in uniform. The abuse shrieked through the room like jets flying low. Everyone was being yelled at, except Iman who got questions, and more questions, and

154

more changes of personnel. She was moved from chair to chair from one side of the room to the other and back again. Iman thought to herself that it was fine, that she had been through it all so many times before. It was all fine, but still one of her hands kept trying to soothe the loose skin of her bent elbow as she sat, her fingers looking for consolation or to console.

'What year are you in at school?' a girl with a puppet sitting next to Iman had asked her, and for a moment Iman had felt younger than the girl and had wanted her mother too, and then the Uzi woman returned and they went back to the questions and the anger rose up again, until she no longer had any idea of who was in charge, what she had told whom, and why she wanted to leave anyway. I just need to get *away* from them. Screw it all. I just need to be away from these people, away from their nastiness, their hate.

And there really was nowhere she could mentally escape to now either. The textured surroundings and tender feel of the place where she used to mentally go to be with Raed, or at least an idea of him, was no more than a burnt-out shell of a room, with nothing to show for it except for his bare, dead feet hanging off a table on a stifling day, and after that the madness of the chase through the streets, being pulled back, falling. The man with the jacket and the gun, Ziyyad Ayyoubi, whose presence there was mortifying to her. That he had seen her run after that man, even though he, Ayyoubi, was really just another one of their heavies, paid to drag men like Abu Omar out of their houses, in front of their families, on dubious second-hand information to further some grudge or another, a feud between families, a political rift at most. Of course, no one liked their neighbour – there was something pathetic and ineffectual about him – but a collaborator? He had lived there for years. They'd known him for years, as long as they had been in that apartment, even back when Sabri had had his legs.

Sitting here like this. Being made to wait, and wait, and wait.

Move here. Sit there. No, there. Get up. Sit down. No purpose to it except for the humiliation. What enemies they had, these masters of humiliation. They prided themselves on it. Well, she could sit it out. They were getting nothing from her.

The cramps had started just when it seemed like it was all over, after they had carted her outside to sit in a bus shelter with all her things on a trolley, guarded by one of the uniformed recruits. It felt as though a lizard was trapped inside her. She felt its teeth and claws as though it was convinced there was a way out at the base of her lower back and it bit and scratched and pushed with a thick tail flaying out at the contents of her stomach. She bent over. *Please. No. No. Not my period now.*

And the bastards had not let her get to her bag for a pad, a tissue, a painkiller, or to visit the bathroom, and when she finally got to the Egyptian side, they had decided to give her their special treatment, which was a room – *God, that room!* No, she did not even want to go there in her head – and a military escort (and it was not as though they could not have spent the money on something else). It was not until Cairo Airport where a cleaning lady had asked if she was OK, '*Malik ya habibti? Salamtik ya habibti*, and given her a stack of tissues, that she had been able to sort herself out a bit in the bathroom.

A shower. I just need a shower.

Chapter 24

Iman's plane had landed over an hour before, but Jibril was counting on his daughter being the last one out. Sensing the prod of Suzi's phantom finger in his gut, he had ordered a skinny latte but it was tasteless, pointless, so he had got the chap to add a vanilla shot and then a touch of cream.

A woman with lilac combs in her hair and matching nail varnish had smiled up at him at the sound of his ringtone: *toot-a-toot, toot-a-toot toot*. A recognisable tune by a nubile Egyptian singer Jibril rather fancied. Charming. He raised his eyebrows at the lilac woman – a look, he believed, that combined a sense of intelligent irony with nonchalant seduction. She smiled back. Ah, maybe he had not reached the end of it all, the end of women. Perhaps there was still time. He did have Suzi, and Suzi was Suzi and there was no trying to undermine that. He was a lucky man. But to know that the door to others was closed for ever? Was, quite simply, terrifying.

It was Jibril's fixer ringing. Telling him that Iman had been held back for questioning. Well, of course she had. What did the stupid man expect?

He ordered another coffee before returning the lilac woman's smile, but she got up and walked off before he was able to take it any further.

It did not take long for the newspaper to upset him. He had read the Sheikh A bin B meets Sheikh B bin A to discuss bilateral relations bit, skimmed the runaway housemaids and discontented manual labourers section, sought and found some hidden nuggets of adultery charges and rogue sexual activity and *(oh joy!)* he even found a piece about further evidence of lesbian activity in school bathrooms. Jibril chuckled happily. Un-Islamic behaviour tickled him to the core.

He braced himself as he turned over the page to the international section, his eye automatically finding the news from home. The same images seemed to have been repeating themselves for years now, the perpetual cycle of violence and diplomatic grins, dead child, stone-throwing youths, exploded car, crying woman outside a demolished house, grinning Leadership, dead child again.

'The worse the loss, the more we grin,' Jibril said staring at a particularly despicable picture of the Leaders standing on a golf course in Texas.

'They treat their dogs better than us,' said the young man behind the counter, gazing at the sprightly Labrador at the President's feet. 'A dog's life would be a blessing compared to what some of us have to live through.' He nodded, this time to the picture of a mother crying over her dead child.

'Where are you from?' Jibril had been having problems reconciling the boy's face and Arabic with his badge. 'Hi!' it said. '*I am ERNESTO. Welcome to Starbright®. I am happy to serve you.*' If he had to guess, he would have said the boy was the same as he was, only brought up in Jordan. 'Mr Ernesto?'

'Oh no, that's only my work name,' the boy said turning to Jibril from the milk steamer that was hawking and spitting behind him. 'HQ designates our names and market research has found that Spanish names are more amenable to the clientele. My true name is Salem Abu Wazir.'

'Abu Wazir? You are from . . .? You are from my village?' Jibril named his village, to which the manager raised his eyebrows.

'You know the Abu Wazirs? You know my family?'

The café was filling out. A woman with prawn skin was leaning down close to Jibril's legs tapping over a chocolate cake with a fingernail, her cleavage a gathering of creases and sunspots.

'*Know* your family? *Know* your family?' Jibril exclaimed. 'I practically *am* your family! I am Jibril Mujahed, the Mujaheds and the Abu Wazirs have married each other for years. Centuries, in fact, since the time of the Crusades.'

The boy laid out a piece of cake on a plate for his customer and looked up, bemused.

'I've heard of you, *Ammo*, Uncle. You were with the Outside Leadership, were you not?'

The boy was a bit spotty. His pimples had white tips and clustered together around his nostrils. Other than that, he would be a fairly good-looking chap if he calmed down on the hair cream a bit.

'I *was* with the Organisation. Yes. Not any more though. Left it years ago. And you're . . .? A manager here?'

'I manage all the airport branches. We had two outlets when I started; now we have fourteen. It's a growth industry.'

'A franchise, I suppose?'

'Of course.' The boy, Salem Abu Wazir (Abu Wazir, eh?), turned back to his staff. A queue was forming of servicemen, businessmen and backpackers. All pushed up behind Jibril to see into the counter. Jibril thought of trying to recreate their village using the salt and pepper pots to show this boy where the Abu Wazir house had been compared to the Mujahed's, but it would be difficult as the village had been built on the slopes of two hills and the houses had been like cubes stacked up the sides.

Jibril could quite clearly see and feel himself as a child in Palestine. When he was there he wore shorts and a dangly belt, always (the outfit had been frozen in a photograph). Behind him, the village was a series of blocks and arches, rough stone straddling from one building to another in semicircles, arched windows, domes smoothed over with sand and outdoor staircases. There were days when the smell of his village would come and sit on his nose like a flirtatious *djinn*. He would wake from a dream and feel himself boyish, a spirit running through alleyways, over roofs, in the olive groves, leaping in the sun, a sun that was always bright but never harsh. And then at other times (it *was* there in him), when he had maybe drunk a bit too much, or been talking to someone who knew his village or a similar village, he would suddenly feel like saying, 'Yes, that place! How about it? How about we go back and see how that place is doing?' as though he had just gone around a corner and if he were to turn back quickly enough it would be there. But it would take less time than the words took to get to his mouth for him to realise that it was absurd. He could never go back to that place, it had been sealed off to him for ever, blown to the sky with explosives then flattened to the ground with bulldozers, built over with tarmac, lived on top of by other people.

People of a faith he didn't have.

He tried to go back to his newspaper, but Abu Wazir, eh? He wished it would stop affecting him. He wished he didn't care. He wished that he were free of it all. It was now almost eight years since he left the Organisation and all political involvement with it, but it still got to him. When Jibril announced that he was leaving, their Leader had looked him hard in the eye. 'You can *leave* the Organisation, Jibril,' he had said. 'Of course, Jibril, we do not want you to leave, for you to leave is your choice. But, Jibril, you must understand that you can *leave* the Organisation but the Organisation will never leave *you*.' Jibril did not know what that meant, but to be safe he had decided to treat it as a threat.

It was true though, people still acted as though he was part of it. 'This is Jibril Mujahed of the Palestine Liberation Organisation,'

160

his Western friends would say, as though they had a piranha in their fish tank, and he had no idea how they knew. The Arabs would just mouth 'the Organisation' at each other, 'Jibril was with the *Organisation*,' they would say with a nod and that was enough.

Enough for some of them, particularly those who had been in Kuwait, to never stop banging on about the fraction of their salary that had been deducted every month to support the cause. 'So, your children went to school in Switzerland, did they? And us? Kicked us out of our homes in Kuwait because of your leadership and then what? Left to rot; the education of our children disrupted. And you? Went to live in Paris, did you? So where's our five per cent? Lost it in the casinos of Monaco, did you? While our families rot in the refugee camps? Bravo my friend, bravo!' He never encouraged any of this talk about the Organisation. No, he never encouraged such discussions. There was nothing he could do, anyway. It was all in the past.

Not for the first time Jibril offered up a prayer of gratitude to this Gulf state that had taken him in despite his background and his papers, or lack thereof, and had allowed him to work. He thanked the glittering forest of duty-free shops around him, complete with their electronic moose heads singing Christmas carols, the three-floor high columns of mirrors, the polished four-wheel drives displayed high on velvet platforms. He even thanked the posterior of the cleaner squeezing out her mop. *I'm so glad to be here. I'm so glad to be out of it.* He had done his bit. No one could hold him to account for the Organisation's mistakes. No one. He had wiped his hands of it long ago.

'I'm waiting for my daughter,' Jibril announced when it quietened down. 'She's coming from Gaza.'

'I didn't know that was possible,' the Abu Wazir boy said.

'Not directly, of course. She's gone through the borders into Egypt and then been flown out. They held her up for days.'

In the middle distance an electronic tape of red dots was revolving around a screen informing Jibril and other potential customers about the discounts in the electronics store, particularly the substantial reductions on portable DVD players.

'You're sure that she got on the plane?'

'Yes, yes. She got on, and she's here. They're just asking her a few questions. Nothing to worry about.'

Nothing that he knew he should be worried about, but of course it was possible that they had picked up on something. The message he had heard was that she, his mousy little daughter, his Iman, named after the belly-dancing star of all stars of the Cairo nights, was trying to get herself mixed up with some Islamic movement. Naturally, there were those who said that she would be backing the right horse there, if she wanted to side with what they thought was the winning team. That lot had been popping up everywhere: elections, coups, guerilla stunts. All action, that lot but not so great when it came to ideas or the bigger picture. Their time was up, Jibril felt and he was ready to celebrate it. He could not stand them himself, so dour and sanctimonious. He had never had any time for religion and saw no reason to change: God had hardly smiled on them this far; in fact he had verily shat upon them.

Problematic generation, Jibril thought, looking at the Abu Wazir boy and thinking of his daughter. They might at best be capable of revolt, but that in itself did not make them capable of revolution; they lacked the sophistication of ideology that was required for that. Silly girl. He would give her a good talking-to. That was all it would take.

More red dots. This time the text stopped and flashed several times before rolling along. Even the main Japanese brands had come down in price. Sixty per cent off the original price for DVDs. *Flash. Flash.* Sixty per cent!

'Terrible,' said the boy. 'How old is she?'

'Twenty-five,' Jibril replied, although he had the feeling he had been saying that for a couple of years now.

'Terrible,' said the man again. 'It appears that it is our destiny to get hassled in these places; airports, borders, checkpoints. That's our unifying national destiny.'

'Yes,' Jibril agreed. 'Yes, yes.' His tongue was dried out from the coffee. He considered buying Iman a present: a shawl, some jewellery, a peaked cap with a designer name on it, a diamante pin, a stuffed camel, a box of dates. She would need so many things that he was not really sure where to start. He squeezed, rubbed and stroked many potential gifts and found out their prices, colours and sizes and had reached the cash till with armfuls of goods when he decided it best to leave it for Suzi to get things for his daughter. She could take Iman to the malls. Lots of time for sorting her out.

Happy with the thought of Suzi's adoption of Iman's upbringing (and feminisation; the girl really should be thinking of settling down), Jibril sauntered into the electronics section, where he remained, haggling over several seven- to eight-inch screens, until the fixer called to say that they were both through.

Chapter 25

It was good to hug her father at the airport, to find his smell of cigar, sweet chewing gum, coffee, sweat and aftershave intact. Held by him she felt small, young, little, and found herself so affected by the embrace that she did not want to talk afterwards, fearing that she might not be able to, but instead would squeak or purr like a baby animal. The hug made her able to overlook (and even to quite like) his shoes, which were a disaster. *Like a pimp,* she could hear Rashid saying. *He looks like a Cairo pimp.*

But by the time they reached his car she was screaming at her father. She was yelling and cursing but none of it could be heard by anyone else except her, to whom it was deafening. The one-way flow of passengers out of the arrivals hall and the finality of the ten dollars and fifteen shekels in her pocket stopped any of it being said because it all prevented her from going anywhere else. *I come here because he demands it of me. I'm held up and questioned for days and when I get here and I just ask is there time to go to the bathroom? I say I need to get something out of my suitcase and get changed. What time would that take? And he says, Oh no, no time for that. But yet he decides to take me to a café to fix me up with a waiter from some family he knows? A waiter? And working in that place? Has he never heard of the boycott?*

Iman, her father and their car were guided into the five-lane traffic jam leading out of the airport in silence. How insensitive was her father exactly? Was it possible that he was quite that dumb? But there did seem to be something defensive in his movements (the way he kept touching his neck, for example) that showed that on some level at least he was picking up on her annoyance with him, or was she seeing things?

It was hard to tell what around her was real. She had seen a skyline of thirty- or forty-storey buildings, blunt blades pointing at the sky, but once she was closer it turned out that they were just outsized billboards. The skyscrapers on the road they were on were real. If she craned her neck upwards she could see their tips, flashing red and white. Some of the other buildings looked like they had been squashed by a giant thumb, to form pads for helicopters, smooth stepping stones for the gods. Where there was a gap between the towers of buildings, it was desert and in the desert a vertical grid of cranes grew up, their uplifted arms creating bulb-lit ladders to the sky. On the sides of the buildings fair-haired girls, hundreds upon hundreds of feet tall, giggled as they ate watermelons and clasped video cameras to their breasts.

The newness and foreignness of this world around her sucked Iman in so much that for the first time she felt herself momentarily broken out of the chase that kept being rerun in her mind: her feet pounding down an alleyway after a man who was about to be killed, her body bent over. She covered her face at the thought that somebody else might have seen her (it was bad enough that the Ayyoubi man had).

'Sometimes the traffic's bad.' Jibril looked out at the silky red banners fluttering down the centre of the road; *Go to the Paradise Isle Where Life is Best,* they enticed. He turned off his engine as did the other drivers. No one was going anywhere. Jibril peered between the cars. 'It must be those construction workers rioting again.' He fiddled around for news on the radio '. . . *The rise of the Islamic party in the Gaza Strip has led to fighting between the Palestinian factions, but as our correspondent points out, this could also mark the* end to the widespread corruption which has marred the rule of the current Authority, the former Outside Leadership . . .'

'Corrupt? Who isn't corrupt in this world? Even the bloody Norwegians are up to it. For that we get this miserable religious mob ruling us? Corrupt? Show me a clean government. What's this latest American war about if not about corruption?' Jibril snapped off the radio.

'What construction workers?' Iman asked.

'Idiots,' her father said. 'Idiots. They'll all get deported in the morning, the lot of them.'

Iman looked for the fresh faces of the giant-sized watermelon-eating girls among the passengers of the other cars, where middle-aged Western men stared hard at the stationary traffic, gripping their steering wheels as though they were about to be pulled away from them, women in black headscarves chewed gum with open mouths, East Asian women in the safari uniforms of the Chinese proletariat held toddlers in backseats, their foreheads slumped against the windows. An open-backed truck slotted into the space next to them, and two bearded men gesticulated to each other from either side of a suspended cardboard disc imprinted with the image of a Lebanese cleric.

Jibril turned his engine back on and the cars started nudging up around each other as though trapped in a dense jelly. 'Don't worry, *habibti*,' he said. 'We'll be there soon.' He patted his daughter's leg. Iman flinched. She had tried to wash out the worst of the blood from her trousers in the bathroom on the plane thinking that it would dry as soon as she arrived, because of the desert heat that she had heard so much about. But the jeans had become too wet and the airport had been freezing. The exposure to un-air-conditioned heat in the carpark had been brief and the outdoor air was perverse; dank and intimate, it wrapped itself about her, seeming to push at her temples and to exhale odours of sulphur and

166

half-baked dough up her nose. It festered in her nose. Sweat released itself from her like pee and slid down her body between fabric and skin. Her jeans had only partially dried and Jibril had felt their dampness. 'Eh?' he said. 'What happened? You spilt something?'

'No, I . . . I tried to wash them: there was blood on them. I got my, my . . . I started bleeding at the border leaving Gaza and they would not let me get anything to sort it out. I was not allowed to go to the bathroom. That's why I wanted to get changed at the airport, I . . .'

'Animals!' He banged down on the steering wheel. He jolted the car forwards into a space that had freed itself up to the right. 'How can they do such a thing? How?'

'I've heard worse. I've heard about girls who've been strip-searched, paraded and laughed at in their underwear, had their pads taken off them . . .'

'They didn't search you like that, did they?' Jibril's eyes were wild and demanded one answer only, which Iman gave.

'No, not this time, but before, at the other crossing.'

'Stop it! *Khalas!* Enough! I don't want to know about these dogs. I don't want to know—'

'You're *angry* with me, are you? Because of this? What could I have done? They would not let me touch any of my stuff. What was I supposed to do? Hold it in?' The traffic was moving now and her father was trying to duck and swerve in and out of it, accelerating and braking in a way that threw her forwards against her seatbelt.

'No, of course not. Damn it. Of course not. It's just the situation. *Yukhrub bait'hum, awlad ars*, goddamn their houses, those sons of pimps. The situation. And what were you getting yourself into, anyway? In Gaza? What exactly were you trying to do? I got a message. Came from the new man, Ziyyad Ayyoubi. I got called into the Representative Office here, with a message about you.

167

Did you know that? Not great, I can tell you, having one of those men coming to the flat.'

Suzi had been in her champagne negligée and they had been having a whisky; they had assumed it was the supermarket delivery boy bringing up some ice and Suzi had not bothered to put anything away, meaning that it was all still there when the official from the Representative Office had turned up in his flat, at midnight. The last thing Jibril wanted was to be brought back into the fold by that lot again.

'What? That Ayyoubi – that henchman from the Authority – he actually tried to contact you?'

'What are you saying? Why are you talking about him that way?' The traffic was still all jammed up ahead. Blue police lights shimmered and multiplied in the mirrored walls of the high-rises. Jibril cut sharply across three lanes of traffic into a side street that they had almost passed, causing a burst of horns around them. 'Who are you talking about? Ayyoubi's exactly what we need. He's very senior, very highly respected. Man of integrity.'

'I thought you didn't believe it was possible to be in the Authority and to have integrity at the same time,' Iman sulked at him. 'I thought that was why you left.'

Jibril stared at his daughter who returned his stare. Too much failed parenting was reflected back at Jibril in her look. He let the comment go. This time, anyway.

'I knew his parents in Beirut, of course,' Jibril said instead. 'Wonderful, both of them. Attention-seeking, people would say, but I always say why not seek attention? If you can get it, take it. Bit snobby too, you know, in the way intellectuals are: Gramsci this, Fanon that, and I don't know what.'

They had driven down a backstreet into a complex, functional part of town strung with wires and pipes; it was like finding oneself behind the back of an extremely large computer screen.

The way he had pulled her around and decided that she should leave. And then contacted her father? Who the hell did these people think they were? Who the hell did he think he was?

'Where are they now then, his parents?' Iman asked.

Their car was jammed in a single line of traffic between two rows of tilting cars parked up on the pavements. Jibril looked at Iman.

'What do you mean, where are his parents? Don't you know who his parents are? He's the son of Mona Zahlan and Khaled Ayyoubi.'

'Mona . . .?' was all Iman could manage. Her skin felt brittle, her hands shaky and cold. She knew this couple. She had never met them; they had died before she was born but she had seen photographs of them with long hair and dark-rimmed glasses. She had read their articles. They were her key examples when talking about the policy to annihilate writers and intellectuals in the seventies and eighties. The fact that they were almost forgotten now had made her able to feel possessive of them. They were hers. They were the parents she had always wanted and should have had.

'How old was he when it happened?'

'A boy, maybe ten or eleven. They were killed in front of him. He went a bit nuts for a while.' Jibril took out the butt of a cigar from the black and gold dented metal cigar case that he carried in his top pocket. He was proud of that case. A king had given it to him. He lit the butt. 'What did you call him? A henchman?'

'He was in charge of the arrest of Abu Omar.'

'And?' Jibril asked. 'And? So what?'

'I hate these arrests. Killing our own people. What evidence do they have? What trials are held? Why don't we have trials for these "informers", these "collaborators" instead of torturing them and shooting them on a whim?'

People were streaming between the cars in the narrow road that they had driven into. A lopsided bus had cranked open its doors and workers in blue boiler suits with stencilled numbers sprayed on to their backs were jumping out of it, swinging multi-layered tin canisters, T-shirts wrapped around their heads, ragged checked scarves tied to their necks.

'It's not a *whim*; there are trials and they always have evidence, information.'

'What? From other informers?'

'Sometimes it is, and sometimes mistakes are made. But sometimes we're right and we get the bastards. It's a war. We can't fight a war without information and if our information is stolen, our people betrayed, we are suffering for nothing.'

We are suffering, are we? thought Iman, looking at the prancing horse embossed on her father's chest.

'And someone like Abu Omar,' Jibril continued, 'well, there's just no way they could arrest him without hard evidence. They're too well connected his family, the Hiyas. No, that rat must've been up to something. No doubt about it.'

If she had known that he was Mona Zahlan and Khaled Ayyoubi's son – it should not have made a difference, but it did. She tried to remember again what had been said, what she had worn, how he was, the sickly pallor, the stepping away from the puddle to make room for her, how he had looked at her, what she had said, but it was all terrible. Her chest filled piteously with the shame of that day: the awful desperation of it.

And for nothing.

Again.

Jibril drove them into a car park underneath a white apartment block with a green trim around its windows. All eight floors were uplit by bulbs of high wattage hidden behind a line of artificial vegetation.

'Here we are. Home.' Jibril spoke with satisfaction as though he were presenting Iman with a valuable gift. 'Home,' he said again, pushing for an appropriate response.

* * *

The glass lift on the side of the building took them up just over three floors then came to an abrupt stop. The city, that had been lowering itself beneath them, went out too. Only the cars were alight, chasing after each other in the new mayhem of the black-out, sniffing playfully at each other's bottoms.

Iman looked at her father under the seedy glow of the emergency light. 'A power cut?' she asked. Jibril hit on the alarm button which rang dutifully, like a school bell. 'What is it?' Iman asked again.

'Yes, yes, just a power cut. System gets overloaded. Grid's not big enough. They're working on it. They don't normally last long. The whole place has just grown so fast, so furiously. It's unprecedented in human history, this construction, this development. It's not surprising that it sometimes hits upon problems, that sometimes it . . .'

'Has a meltdown?'

'Has glitches,' said Jibril, staring out at the race track below them, willing the tray of electronic circuitry that was the city to relight, for the crystal buildings to glow, the antennas to blink, for the up-lighters to illuminate his building. They didn't. He looked at the floor. 'We might as well sit down,' he said, pushing the suitcase against the door. 'Could be here for a bit.'

It was starting to get hot. They sat next to each other on the suitcase, their arms sucking at each other's sweat.

'Suzi'll take you out tomorrow. To get fixed up and everything,' Jibril said after a while.

'Who's Suzi? And get fixed up how, for what?'

'Suzi's a friend. It's Sousan actually, and you know, she'll do women's things with you, shopping and all that. You'd like that, wouldn't you?'

'Sousan? Where's she from?'

171

'Like us, but from Lebanon. From the camps actually, but don't let her know I told you that. She doesn't like talking about it.'

'What's that?' Iman asked as Jibril placed the rectangular object he had been carrying down by his feet. It was wrapped in the thick plastic bag that said *BUY! BUY! BUY! FLY! FLY! FLY!*

'Oh,' he cleared out his nose, 'just a DVD player.'

'Small,' said Iman after a while.

'Oh, it's much smaller than that. That's just the packaging. It's very neat. Very compact. Seven inches and weighs less than 1.2 kilos. It's just the box makes it appear bigger. I never know what to do with all these boxes. You want to keep them in case you move; you want to throw them in case you don't. Boxes, boxes. Seem to have rooms full of the things.'

There was more traffic now below them and it was getting slow and frustrated.

'Where's everyone going during a blackout?' Iman asked.

'They're not going anywhere. They're just escaping their houses, driving around in their cars so that they can use the air conditioning. If they're going anywhere it'll be to the petrol station to try to fill up.' Jibril pointed to a mass of traffic stuffed into a station across the road.

'And after his parents died, then what?'

'What the boy, Ziyyad? He went into one of the fighting forces, you know, the youth ones – the Lion Cubs and what have you. I forget the names now. Fought throughout the war in Lebanon. Held a good position, of course, a sort of officer role over those camp boys.'

'Why of course? What did he do?'

'He didn't have to do anything. His parents were assassinated, weren't they? Ibn Shaheed, the son of martyrs and all that. When do the sons of martyrs have to do anything? But to give credit to the chap he seems to achieved a lot.' Her father hit at the lift alarm with his fist.

'Rashid got a scholarship,' Iman said.

'Yes, yes.' Her father hit at the alarm again. *Brring!* 'Damn it!' he said, kicking at the glass wall. 'Damn it!'

The city flashed on below them, hesitatingly at first and then it was resolutely on, blindingly so. The lift dropped several inches before it lurched itself up again to the seventh floor.

'What's that?' Iman asked about the scurrying noise and the tinkle of bracelets as they came into the apartment.

'Must be the girl,' Jibril spoke absently as the apartment began to start itself up again and a blast of air and dust came out of the vents.

A butterfly constructed of webbed cane and gilt hung behind the sofa in the sitting room, clattering in the draft from the air conditioning. Rounded stones were gathered together across the floor. Huge bowls supported significant quantities of sand and shells on the coffee table.

'Eh?' said Jibril, as though he had just had a fine meal presented to him. 'Eh?' he said again, hinting heavily that he was also presenting something to Iman. The sound of running water from a small fountain in the corner of the room made Iman need the bathroom. 'Suzi designed it for me. You'll meet tomorrow, eh? Tomorrow she'll come.' He continued to smile but Jibril found that the living room did not seem so pleasing now that his daughter was looking at it.

Iman's room had the hostile smell of new paint. In the corner a tall pile of cardboard boxes teetered on to a shorter stack. The insides were covered in print: bullet points itemising the features of their former contents: 32' flat screen, rotatable blades, spare batteries, stereo speakers, adjustable headset.

The water for the shower ran brown orange with rust before it cleared.

Akheeran. Finally.

Chapter 26

How did one ascertain the cost of waxing half a leg and half a bikini? Was there even such a thing as half a bikini? Settling the bill at the beauty salon was not straightforward and Suzi was not one to accept being screwed over by anyone.

Iman had walked out. Walked out halfway through the treatments and was standing outside (no one stood outside), her face in the sun, her mouth and brows livid from the threading. It was unacceptable.

It had all seemed fine earlier that morning. The girl had worn the clothes that Suzi had left for her: a pale blue T-shirt that had gold loopy writing and some pink-trimmed jeans with a rabbit-fur feature on the belt. 'Thank you, Auntie,' Iman had said when they had met that morning, covering her chest with her bare arms, seemingly uncomfortable with those parts of her body, 'for the clothes.'

Exfoliation had been the first item on Suzi's agenda and upon seeing Iman she had estimated that this would take some time. Her hair was dishevelled and curly (like an Israeli, Suzi had thought, that loose way their women wear it) and her eyebrows were sprouting hairs every which way. 'Full wax, leg and bikini, thread, blow-dry, manicure, pedicure,' Suzi had tapped off the items on her fingers to the slip of a girl in tight jeans and a T-shirt saying, *Condo Heaven*, who had scurried around the beauty salon at Suzi's heels.

'Of course, Madam,' the girl had smiled at Suzi's chest, at Iman, at Suzi's bag, at the counter, until she ran into the kitchen where she screamed rabidly at the rest of her team of women chewing around a plastic table all of whom were dressed in broken plastic slippers, jeans and message T-shirts.

Suzi had been pleased when she had peered through the curtain and seen Iman lying flat on her back, stripped down to her T-shirt, with her knickers pulled up between her legs. Iman's figure was not bad, she was fairly slim and her legs were decent. Suzi had been debating whether to take the time to get the girl's highlights done when the glow of benevolence had come over her. It was similar to the sense of satisfaction she got when she dropped coins into the lap of a beggar, the magic of seeing an object expand in value dramatically through the simple act of transferring ownership.

But Iman had caught Suzi looking through the curtain and sat up on the bed. 'What do you want?' was all she had asked. But in *such a way*. The *malice* in that question. Suzi had tried to appease her. *Jibril, Jibril*, was all she had thought, *to hell with the girl*, but *Jibril, Jibril*. His anger. That was all Suzi could think of. But nothing she had said helped. Iman was already up, throwing off the two girls working on her leg and the one on her armpit. The salon's floral skirt of cloth gathered together by an elastic cord was still around her waist; a strip of wax hung from her leg. Iman ripped it off viciously as she stood leaving lines of hair wax on her shin. Then she had pulled on her jeans and gone to stand outside.

Outside! No one stood outside.

Iman had not spoken in the car or at the mall. She had just hung around the shop entrances like one of the delinquent *shabab* who came over from neighbouring countries to gawp at women. She seemed completely disinterested, only waiting for Suzi to finish, when the trip had been for her. It was hopeless.

'Now we shall lunch.' Suzi escorted Iman along with steely camaraderie. Suzi's large shopping bags were carried low, hiding her legs in a way that made it seem like she was gliding.

The café was in the mall's atrium. The reflection of a glass dome held up by an exoskeleton of white piping created a goldfish bowl of sky and sunlight in the polished marble below their feet and the pipes' shadows cut through everything under them. Suzi identified a table under a canopy to protect them from the air conditioning.

Iman found the mall overwhelming. The amount of glass for a start. Even a weeny little bomb, Iman thought, would lead to carnage in there. She saw large jagged panes of it dropping down on the croissant eaters, the lipsticked smokers, and the backs of adults bent over children.

Oh God, Iman thought again. *What had she done? What had she nearly done?* Walking with Suzi in the mall she kept finding herself stopping and being there again. Chasing the man (and in this vision her limbs flew out, the street gawped) or with that man, Ayyoubi, in the porch explaining to him why, why she had got to that point, why. But she hadn't explained anything to him. What could he think of her?

'How is your brother?' Suzi asked to get Iman to look up. Iman was weaving the salt and pepper pots in between the flower vase, the disk showing that they were on table twelve, and the olive and chilli oil dispenser. In, round, and out again.

'He's in London,' Iman started. 'He needed to get out.'

'Everyone needs to get out,' Suzi said, dabbing at the oil on her lips. 'Everyone.' She waved at the waiter to come back. There seemed to be something wrong with her salad.

'I don't agree with that. We can't just run away. It's our land. Our people. We have a duty,' Iman said.

'Your duty is to yourself,' Suzi replied. 'That's what I have learnt. He'll stay in London, you think?'

'He would not be able to; he'll come back, but with his master's and by then, if things have improved, you know, he might be able to get a job – But with duty, I don't agree—'

176

'And you? What are you going to do?'

'I – I don't know. I needed to leave for a while.'

'I heard.' Suzi spoke with distaste as she dabbed at her lips with a thick napkin. She had eaten the mozzarella in her salad, but now was not sure whether that sort of cheese complemented her blood type or not. It needed to be changed for goat's cheese. Did the waiter understand that? Cheese made from the milk of a goat, not a sheep. If he didn't understand she would explain it to the manager.

'Rashid was doing some work with Khalil Helou at the Centre they set up in the camp—'

It was almost insulting for Suzi to hear Iman talk of refugee camps. The girl knew nothing about them. Suzi knew about camps. She could tell Iman all about them. At first, when she was a child in Beirut, the camp had been their womb; it was home to all of them and there was to be one birth and that birth was return. Return and only return. But there were others who didn't want this to happen. Many powerful others and they were determined to stop it. And they did. They stopped it. No birth. No return. And then?

Suzi did not want to dwell on it. She wiped her lips and reapplied her make-up. They go on in Gaza about bombing this, closure that, but compared to what she'd seen? Nineteen eighty-two in the camps of Lebanon, screams of women being raped, stabbed, shot, bodies heaped the way sacks were piled when you wanted to prevent a flood, bodies crawling with flies, women with their fingers chopped off at the joints, bodies . . . Enough! Suzi snapped her mirror closed and explained goat's cheese to the manager.

The newspaper headlines caught Iman's attention: *Strike Kills 4, Injures 25 as Islamic Parties Rise . . . Peace Process Not Dead Claims President of the . . . Internal Strife Claims 3 in recent outbreaks of fighting . . .* The owner of the newspaper lowered his paper to find Iman staring at him.

'Please,' he said, offering the main section of the paper, 'please, take it. I've finished with it.' He smiled at Iman and Suzi decided that she should at the very least point out to Iman how much a blow-dry would complement the lines of her face even if she had refused to have one that morning. The man smiled at Iman and an awkwardness came over her. The girl was so gauche. Her arms kept crossing over her chest and she hunched herself up as though there was something to hide. Her hands kept holding at her upper arms as though it was her *breasts* that were bare not her *arms*. She moved with the jerkiness of a baby camel. At the end of the day there really was no woman in this girl. No woman at all. The man pushed the paper across the table before standing up and leaving the food court.

It was him. Ayyoubi. In the picture on the front page. His back turned. The green jacket. He was everywhere. Even there, in the mall.

'*Smile!*' Suzi commanded with the sharpness borne of the knowledge that she had been far prettier than Iman would ever be. Iman, the paper tight in her hand, slowly turned to Suzi.

'You want to get me to dress up and smile at men? Is that what you and Baba want?'

'We just want the best for you,' Suzi snapped back, 'and if you take my advice you will start to work on developing yourself as a *woman* rather than . . . whatever it is that you are trying to do. You want to be a *politician* of some kind? Or an *activist*? Is that it?' Suzi disregarded Iman's stare. With this type, Suzi decided, it was far better to just be rude. '*Yallah! Allons-y!*' Suzi brushed the bread-crumbs off her herringbone skirt. Come now. *Allez!*' Iman folded the newspaper section up again and again until it was small enough to be pushed into her back pocket, 'Maybe a little bag, too? You seem to need a little something like that,' Suzi suggested, re-armouring herself with her shopping before she took Iman's arm and led her back into the shops.

Chapter 27

Iman had come to accept that he was everywhere and now he was there in her room, in her father's flat, in this oasis of boredom. In her hand she held a piece of evidence that that world of meaning and horror still existed. He was in the newspaper she had stuffed into her jeans pocket. Of all the objects that she had brought back with her to the room from the mall, it was only the newspaper that was meant for her. She took it out of her pocket, unfolded it and stood next to the window so she could see the picture clearly. It was definitely him: the green jacket, the slight stoop. It was not clear what story the photograph was linked to, whether it was to illustrate internal strife or the well-being of the peace process. Whatever it was, it showed that he was there and she was here. And that there was a link.

How fickle was love. Or at least how fickle was Iman's experience of it. These men she hardly knew, had not really even touched, had barely spoken to, who expanded to take over her brain, the core of her purpose, who had filled out into idealised figures that she was free to adore for a period, until for some spurious reason they would disperse as quickly as they had entered, without leaving a trace. Raed she had barely thought of since that day, since his death. She had not just forgotten him because he was dead. There had just been so many other things that had happened since then, but now, and she was shy to admit it even to herself, the man Ziyyad was taking over space in her mind.

Outside, a stream of traffic made its way down from the ports: trucks carrying shipping containers blocked the road as far as the eye could see, grinding and beeping forwards under a low net of electricity cables. On a diagonal to the road stumpy pylons stretched far into the desert, lined up like crucifixes after a slave uprising.

She knew now that he had been right. Right about Manar and Seif El Din. Right to stop her and to send her away. She had been manipulated and she had been stupid. Her lower lip was sore from being pulled at and now it bled. She looked again at the picture of him. All she could make out was some green jacket and a blurry hint of his profile. But still, there was something in it.

She could trust him. The secret of her stupidity was safe with him.

The skin around her mouth still burnt from the threading. She had been dressed by Suzi and had agreed to being made up in a department store in one of the malls. Grains of mascara were stuck in the edges of her eyes. She wanted to scratch at herself, to get herself out of all this frippery.

You should concentrate on developing yourself as a woman.

What did Suzi mean? The hell with Suzi and her father telling her to get fixed and settle down as though she was a dog needing to be neutered.

But there were the phrases of the Jahali poetry that sometimes ran around her head, *body lapping, hair pulling*. What did it feel like? Why was she the age she was, where she was, with no experience of these things at all, although she felt inside her that she had lived all of them in another life? She was not surprised that her lacking showed; she felt it everywhere. It almost hurt.

She would have to get a job to get out of there. For all the shopping in the world piled up in her cupboard, without her father she still had just ten dollars and fifteen shekels.

As a woman. What did that mean? What had Suzi picked up on? Suzi knew, she was sure of it, of her inexperience and ineptitude in *that* way, in the sexual way; women like Suzi could sniff these things out.

She could not sell the shopping for a flight out of there. She could not sell anything. No job. No money. No visa. Stuck.

She looked at the newspaper photograph again: Ziyyad Ayyoubi. He had treated her like one of his deputies. He had spoken to her, not as a girl, but as someone of significance in all of this, even though he had seen the stupidity and the madness of that day. He had seen her deranged with grief and caked with mud but yet he had treated her as though she had the balls of a man. Iman folded the sheet of newspaper and fed off the exhilaration of it.

The air conditioning, which had stopped earlier, started up again and the bags of shopping rustled in its first gust.

The place was deadening. Iman kicked out at the wide-bottomed office chair left in the deskless room, thrashed out at the ghost of a fat-bottomed executive who sat there. It swung around and knocked into the towers of cardboard boxes behind it. They started falling and Iman kicked again. She wanted the whole lot to collapse. They fell incompetently: some backwards, others forwards, one tower staggered on its base until it finally toppled. At the top of the pile was one shoebox, heavier than the others, and this tumbled to Iman's feet, spilling photographs on to the floor.

There were photographs of them as a family in Cyprus and Geneva, several of her father standing next to his Lancia in Monte Carlo, others of her and Rashid at school in Switzerland. There were some enlarged ones of Sabri and Lana by their wedding cake that she passed over quickly, two of Naji as a baby, and then in a brown envelope scribbled with rough calculations were photographs of her mother. These were professional photographs on thick card with clipped decorative edges and in them her mother was wearing fatigues and standing in the desert with a Kalashnikov. Iman switched on the desk light and checked the pictures. She looked from one to the other until she was absolutely sure of what she was looking at. The badge on her mother's sleeve was that of the leftist group, the Front, and her mother's nose had since been completely altered by plastic surgery.

PART IV

LONDON CROWDS

Six months later

Chapter 28

London was quiet to Iman. The traffic, planes and people worked along allocated channels. They moved along the grooves cut out for them. It was not a world shaken down and cut through night after night. The noise was conformist and the talk and expressions appeared to operate on one level only. People behaved in ways that seemed unconnected to others. Their actions had repercussions only for themselves. There was an enviable ability to relinquish involvement in the bigger picture, to believe that it was all under control, that somebody with your interests in mind was looking out for you.

But close up the whole place was talking. London was babbling. The air was crossed through with questions and fragments of sentences, the tails of the kites of conversations that flew elsewhere:

. . . *so I said to Nisha* . . .

. . . *could always do Ibiza if we can't do Goa* . . .

. . . *machine-washed my dinner jacket three times already* . . .

. . . *knocked through into the dining hall* . . .

. . . *like a crêpe rim around the bottom* . . .

. . . *he just won't talk to the children* . . .

. . . *she's a dancer, doesn't have any fat on her* . . .

. . . *I told him about the Viagra* . . .

. . . *her mother sang at the Sydney Opera* . . .

. . . *it's a mini form of typhoid* . . .

To get more of their lives, Iman followed strangers, fascinated by the directions that the mind's interests took when no longer consumed by fear. But then her world caught up with her and she could not do it any more.

The news became so terrible: an onslaught on a West Bank town, rumours of a massacre, of mass graves, and yet the chatter did not ease up for a second, there was no pause. The humanitarian organisations were being refused entry. The dead were rotting in the streets.

. . . it was bliss, it really was. Sailing on Thursday? . . .

. . . no one's going to go near you when you're breastfeeding . . .

. . . she does it to wind me up, every morning . . .

Food could not get into the town and the water was dirty; medical professionals spoke of the spread of cholera and typhoid.

. . . if I were single and could still get it up . . .

. . . he has the same land but better money . . .

The UN monitors still were not allowed to enter. The numbers of dead flew between the tens to the thousands. Day after day the town was pounded by missiles, hit by tank shells, mowed down by bulldozers.

. . . are you taking your camera on holiday? . . .

. . . you are always in my heart . . .

. . . the most amazing curtains . . .

The chatterers that filled the streets became complicit with each missile that blasted the town, each sheet-wrapped body thrown into a mass grave, each child screaming outside a demolished home. As soon as Iman had the satellite wired up to bring sympathetic commentators to her, she no longer felt any desire to be out there, in streets delirious with inanities.

Chapter 29

Rashid found Iman in the same position that he had left her five days before, curled into a ball of blanket watching the news. The coverage was in English now: *'The Israeli forces are engaged in a firefight with armed Palestinian militants . . .'*

'How? How, you son of a bitch, when we have rifles and you have F16 fighter jets, how do we *engage* them exactly?'

Iman was surrounded by screwed-up tissues. Rashid moved some cushions to sit next to her. The screen showed night footage, spitting lines of gunfire shot into buildings so continuously that it looked like the town was being pinned down with needles. Then the pile of a town burst into smoke and fire in three places. Iman jumped.

'It feels worse to watch this being here. Seeing these people just walking around without a care.'

'I know, Iman. I know,' Rashid assured his sister, who was on the verge of tears, or had just come out of them. He couldn't tell.

'Like my pointless flatmate. Not a clue. Forget the Middle East, she doesn't even care about the politics in her own country.'

Isn't that how it's meant to be? Not to care about politics? Rashid thought, but decided against saying anything as the commentator had started again, *'. . . the Israeli Prime Minister is sticking to his promise of tough retribution, saying only last month, "The Palestinians must be hit and it must be very painful. We must cause them losses, so that they feel the heavy price."'*

'When did you last leave the house?' Rashid asked.

'I went to the shop for some bread.'

'The shop doesn't count. It's just downstairs. When did you go anywhere other than the shop?'

'A week or so ago,' Iman replied vaguely.

'Exactly when?'

'That party you took me to.'

'That was weeks ago.' Rashid took the cushion that Iman was holding to her stomach and pulled the rug wrapped around her legs away before he got up to turn off the television. 'I know it's horrific but you can't just stay here just watching this all the time. You've gone yellow. Have you even eaten?' Iman nodded her head at a plate on the table with some crusts left on it. 'I'm taking you out with me.'

'Go out where? I can't go out. Neither can you. It's the demonstration this afternoon. Khalil's coming down from Leeds, remember?'

'Of course I remember. But this isn't going to take long. We have to go – there's a document at the Public Records Office. The file that Sabri is insisting that we get for him is back from their reviewers.'

'The file that was locked away for years and years?' Iman asked, sitting up.

'Thirty years. Yes, that one.'

'It's about Mama. It's to do with the photographs. She was in the Front. The file's about her. She must have done something that interested the Brits.'

Rashid seemed to be refusing to get the significance of the photograph of their mother. Her excitement to show the picture to him had dispersed when he had blithely looked at her and said, 'It just means that she was in a training camp or something for a while, that's all.'

'That's all?' she had replied. 'It's more than that. Why would she have changed her nose?'

'Probably just broke it jumping over a ditch with that gun.' But it was always fractious between Rashid and Mama and had been for as long as she could remember.

'Sabri would have told us if it was about her,' Rashid said, protective now. This was his news, his quest, his mission for a family member. 'He just said it was for his research.'

'No, Rashid,' Iman replied, not sure how far she should push it, 'What he said in his email was, "*Your Mama and I* are in agreement that the time has come for there to be greater knowledge of our *own circumstances* and the *roots of the divide*." That's what he said, and I showed you the photos I found at Baba's. When he says "divide" he's either talking about the divorce or the fact that she was in a different party to Baba. You saw for yourself that she even had her nose fixed. Look.' Iman pulled out the photos that she had wedged between the pages of the paperback in her bag.

'That in itself doesn't prove anything.' A woman as old as he was now smiled at Rashid from the pictures, triumphant. He doubted whether he would have got on with her even then. The gun she was holding had become so iconic that it made the photograph seem like some kind of spoof.

'They could not tell you anything else about the file?' Iman asked.

'I am sure they could, but let's just go and see it for ourselves. Get in the shower. Get dressed. You need to get out.'

'What, now?'

Iman had established a reliable three-pointed routine, with her bedroom, the television and the kitchen delineating her movements. Occasionally, she ate or went to the bathroom. Her flatmate moving around interrupted her patterns slightly and sometimes she had been forced to go outside to shop for food. But she had just gone to the shop and now had enough food for at least another three days. She had not planned to venture out again apart from going to the demonstration, which was different anyway. What was the point in going out and hearing people worrying about redecorating living rooms and broken-down boilers in ski chalets? Her triangle of life was about as comfortable as it got. It was all she needed.

'You want to go out right *now*?' Iman asked again.

'Yes, I do, and you are coming. What's the problem with that? The demonstration doesn't start until two. They'll let us copy the file so we don't need to be down there for long. There may not be anything in it.'

'What's the weather like?'

'Who cares? It's London; it will be different by the time you are ready to leave. Just get away from the news. *Khalas*. *Bikafee*. Finished. Enough. There is nothing you can do right now. Crying is not going to help. Come on. Move it.'

Rashid picked Iman up and carried her into the bathroom as though she was a bride he was about to dump over the threshold.

'OK, OK,' Iman almost laughed. 'Leave me alone, I'm up. I need my clothes. Let go.'

There were books from Iman's teaching course with uncracked spines lying on the table. The carpet had coffee and red wine spills on it; the ceiling was low and grey, but the walls had been painted recently and the view was not bad. Rashid opened the window to the blunder of lorries, clouds of birds and bursts of Bangla and rap from the cars. There was an anguished warmth outside. Spring was arriving in jolts. It was there for a couple of days and then it left without a trace. When it came, it made London all the more extreme. The sky, the grass, the parks became florid and this fest of colours throbbed with the jauntiness of bare flesh and loud laughter. The vigorous bounce of it was bewildering and then within hours it could be dark and rainy. Street lamps would flatten the faces of the office workers who hurried from their buildings to tubes and buses that stacked and squashed them up so that they could be transported home again, ill-looking people in need of a rest.

Rashid waited until he could hear the shower running before he turned the TV back on to listen to the rest of the news.

In the bathroom, Iman received a sign: a thin line of sticky pink in the gusset of her pants. She closed her eyes and sat on the toilet seat, rocking her knees a bit. It was going to be fine. She had done what she had intended to do and there had been no negative consequences. She was OK. It was OK. She had done it and got away with it. The shower was strong and the water made her hair jump with curls and stick its fingers up at Suzi and her Philippino girls with blow-driers and tongs.

Rashid waved a leaflet for a charity at Iman as she came out of the bathroom.

'It's not me; it's her, Eve my flatmate. She does charities.' Iman went back into her room wrapped in two towels. Rashid turned the sound of the TV up – it was news from home again. The journalists were nowhere near the town, they were all pumped up with the military on the outskirts, wearing the Occupier's flak jackets and donning its vocabulary: 'tactical strikes', 'guided missiles', 'armed militants'. *Baf!* Another missile. *Baf!* '. . . *unconfirmed reports of mass killings . . . fierce resistance . . .*' He turned it off.

'But I thought your flatmate doesn't care about anything?' he said when Iman reappeared from her room dressed in jeans and a winter coat.

'Eva? She can manage charities. They make her feel good, but she doesn't actually do or care about anything.' Iman threw some things in her bag: keys, wallet, travel card, apple, and the poetry paperback that concealed the photograph of her mother.

'Glad to see you're still into your ancient Bedouin porn.' Rashid smirked picking up the book of poetry. Iman kicked out at him.

'Shut up, Rashid. It's not porn,' she said before she turned on him as though she was going to launch straight into the heart of the matter. 'It's all right for you.'

'What's all right for me?'

'Nothing.' She retreated. It was impossible. She was sulking now. 'She just does charity; that's what I was saying.'

'Charity's better than doing nothing.'

'Charity just supports the existing system.'

'You sound like Mama.'

'Are those hers?' Rashid pointed at a white coat and a stethoscope hanging on a hook together with a mangy scarf.

'She's a medical student.'

'Can't be that stupid then.'

'Not stupid, just disinterested. It's worse.'

Iman hugged at her brother's arm all the way to the station and carried on hugging it until they found seats on the train. It was too hot for her coat. She took it off and hugged it too.

'I am not convinced it was worth it.' Iman spoke once they had sat through two tube stops in silence.

'What wasn't worth it?'

'Colonialism. Two hundred-odd years in India, another hundred or so in Egypt, thousands of years in Asia and Africa. If you stack them all up on top of each other it's feels like the whole history of civilised man, and for what? To create this place?' Iman seemed to be talking to herself. 'And people like Eva. What's the point?'

'What is your problem with Eva? Why do you keep going on about her?'

Iman stopped and pulled a face. 'I made her cry this morning.'

'Why did you do that? What's she to you, Iman?'

'She was trying to talk to me about what was going on in the news and she kept trying to do this supposedly objective BBC thing of being so intelligent and always looking at the other point of view, and she kept using their terms: "*terrorism*", "*democracy*". I flipped.'

'What did you say?'

'It doesn't matter, but I made her cry, all right? I hate these people who try to stay neutral in times of crisis.' Iman was picking at a sticker on a railing and wasn't looking at Rashid. 'I told her that she didn't understand anything. I told her about what happened to Taghreed and Raed, all the other bombings and how all her charity stuff was a waste of time and she had never really done anything to make a difference to anyone.' Iman looked at the toes of her shoes. 'I regret getting personal. I was just so angry. I know. It wasn't really fair.'

They got up to change trains, squeezing past Saturday shoppers and women with pushchairs. The air was sticky. On the platform, Rashid found a dented drinks can and kicked it around for a while. He considered telling Iman to apologise to Eva, but he knew that that wasn't something that she was likely to do, even though he could sense that she was urging him to tell her to do it.

'You're not worried about missing Khalil?' Iman asked.

'We'll meet him at the demonstration.'

'And Lisa?' Iman had been waiting for her brother to mention Lisa and was pleased that he had not. Rashid found some dead skin on the side of his left middle finger and bit at it.

'Don't do that.' Iman pulled his hand away.

'She's fine. Fine. She's just been really busy organising speakers for today's demonstration. Ziyyad Ayyoubi will be speaking. Do you remember that name? The fighter from the Patriotic Guard?'

'He's coming? Here?' But of course he was; he had to be, she decided dramatically, he was here because of her. 'He can't be here. Why? Why did Lisa ask him of all people?'

'It was a last-minute change of plan by the Authority; they switched him. But it seems he has a foreign passport of some kind so it's easier for him to attend. What's wrong with you?'

'Nothing. Why does he have a foreign passport?'

'How would I know?'

Two girls in matching outfits with soft stomachs and hard, moving jaws got onto the train.

'Do you know he's the son of Mona Zahlan and Khaled Ayyoubi?' Iman whispered.

'The couple who were shot in Beirut? No, I didn't know that.'

The girls sitting in front of them were sharing earphones plugged into a phone. One of them had caught Rashid's eye earlier and had wiggled her bottom a bit in her seat, crossed her legs this way and then the other way. For him.

Who cares? thought Rashid annoyed by this Ziyyad Ayyoubi. *It's not him. It's his parents. Why should being orphaned make you a better person? A braver person? A more worthy person? More likely to just fuck you up.* He could see it impressed his sister though. He wasn't going to get into that one with her. She could be so predictably like Sabri. Like his mother. They were a family. He was the outsider.

'I feel we haven't caught up on anything since you came. I've hardly seen you. How's your course? You still haven't told me about it,' Rashid asked.

'Expensive.'

'Worth it?'

'Not in the least. I told Baba that he was crazy to send me here but he was insistent that I don't go back to Gaza.' Iman made another face. 'He was also determined that I didn't stay in the Gulf.'

'What exactly was the fallout about with him? What happened?'

'Nothing *happened*. I didn't make a fuss or anything. I am just not really Suzi's type and I started making excuses not to go to coffee mornings and ladies' lunches and then she stopped inviting me.'

'Was that it?'

'Nearly, but the final blow was a date that Suzi had lined up for me with this Palestinian American guy. Rashid, you should have seen him . . .'

'Ugly was he?'

'No, I mean you had to *hear* him. He was just . . .' Iman waved her hands about. 'I got this long lecture about how we deserve the fate we have got, how Arabs are immature and don't think logically, all these quotes from UN reports about our underdevelopment and cultural backwardness.' Iman waved at the air. 'Oh, yes, and how we just have to believe in the Peace Process as it is the Best that We are Ever Going to Get. All this from a guy wearing a tweed jacket in fifty-degree heat who has never even *been* to Palestine.'

'You didn't get personal, did you?'

'No, not personal but just . . . you know, I went through the history of the Arabs, the effects of colonialism, the need for resistance. You know, standard stuff. It would have been fine, but he went back and told his mother, who told Suzi, who told Baba that I was a militant communist who held dangerous beliefs.'

Rashid started to laugh. 'Was he in the CIA, too?'

'Could've been. I don't know. I thought it was funny but Baba went crazy. Started screaming about his reputation and my reputation and who the hell was I involved with in Gaza anyway? Basically that was that; there was no place for me in the Gulf. I thought he would calm down and get over it. And he did calm down but he didn't change his mind. He went off and found out about this teaching course, applied for a visa and here I am. Never seen the man as determined about anything.' She shrugged. 'Great that you're here though.'

'It's good to have you here. Not that I seem to be able to get to see you. What happened to you at Steffi's party? You just disappeared.'

'I was tired, I got a lift home.'

'Who with?'

'This English man.'

'We're in London. There are lots of English people here. Does this one have a name?'

'Charles.'

'Charles Denham?' Rashid asked, remembering the name from the thick crested card. 'The civil servant? The stiff guy? You were talking to him for ages. You liked him?'

'He's not stiff; you're just saying that because he's English. Typical stereotyping on your part. He's OK. Look, this is our stop, isn't it? Come on.'

Chapter 30

The voice on the intercom had sounded harassed and urgent, 'I can't hear you. Sorry, I can't hear you. Can you just come up?'

Khalil had pushed himself into a hallway walled with bicycles and plastered with takeaway flyers and made his way up a muddy, once pastel carpeted staircase to the top floor flat where a shabbily dressed girl with marble skin and weak eyebrows stood against the doorway. She looked exhausted.

'I'm Khalil, a friend of Iman and Rashid's.' Khalil was out of breath by the time he reached the top.

'Oh, you just missed her. Iman, unusually for Iman, has just gone out. I don't know where she is.' The girl was about Khalil's height, and wore bent glasses. 'You're unlucky because she hasn't so much as left the house for the last week or so.' The girl had a slight twitch in her nose and seemed to be suffering from a cold. She looked at Khalil's bags, a small canvas rucksack and a sizeable sports bag. 'Where did you come from?'

'Leeds. But I've known Iman and Rashid all my life. We live in Gaza together.' Khalil felt a need to explain himself, to be clear in his English. 'I can't understand why they aren't here. I only came down to see them and because of the demonstration. They were the ones insisting that I attend it.'

'You better come in and wait,' Eva said, opening the door wide, 'or leave your bags at least?'

Khalil removed his shoes and placed them outside. They both looked at his feet in his electrician's socks.

'I don't really know what she gets up to,' Eva continued. 'Sometimes she's gone all night. Other days she's just holed up in front of the news for days on end, particularly this week.'

Khalil was still holding the door open. This girl seemed to be on her own in the flat. If he were back home he would leave the door open, to show the neighbours that there was nothing going on. He waited for a while, to gauge her possible reaction before he shut it tentatively behind him. His embarrassment at their isolation together did not seem to be felt by her. She offered him the TV remote.

'You want to see what's going on?'

Khalil took in a large Gauguin print in a clip frame and a wrinkled apple in a fruit bowl.

'I was just doing coffee,' she said, indicating the kitchen, 'if you'd like?'

'Yes,' Khalil was unsure about what to do. He could study while he waited he supposed.

'You're Iman's flatmate?' It didn't feel right to ignore the girl when she was making him coffee.

The room was vibrating with traffic noise: revs, car stereos, brakes, accelerations, the scream of sirens. Eva dulled it by pulling down the sash window, leaving them with the sound of the neighbour's music through the wall.

'In a way, but I don't think Iman would have *chosen* me as a flatmate,' she said with a fake-sounding *hah!* 'It's more of a flat-share arrangement by the university. We didn't know each other before we moved in.'

Eva swatted at some fruit flies buzzing over the apple, momentarily disturbing their orbits. She sat on the edge of her chair as though she was Khalil's guest and was not quite sure what to do with herself.

'Why wouldn't she have chosen you?' Khalil had thought about going through the notes from the workshop he had just attended and had pulled them out, but then he changed his mind and shoved them back into his bag.

'She doesn't approve of my politics, or rather my apparent lack of them.' Eva gestured with her hand and snorted slightly.

'Oh, really?' Khalil smiled at the idea of Iman flipping out, 'Don't worry about Iman. She's a bit hard on people. She's probably just upset about what's going on.'

'You think so?' Eva picked a piece of skin off her lips and bit at it.

'Completely. I've known her since we were kids. She does sometimes give the wrong people a piece of her mind at the wrong time.'

'Oh, really? I thought it was just me.' Her eyes disappeared as the steam from the coffee covered her glasses. She took them off and rubbed her eyes. 'Does she know you're coming?'

'Her brother Rashid definitely knew. We set it up weeks ago. There's this huge demonstration starting at two. But I can't seem to get hold of either of them this morning.'

Khalil took off his jacket. Eva rubbed her nose with the back of her hand. Khalil gestured at a chair, even though it was her place, but she seemed to want to talk.

'What was it you said that set her off?' he asked.

'That Israel was the only democracy in the Middle East. That's bad is it?'

'Unforgivable,' Khalil replied sternly, 'and no longer accurate either.'

'I only said something because she seemed so distressed. I wanted her to explain. It is such a dominant conflict in the world. To have the kind of limited understanding of it that I have, is kind of sad.' Eva looked appropriately miserable.

'You need to come to the demonstration then,' Khalil said as though it was an obvious conclusion. 'The speakers are excellent.'

Eva was about to object. She had her finals coming up. She had 124 pages left to do that afternoon on blood. She should be studying. Demonstration? She had never been on a demonstration. She didn't know this man at all. Going on a demonstration about *the Middle East*? No. That just was the kind of thing she did not do. Khalil looked up at her again, his eyebrows raised a fraction, just enough to make her feel the challenge in them.

'Yes. Yes. OK. I'll do that.' Her mouth expressed that she had resolved something of significance.

'Good. It starts at two. We'll go together.' It being agreed, Khalil and Eva sat together in silence. He had never managed to master small talk. He thought of his papers. 'I could show you some maps that would help to explain the background,' he said, not wanting to push it. 'If you are interested that is.'

'Yes,' Eva said. 'Yes, that would be good.'

'These maps show it graphically, which is the most important thing, and you can see here that the whole conflict is about land and the depopulation of that land of one group of people for the benefit of another. Ethnic cleansing, basically.' Khalil pulled out a book and bent back the spine to show three dated maps of the same land with different borders and blocks of shading. 'Here, in 1917, we have a hundred per cent of the land under the Mandate. Go to 1947, the recommendation is that we should have thirty-three per cent. Currently, what we are actually given is less than five per cent of the land, and then no real autonomy in that part . . .'

Eva looked at a solid elongated country with its hatched grey land becoming blotched with amoeba-shaped patches of the same colour. She also looked at the hands holding the book open to her, delicate male hands with noticeably clean fingernails.

Chapter 31

'You knew about this, didn't you?' Rashid was asking. 'You knew and you didn't tell me.'

After filling in multiple forms, Iman and Rashid had been taken into a room with bright blue carpet tiles and lined with empty shelves the colour of bleached oak. They had read the memo that was on the top of the file twice and had looked at the one photograph clipped on to it of their mother challenging a cameraman with a gun in her hand.

'They told you, didn't they? Sabri and Mama? They just decided that it was me who shouldn't know.'

Rashid's internal tumble and slide to somewhere below and apart from the rest of his family was quick and brutal. The sense of being punched out from the group was not a new one and once the realisation (and the shove that came with it) that they had been in on this together came to him, it felt obvious, as though it was something he should have always have known was going to happen. It was an eternity ago that he had had any expectation that it wouldn't. His family were on a piece of ice that had broken off and was scudding away from him on a different current. He was no part of it, no part of the struggle and no part of them. He didn't know why it had taken him so long to understand that this was the case.

'I had no idea that the photographs meant this,' Iman said. 'I honestly had no idea, Rashid. And I did try to discuss this with you. You just didn't want to know. I guessed these documents would be to do with her, because of the photos that I found. I knew no more than you did. I would never have guessed that she was . . . well, that she was someone like *this*. I mean, would you? No, obviously you didn't, but there's no harm . . . I mean, really, it's amazing, isn't it? Rashid, sit down. Don't just stand there staring at me like I've harmed you in some way.'

'This is the way that they decide to tell us, well to tell me anyway: to send me down to a Public Records Office to find a document that has been released after thirty years. What would they have done if this document had been held back for fifty years or a hundred? Do you think they would ever have told us what she did? What she was? I mean, she is our mother after all.'

Rashid flicked at strip of laminate that had come loose from the corner of a shelf.

'She would not have been able to tell us for security reasons. Probably nobody knows; I mean, everybody knows about her, about the person she was, but she had to keep her identity secret from everyone. I mean, it must've been really dangerous for her if she had to change her face and everything. And Sabri needed the documents for his research.' Iman moved to get up.

'It's always about Sabri, isn't it? Always about Sabri needs this and that and whatever . . .' Rashid tugged at his jacket and remembered what he had left in his pocket from the night before and the proximity of it to his body was like contact with a sensual presence, like the touch of the lover whom you were not aware was in the room. 'I'm going outside for a smoke. I'll be on a bench or something, if you want me.'

Iman let him go, she wanted to stay with the file for a little longer, to rest her hands on the memos written by the men of Whitehall that her mother had thwarted. She smiled at the carbon-copied documents and the notes scribbled in the margins, the codes of numbers and letters. She read the top memo again, settled into the pride of the heritage it bestowed on her:

Re: Palestinian Leftist Groups Hijackings
Profile: 'ASFOOR' or 'The Sparrow'
Date: 11 December, 1971

It is believed that this is the only existing photograph of this female member of the communist Popular Front for the Palestinian Struggle for Liberation ('PFPSL') who is known by the name of 'Asfoor' or 'The Sparrow' in the popular Arab press. For security reasons it has been decided that this photograph should not be made public, although its broad circulation to our security forces and those security forces with whom we have signed the Agreements on Security for the Co-ordinated Response to the Hijacking of Aircraft as well as our intelligence and Foreign Office branches is to be encouraged.

This photograph was provided by an unnamed source that has declined to provide any further information about this suspected terrorist.

Little is known about the suspect. She is in her late twenties, of dark appearance, with a noticeable gap between her front teeth. She is approximately 5'4" and of slim build.

The Sparrow has been turned into a heroine in the popular Arab press due to the PFPSL's hijacking of Flight 432 from Athens to Tel Aviv on 23 September, 1971. Details of the hijacking have been documented elsewhere (see Memo to HQ of 28 September and 12 October, 1971 and the Intelligence Report of 8 January, 1970), it suffices here to report that the hijacking was considered by the PFPSL and the popular Arab press to be a 'success' for the PFPSL and Palestinian resistance in general, their demands being met by the Israeli government and all of the hijackers having escaped arrest. The mystery surrounding The Sparrow's origins appears to have added to her personal appeal.

Our intelligence services report that The Sparrow is dangerous. Although she is not reported to have harmed any of the passengers on Flight 432, she was armed and threatened passengers with the use of force. There are warrants for her arrest in three jurisdictions (Israel, Greece, Jordan) due to the criminal nature of the hijacking itself.

As far as the security and intelligence services are aware, Flight 432 is the only known terrorist activity that The Sparrow or PFPSL has been engaged in.

All further information on The Sparrow should be reported to PV456 in the Middle East Department of the Foreign Office and DV342 in our Intelligence Services.

Chapter 32

The way she remembered Steffi's party was him standing by the table with the drinks on it, sipping red wine out of a plastic cup. His manner, she decided later, was one of bemused humility. He had latched on to her as soon as she walked in and watched her with a gauche lack of subtlety that was almost exciting. He'd stared at her. Wherever she went in the room he had watched her.

To hell with Suzi, Iman had thought at the sight of the English man fixated on her, *to hell with her*. Develop yourself *as a woman*. It bugged her immensely that despite the disrespect she felt for every aspect of Suzi, the judgement had resonated and caused so much self-doubt. Iman felt as though her inexperience had been branded on her forehead with a cattle iron. She wondered about the visibility of her sexual immaturity continuously. She scrutinised photographs of herself from a new angle, analysed reflections in shop windows and mirrors with a new critique. But mainly she tried to weigh up the possible impression she made on people, particularly men. Did they see it, too? That *lacking* that Suzi had hinted at, the *naivety*, the *inexperience*?

The man waited until Iman was closer to the drinks table before he held out his hand. 'Charles Denham,' he announced, shaking her hand repeatedly as though they had just settled a deal.

Leaving the party with him had not been difficult – he had suggested it – but the rest of the plan that she had decided upon during her second glass of wine was not going to be as easy.

He didn't have a car and she liked that, particularly after the fussing she had experienced in the Gulf: those men who paused expectantly in front of their vehicles waiting for her praise, her awe, the instructions she had been given about how to raise and tip and slide her seat forwards using pointed electronic controls, the irritated commands, 'Careful when you get out', 'Don't slam the door', 'You only need to twist it once'.

'I can only ride a bike,' Charles said as they got into a black cab.

He had tried to direct the taxi towards her flat but that had not been what she had decided upon. 'Can't we just see London for a bit?' she asked. 'Drive around?'

'Of course.' Charles followed a look (of relief perhaps or was she flattering herself?) with a long string of directions communicated to the driver, which the driver barked back as though they were about to parachute behind enemy lines. The taxi swayed around a corner, moving further away from the traffic, through the gates of a park, past fountains sprouting cherubs and chariots. Charles pointed out monuments and streets, parades for royals and palaces for princesses. In between landmarks, they carried on their conversation from the party about the situation back home. He did not ask about specific people, or even particular groups or movements but seemed more interested in her thoughts, ambitions and beliefs for change. He did not drag her into the mire of existing ills that such conversations normally wallowed in.

'Where do you live?' she had asked. He named somewhere that she had heard on a domestic news report.

'It's not really a residential district; it's where all the government offices are.' He cleared his throat. 'The flat was left to me by my great-aunt. It's very convenient for work. It's a bit dark, being a basement, but I'm rarely there during the day. Can't complain.'

'Can we go to your place?'

She had almost laughed aloud when she saw how much this

question threw his reserve. But then he was back on his saddle, back into his role.

'I'm with you, sir,' the driver repeated the change of direction tonelessly. The last thing Charles pointed out before they arrived at his flat was the headquarters of the intelligence services just across the river.

Chapter 33

The swell of demonstrators was growing, strengthened by pedestrians and passers-by who streamed down from alleyways, emerged from tube stations and off-loaded from coaches. Police helmets and shields wobbled out of line with each other along the sides of the road. Armoured vehicles rolled up between the surveillance vans on the kerbs. Spy cameras on hydraulic brackets were manoeuvred to examine the crowds. They focussed in, pulled back, moved inwards again as they were adjusted to scan, identify and pinpoint.

His mother's file had been a betrayal to Rashid. It was not just that his family had hidden something so significant from him for so long, but that they had had him find out in such an offhand way, as though Rashid and Iman reading the file was merely incidental to Sabri's research – yet another snub from his elder sibling and his mother of the type he was unable to get used to. He rejected it. He didn't see why he should have to take it, just because of what Sabri had been and because of what he had become, nor because of what his mother had been.

To Rashid the whole thing was a deliberate slur against him.

But to Iman, it was none of these things. To her, it was a discovery of a legacy that she deserved. It gave her the legitimacy that her father's spineless involvement with the Outside Leadership, followed by his ignoble and unexplained defection, had sapped them of. She knew that if the release of these documents were to reveal her mother's identity, it would do Iman no harm, in fact the opposite. No one would interrupt her in committee meetings any more for a start. It was a cry for recognition. She was knighted by the revelation; London was humbled by it.

The demonstration was in her honour.

'Yo! Rashid!' A yell came from behind a sheath of red banners, an army of black rubberised boots. 'Yo! Over here!' Ian was waving with gusto from behind his militia of revolutionary workers. 'What do you think, brother? Not a bad turnout, eh? We did a lot of the work, you know, although, of course, it will be others who take the credit.'

The crowds spanned out across the street, stood up on the kerb, they eased themselves around the corner. The procession swayed, jangled and bristled like a Chinese dragon. Their flag, Rashid's flag, Iman's flag, the until-quite-recently banned flag, flew above heads, reproduced again and again, with Arabic writing, Islamic scripts, with calls: *Freedom! Justice! Liberty! Against invasions! Against occupations!*

Rashid wanted to cry in happiness or in despair. He was not sure which. He could cry on anyone except Iman, because at the moment she was making it feel so much worse. He could even cry on Ian, because there was nobody else and Ian was now there standing in front of him smiling like the twit he was, and looking like he had been waiting for an eternity.

'Who's the girl?' Ian nudged Rashid to indicate Iman standing imperiously as demonstrators poured around her sides along the road, tramping on drains and on dropped flyers, skirting under banners while lifting their own.

'Iman. My sister.'

'She's hot. Want to introduce me to her?' Ian asked, looking past Rashid until he saw his face and changed his tone. 'OK, OK, chill, chill.' Ian's big hands flapped downwards before Rashid's face. Palm leaves before a ridiculous emperor. 'I was joking. Now is the time to overcome your patriarchal baggage. Calm down, OK?'

A lone Buddhist monk draped in red stood out against the black and denim swamp of the crowd. His jangle of peace bells and the rap of his tambourine were drowned by the shouts, the milling and the pure noise of the throng. Iman wanted Rashid to get a move on. Ian waved coyly at her from behind Rashid before she turned away.

'Look, Rashid. Look.' Iman grabbed Rashid's arm and pulled him further into the crowd, past small groups chatting as they walked, women with pushchairs and men with babies on their shoulders. She pointed to a makeshift placard with a black-and-white photograph on a stick. It was the hospital with the words, *'Who were you bombing on 8 August?'* handwritten above it with a black marker. Pictures of Raed and Taghreed were among those displayed at the bottom of the poster. Rashid could not help but be lifted too by the acknowledgment of injustice and the demand for it to be adjusted. He wanted to embrace the pale, bearded bearer with his Jesus sandals.

'Where's Khalil?' Iman asked.

'He's down by the main square. He sent me a text cursing us both for not being in this morning. He brought your flatmate, by the way.'

'Flatmate? You don't mean Eva?'

Rashid shrugged that he didn't know. How would he know, anyway? It was just a text. The prospect of moving into the square with this energised crowd was starting to make him feel weak.

'And Lisa?'

'Somewhere down there, too.' The knowledge, Rashid indicated, was with others and not with him.

Chapter 34

When they had arrived at Charles' flat over a fortnight before, the dark street had been pulsing with the blue lights of stationary police vans. His door had unstuck itself with a crack as he had forced it open. 'PM's just around the corner,' he had said in a way that suggested he always said it to himself or others as he stepped over the threshold.

The flat smelt old and felt unused. If it were not for the contemporary mess on the surfaces, it would have been possible to believe that it had been sealed up for decades and preserved against the century's turmoil. Charles strode ahead, trying to scoop up odd pieces of paper, a pair of trousers thrown over a chair, a cold mug that slopped something greyish on to the floor. He bumped into the lampshade causing a yellowy light to swing over the faded surfaces. It was furniture built for tight spaces and limited heat, for rooms where visitors stayed for a purpose and did not expect to be indulged. Books lined the walls around the fire and were stacked up on the floor. Several lay open on a polished wood and leather desk that seemed too small for a grown person. Swirls of flowers adorned the low sofa, the short curtains, the tapestry cushions.

'It's like my brother Sabri's room,' Iman said.

'Really?' Charles found it difficult to reconcile old-world chintz with new-world Gaza.

'The books,' she added. 'He has books everywhere. They even prop up his mattress.'

Charles thought fleetingly of a cartoon character, a worm or something, that had all its furniture made out of books. Bookworm. He was going to try to joke about it, but didn't think it would work. Her profile really was quite something. Great smile. He had always found gaps between women's front teeth rather thrilling. Stemmed back to reading Chaucer at school. Lascivious. She had that pre-Raphaelite thing going on, too. Charles flicked through some images in his head to try to find one that matched, but found none of them entirely satisfactory. There were also those rather lovely paintings of the bare ladies by the pool, fabulous detail of the blue painted tiles, Delacroix possibly? A bit out of fashion now. Should not be mentioned. Orientalist probably.

'A drink? Or tea? Do . . . do sit down, make yourself at home.' Charles took some papers off the sofa and patted it so vigorously that dust rose from the fabric.

'What are you having?'

'Scotch, I think, but I also have some liqueurs, if you are not partial to strong tastes. Or I could pop some ice in it?'

'That would do.' Iman looked over to the kitchen, where Charles was noisily washing two glasses. The cabinet doors had been removed and two chrome replacements leant against them. An orange cloth hung over a pipe under the sink. Charles walked into one of the spare doors.

'Trying to fix the kitchen up,' he said. 'Just never get the time to finish it. This girl I was seeing was very keen that I revamped this place.' He wished he had not mentioned another girl. He did not want to have that conversation: the one about exes and where it had gone wrong. She was bound to ask now. But Iman did not ask and Charles surprised himself by feeling a little put out by her failure to do so.

Iman could see some of the titles of the books: spy books, war books, books about dogs and the countryside. A whole shelf of books about a place called Blandings. There was a book about etiquette and several about the lives of Hollywood actresses who had grown fat or died. The walls had a lot of detailed etchings and lithographs, hunting scenes, Captain Cook landing among the natives, an Indian war scene entitled 'The Battle of Krishnapur 1845' with a jolly italicised caption underneath it about bivouacking.

'Bit of a collector, my great-uncle, liked the old military stuff. Arms dealer himself, you see.' Charles handed Iman a glass that was wet on the outside and sticky on the inside. He spoke to the crossed swords over the mantelpiece, because they knew him better than Iman did. 'Not really my cup of tea, but just don't know what to do with the stuff. No other relatives. Can't really just sell it all off.'

There was an extra 'r' in the last word that Iman had not heard others use before. *Orff.*

'Why not?'

'Well . . . well, I suppose I could. It's just not really done. It's not that it *can't* be done, I guess you could say, but it just *isn't.*'

Charles felt an anxiety with Iman in the room that he was not sure how to resolve, he did not want to be obvious about it but felt that really one should not be too indiscreet. He had left some confidential documents out which he didn't want to be too careless about. He placed his Scotch on the coffee table and got up to move his work papers back inside the desk and close up the flap. He sat back down.

'There, looks a bit neater like that. Bit of a mess really. Cleaning lady only comes on Mondays.'

Iman was quiet now, but at the party she had got heated about some erroneous supposition he had made. She had become fiercely aggressive and tremendously beautiful.

Charles tried to find something else that was as easy to fix as his desk, but could not see anything else that was as easy to remedy. He drank his Scotch in one go instead. *Ha. Done.*

213

Iman had come into the flat with a purpose, but then with a stunning suddenness, like a floodlight coming on to a stage she realised that she did not know what it was that she was supposed to do. She had no lines to utter, no directions as to which moves to make. She was a woman alone in a flat with a man. But still nothing had been resolved. Her message was not being picked up on. Normally just to *talk* for this long to a man would be enough to make her intentions clear. The drink stuck all over her mouth and her hands. It seemed to glue them all up. She felt a bit sick. She had not been drunk since school when the girls in her dorm had smuggled in some sweet wine. She had spent most of that night vomiting into the shower tray. Sometimes she had sipped *arak* with Sabri but that was not the same.

'Another?' Charles took the glasses and came back with them full and tinkling. 'Not quite the right shape, I daresay, but it will do, no? Better for brandy that one.' Charles moved across the sofa so he could see Iman. 'See, we are searching at the moment, at the FO, for a so-called Partner for Peace. It would be a cross-departmental collaboration; we'd be working with the development people, just at the non-governmental level, you understand. Now, I suggested Abu . . . someone. Well, whoever, but I have had some discouraging reports.'

Iman guessed a name and got it right. She smiled at it. She felt more comfortable now in this safe little hole underneath the centre of London's government, this flowery little bunker, unchanged for over a century or two, filled with the regalia of the past. There was comfort in victory, in the silence that it brought. The knowledge that the bed you slept in would always be yours in the morning. She could see Charles' confidence coming back with his subject matter. He furrowed his brow and small freckles found each other and merged into a tanned splat on his forehead. He had a habit of pushing his glasses up his nose as a sign of concentration.

He did this now although he had already taken them off.

'So, what I would like to put to you is, what would you do? Hmph? I have been, you may have noticed, skirting around, flirting with this issue all night, but tell me, what would you do in that role?' He spelt out to her the mandate, the proposal, the limitations, the freedom, and the possibilities.

Iman found the muscle in her tongue and spoke of ideas that had knocked against her head in her room, had been interrupted for 'points of organisation' at her women's meetings, would be taken as givens by Khalil and Sabri. Things that they all thought, that everyone knew.

'I see. I see. Excellent. Excellent. Well, let's see what we can do.'

Had she had one glass or two sitting there? Whatever it had been, even if it had been more, they had both gone into her brain and seemed to have both fouled it up and bedazzled it at the same time. The desire to giggle at her host and the pictures which surrounded him flooded through her. She fought an urge to stick her toe up his trouser leg to test for a reaction. A rush of opportunities all presented themselves to Iman at the same time. She thought of the things that had made her laugh, the bawdy Jahalia poem found by the Israeli border guards about the man's key wilting in its lock (how could she even try to translate that?), the men that Suzi had tried to set her up with and even (in a really warped way, that she had not thought possible), the sheer weirdness of that day when Seif El Din was murdered and Abu Omar arrested, that man Ziyyad Ayyoubi outside the house. It was quite a story to be told. She was about to start recounting it all, in all its hilarity and horror, when she was overwhelmed by a feeling of fatigue and loneliness. She could not see the point of any of it. He would not, he *could not* understand. She didn't know what she was doing. She had forgotten what the point was any more. She didn't even know where she was.

'You look a bit bushed.' He leant over enough so that he could stroke her cheek. He could not help it. Her hair against the sofa's pink roses and curling leaves made such a contrast. He would not get the sofas upholstered like his ex had gone on about; he didn't need solid colours. They were beautiful sofas. Exquisite. 'Shall I get you a taxi? Or I could make a bed up for you, I have this old camp bed that I can pull out and sleep on. You could have mine?'

'No, no, I'm OK, really.'

Iman stood up clumsily as though heavily pregnant and walked over to the bookshelves. He followed her and took her hand as he gave a commentary on the titles. 'A lot of it was here when I moved in.' He pulled out a red leather-bound copy of the *Rubaiyat of Omar Khayyam* and she flicked through its pages, marvelling at how there was much much more curiosity back then than now. He moved behind her and kissed her near her ear. She stayed still and waited for kisses until they compelled her to respond and it was all so much easier than she had thought.

The bed had been narrow and soft, a child's bed, pushed next to a wall and sunken in the middle. He had been courteous and she had refused to be shy. It had not hurt as she had been told that it would, nor had she bled, but his skin was foreign and on it his sweat had the smell of wet potato peel.

Chapter 35

As the march entered the square, Khalil was standing, as agreed, by the fourth lion in front of the burger place. He blended in better here, Iman thought, seeing him up there in his black jacket, than he did back home. Behind him, banners waved and in front of him a row of speakers sat on fold-up chairs on a platform. Lisa was to their side, writing on a clipboard, a phone squeezed between her shoulder and her ear. An elderly politician, his legs crossed, smoked a pipe.

Ziyyad Ayyoubi had been on the stage when they came into the square. There had been some applause when he had finished a point and then he had started another one before he looked down, and she knew it was ridiculous to think this, as it was hardly possible, but she thought that he had seen her. He had stopped mid-sentence. The audience waited, but instead of continuing he had stepped off the stage. The audience held on, murmuring and speculating loudly until a poet in an anorak stepped forwards, silver hair lifted around his head in a static cloud.

Iman could not see Ayyoubi once he had left the stage and she found herself looking for him until she realised that Rashid, who had been at her side when they entered the square, had also disappeared. She pushed through the crowd towards Khalil thinking it was the route that Rashid would have taken.

'I thought he went ahead to find you,' Iman said to Khalil when she found him.

'Is he avoiding me or something? I told him I would be here today.'

'I expect he just went to get something to eat. He's like that when he gets urges, he just shoots off; whatever it is, food, sleep, needing a smoke, he doesn't tell you or ask you, you just turn round and he's gone. You know Rashid. We went to the Public—'

'I know. You were out. I went to your flat.'

A choir in red T-shirts were now on the stage.

'What happened to your hair?' Iman asked.

'My father insisted on me cutting it. No, in fact he bribed me into it, true to form. I needed a pass to get to see Jamal in detention and he wouldn't help me out with getting one unless I cut my hair off. I know, it's outrageous, but you know my father.'

The red choir threw their shoulders back and formed a line of 'O's with their mouths on stage.

'You came with my flatmate?' Iman raised the tone of her voice to something a bit jokey, a bit mocking, which Khalil declined to pick up on. He answered her question seriously.

'Eva? Yes, I sent her off to talk to one of the speakers from the Medical Union of Healthworkers and one of the other medical charities.'

'Oh, good, good. Great idea.'

The crowd, muddy coloured and anonymous from afar, appeared diverse and Technicolor up close. People spread around the fountain and along the stairs. They stood in the roads; tourists photographed them from the top of buses; faces leant against windows to watch them pass. Some of the groups around her carried placards: *Socialist Jews Against War and Occupation*, *Muslims for Palestine*, *Welsh Singers for Peace*. Khalil acted as though he was entranced by the round-mouthed singers with their low-slung breasts (*Aaah! Peace! Aaah!*).

'Did you see Ayyoubi?' Khalil asked.

'We arrived just as he left the stage.' Iman checked Khalil's face to see if somewhere behind the diplomatic manner of his father he was mentioning Ayyoubi specifically to test her. She could not see anything like that.

'Strange. He stood up there staring at the sky giving a very impressive talk and then in mid-stream he just stops and goes. Gone . . .' Khalil continued to look around him. 'Where is Rashid? I was really looking forward . . . Is there any point in waiting for him?'

'He'll turn up. How's Leeds? How's the course?'

'It's not bad. It's nothing that I need to know, but they want to vet me for their own processes. I don't have much choice if I want to apply for a grant. Most of the funding for our type of work has gone. They're more interested in peace initiatives, "building rather than critiquing" in their words. Where is Rashid? I've missed the bastard.'

Khalil tried phoning Rashid as he looked around and up at the row of policemen and vans standing at the top of the steps, the rows of hard Perspex shields near the black-booted revolutionary workers. But Rashid was not down by the fountain or up by the museum, nor was he in any of the groups standing at the front of the stage. Pigeons fluttered around them pecking at the ground, unperturbed by the thousands of pairs of moving feet. Surveillance cameras focussed in on the faces of the crowd, twisting their hydraulic necks in order to record their images for ever.

'At least we can see that he's not with her.' Khalil gestured with his head at Lisa sitting primly up on the stage.

The crowd by the stage was too compressed for Iman to make her way through it and she didn't think it was Rashid's style to push himself up to the front. Some flyers caught on her feet. She slipped slightly on a ring of fried onion. A voice called out 'Yo!' from the brigade of black-shirted revolutionaries and she recognised Rashid's friend sucking on a rolled cigarette. He jumped forwards to meet her.

'Have you seen Rashid?' Iman asked.

'Not since earlier. We haven't met by the way. I'm Ian.'

'Iman.'

'Cool name. Does it mean anything?'

'Faith.'

219

'Beautiful.' Ian indicated his approval with a half-smile and a contemplative nod.

'So you haven't seen him, then?' Iman asked again.

Ian clicked the side of his mouth. 'Nope. Sorry. Rollie?' He proffered a squashed box of foil at her but she had already gone.

She moved towards the edge of the square where the traffic was still moving and she became pressed against people, bags and the sticks of banners until she came to a side street. There were so many dark heads, so many leather jackets, short sideburns and high fore-heads; it would be impossible for Rashid to stand out in any way.

An alert-looking Eva stood by the Medical Union stall. Her right hand was full of leaflets and booklets. Despite the hazy light, she looked brighter and healthier than she did indoors, but her internal light seemed to flicker as she saw Iman approach.

'Eva, about what I said this morning. I'm sorry I upset you.'

'Thanks for saying that, but it's OK. Really. It turned out for the best. It's totally OK. I think you were right.' Iman looked again at Eva. 'I mean, it really got me thinking and I had this *amazing* conversation with your friend, Khalil, who is just *incredible*, and he suggested coming down here, which I really didn't think was my kind of thing, but I did it and it's just been so, so *interesting* and I've met these really *awe-inspiring* people from the Medical Union and this other direct action campaign. It's been *amazing*. So, no, please don't apologise.'

Iman nodded at the doctors by the stand and wondered whether they knew her. 'They do good work,' she said.

'They're outstanding.'

Eva looked around her, and Iman tried to join her enthusiasm, struggling to recreate the sensation of elation she had felt earlier. Maybe she should tell Eva who her mother was.

'The number of people . . .' Eva continued, '. . . I mean, the *belief* they must have, and so many of them are just like me, no connec-tion at all to the place yet still they are here and, I don't know, I've never been on a demonstration before, but it's *incredible*.'

'Eva, you've met my brother, haven't you? You know what he looks like. You haven't seen him, have you? I can't find him. We were together and then he just disappeared.'

Someone from the direct action group had come up to speak to Eva and was anxious for Iman to leave. Eva smiled at the volunteer, before turning back to Iman. 'Oh, no. No. Sorry. I don't think so, but I'll look out for him.'

'Get him to call us if you see him.'

'Sure. Sure.' Eva stopped and leant close to Iman as though she had seen a spot on Iman's face that she was tempted to squeeze. 'You've known Khalil for a long time?'

'We grew up together.'

'I see. Over there?'

'No. Our fathers used to work together so we were together in Scandinavia, Switzerland, different places in Europe mainly.'

'Europe. I see. So he's like a good friend to you then, Khalil? That is . . . you're not together or anything, are you?'

'Khalil? No, no.' Iman tried to laugh but she could not help thinking of Lisa and it made her want to claim Khalil as hers. She struggled to be bigger than herself. 'I'm glad you came. I must say, I was a bit surprised when Khalil told me that you were down here, but I'm pleased that I got you wrong.' It was a dauntingly difficult thing for Iman to say, but Eva had already been taken over by the direct action group and had missed most of it. Standing next to Eva all wired up and enthusiastic did Iman no good at all.

Iman joined the stragglers leading into a side street. Smokers hung around in groups to chat; people made phone calls out of the noise of the speakers; some parents changed their toddlers' nappy in a doorway; couples drifted away from the mêlée for a late lunch, a stroll by the river, afternoon tea perhaps? It was muggy and close. The sky was taut and anxious to be released from its rain.

Chapter 36

They had just joined the demonstration when Rashid's gut filled with pangs that rose up in him and diluted the purpose of his body. A mussed-up haze had fallen over the demonstrators and the heat of them, the street and the tarmac was now trapped solidly between the buildings. It was dull and debilitating and the ligaments of his body were weak with the cravings of his stomach for it was a laborious ploughing that he felt he was doing through the crowd, stuck in place and barely shifting. He found himself unduly attracted by advertisements for food, the counters of small restaurants, biscuits being fed to children.

Once decided upon finding food, he nearly blundered into the wrong hamburger joint before he remembered the boycott, and the demonstration that would remind him of it if he broke it. He pulled himself away around the corner into a small café with a glass cabinet piled with sandwiches, each one the length of half his arm. He stuffed buttered meats and soft bread into his mouth, closing his eyes at the relief of it, and shoving and stuffing until it was all gone, bread, butter, slips of meat and crisps. He felt his body become braced back into place enabling him to feel relaxed enough to take in where he was, which was on a wicker bar stool under black and white photos of 1950s cars and girls in red plastic frames. A stream of demonstrators slunk away from the square to his right and from the square the speeches railed and crackled. He cleared out his nose and felt a whole lot better about everything.

There were four of them that came up to him as he left the café, or it could have been five. A lot of them anyway. Only two of them were uniformed. The one who was talking had a dark red mark across the bridge of his nose where some glasses had been and one of them had eaten garlic. Rashid knew that much because they were very close and piled into him, grabbing at his arms like he was going to try to get away, and saying a long name which sounded familiar and vaguely Arab. Inferences. The one with the takeaway breath was talking about inferences. There was a brusque closeness that was foreign and repulsive to Rashid; he wanted instinctively to hit them away but they had him pinned and stunned with his hands cuffed behind his back before he could possibly respond.

They led him towards a van on the side of the road while someone screamed and swore, but then he realised it was him. No one else, and those streets were full of people. Not one of them so much as raised an eyebrow at the staggering, blundering injustice of the whole thing.

'The suspect under surveillance is in our custody,' one of the uniformed policemen told the radio held to his chest. It had to be some kind of joke. Rashid's wrists were too large for the cuffs and they had pulled on them as though he was a reluctant cow, a prize cow.

What had he done, for fuck's sake?

'You've got it wrong,' he said. 'I haven't fucking done anything. Get off me.'

The van wailed as it spun around corners and more corners as though it was roped on to a central pivot around which it rushed and spun, bumping up and down over kerbs and cutting through lights, barging through stationary traffic. Without the use of his hands he was thrown across the back of the van, off his bench and on to his side. He pulled himself up and tried to find a bar for his fingers to catch on to.

Fucking calm it down . . .

And when they could be bothered to turn to check on him, they laughed at him through the thick soundproofed glass, their mouths going on about something inaudible but definitely hostile and personal.

When the van stopped and his feet had stationary ground under them again, they took him inside the station and removed all the contents from his pockets and placed them in see-through plastic bags. A man behind a high desk recorded it all and read out the list to Rashid, who did not hear anything.

A more senior-looking officer saw Rashid's name on the form, and looked at the custody sergeant behind the desk and said, 'That's who he says he is, is it?'

'Same on his student ID, sir.' The sergeant was a pointy-nosed little man with an air of diligence and mischief.

'Get one of those made in five minutes,' the senior officer replied. 'Take him down and we'll look at what we've got on him.'

He was allowed one phone call and he wasted it trying to call Lisa. Her phone was off. He left a polite but desperate message for her. Even if she wasn't his girlfriend, as she had seemed to want to stress was the case, she would still help him out of this, wouldn't she?

The room he was put in was about one and a half metres by two and had two plastic-covered mattresses at knee height at either side of it. There were no windows, only a small sliding opening on the door. The door was thick and covered with bolts. The cell smelt of piss, old smoke and sick men. There was something final about the smell.

'Get me a lawyer,' Rashid shouted through the grill. 'I should be able to see a lawyer.'

He kicked at the door until a very large officer came up to his peephole and looked in on him. Rashid promptly shut up.

'Better get him the duty,' he could hear someone say down the hall and he was sure he could make out the words, 'Bit of a fuck up.' *Bit of a fuck up?* Of course it was a bit of a fuck up. He had known that all along.

Rashid wanted to remember all of this, to mentally document it. He wanted to ensure that any tale told later to Khalil, for example, would be detailed enough. Now that he thought he had confirmation of what he had already known (*a bit of a fuck up*) he was able, for a while, to contemplate the cell with detachment. There was something almost desirable about the drama of the situation. It was so familiar to him from films and TV that to find himself in it gave him the sense that his life had taken on a dramatic purpose, that he had actually (finally) reached the level of being able to not just feature but to *star* in a narrative of some interest. This voice was convinced, no it just *knew*, that it was a mistake that Rashid had been arrested. It was an aberration. The chatty story-telling voice in his head would not contemplate any other alternative as to do so would deflect from the entertainment value of its own mission.

He continued to feed this perkily amused narrator in his head. It made him feel better and he was sure after the fuck up comment that his sense of this was the right one. He provided the narrative with details of graffiti from the walls, counted the cigarette burns in the thick mattress covers and touched the shiny hardwearing surfaces of the cell. He had sat back against the wall that was far too cold for a hot day, his feet on the mattress, waiting for Lisa, waiting for his lawyer, waiting for the policeman to come down the corridor and tell him that they were very sorry sir, but they had made a bit of a mistake. They just needed to clarify that there was a *bit of a fuck up, sir. Do apologise.*

Rashid resolved that he would be very gracious to the officer when he came.

Chapter 37

Iman was avoiding Charles. Although most of what had passed between them had been no worse in terms of embarrassment than border strip searches and medical examinations, the memory of the shudder that had run through him when the act had culmi- nated, as though he had released a great sneeze into her (a liquid sneeze that had actually spread wet and warm onto the sheet under her) was hard to deal with.

'What are you looking so pained for?' Khalil asked Iman. 'Squeezing your phone won't turn it off. There's a button for that.' Khalil had thought he had lost Iman too as the long, low light of evening had come in and the blocks of elongated building shadow were joining together. Eva had become ensconced with the direct action group, Rashid had never materialised and Iman was in a daze.

In the half-light the square looked as though it had been rolled upon by the demonstrators; it was strewn with miniature flags, crushed paper cups and abandoned flyers. The lines of police had broken into ambling groups, boarded on to multiple vans, and dispersed.

'No sign?' Iman asked.

'None. I don't get it. He sounded so keen to meet; I didn't think he would just go off. Did you ask Lisa?'

'She left with the VIPs before I had a chance to talk to her.'

'Some of the guys who came down here from Leeds want to get together for a bit.' Khalil indicated a group of men with banners declaring: *Muslims Against the Occupation*. 'I'll come over to your place later if that's OK? I left my bags there.'

'That's fine,' Iman said. 'I'll be there, or at least Eva will be. She never normally goes out. She's got her finals coming up. I'm amazed she came to this, to be honest. She's been studying through the night for weeks now.'

'You're going out?' Khalil looked dejectedly at Iman. She had not really decided what she was going to do; she just really didn't feel like going home. 'We need to catch up. We haven't even talked about the Gulf or anything. How's your father?'

'Baba now wears square-tipped shoes made of imitation snake skin. Yours? Is he still into lemon-yellow ties?' Iman asked.

'More of a lime green at the moment, but yes, he's the same.'

'I need to find Rashid.'

'Bastard.'

Iman and Khalil did not hug when Khalil left because Rashid was not there, that was their unspoken rule on it. Iman watched Khalil approach the group who were waiting for him. As he came close to them these brothers (for she was sure that was that they would call him) reached out to place their palms on his back as though it was the side of a holy stone.

The drawn-out, muggy weather felt like it was working on something, storing it to burst. The demonstrators had almost all dispersed. Iman wanted to go before the tourists moved in around her with their pointlessness, which she feared might be contagious. She found herself heading towards the river, down the street where Ayyoubi had disappeared. The side street fanned out into a small square, with its embellished greenery and a handful of wooden benches.

As she walked down the side street, Ziyyad Ayyoubi stepped out from behind a bush. She nearly laughed at the shock and absurdity of his appearance. It was nuts for him to pop out like that. Had he been hiding behind a rose bush? Behind him a mass of yellow green laurel leaves pushed up against the railings. There were rosebushes too and Ayyoubi appeared surrounded by a profusion of petals and lusciousness. The air hung heavy with the rain to come and the scent of blooms. It was all so different from the last time they had met. But he was the same: the same jacket, the same stance, and the same look of intense interest in her. This time he was not carrying a gun, but she felt she could see it on him anyway.

'Miss Iman,' he stepped towards her, and she smiled awkwardly as though she had been caught out doing something wrong, skiving in exile possibly. She realised that when he was close to her he had the not unpleasant effect of making her feel small. She could not say his name back to him in return. Since they had first met she had found herself addressing so many explanations to a spirit of him that his name – *Ziyyad Ayyoubi* – had become both irrelevant and far too powerful at the same time. It seemed almost degrading to reduce the sense of him to something so limited and arbitrary.

They were noticeable standing there. Everything and everyone she felt, must have stopped to observe them, the solemnity of them, the profundity of them being in the same space. It was remarkable. It had happened. They had done it. They were there. Together.

They stood as though they were waiting for someone or expecting something. He was smiling as though she had brought him news of great importance that would affect them both.

'I'm looking for my brother.' She wanted to dislodge his expectation although she needed it at the same time.

'I hoped you might be here.'

'You haven't seen him?'

'Your brother? No, I haven't. But someone mistook me for him. An English guy wearing black.'

'I think I should look around the square again.' It was too heavy between them. She was not even listening to what he was saying. Was he saying anything? Something was definitely being

communicated to her. She was concentrating only on his movements and the way he said things.

'Yes.' He shrugged but otherwise didn't move.

Perhaps she had got him wrong. He seemed scared of something
now, moving back into the bushes and the trees, away from the
thin traffic of people. She had imagined telling him that he was
right and that she had made a mistake on that day and had been
stupid. She had already apologised to Eva, she might as well apologise to him as well. Have a day of apologies. Get it all over with in
one go. Perhaps she should thank him for pulling her back like
that from the explosion. *You saved my life. Ha!* She had gone as far
as to think of apologising for the way she had addressed him then
and afterwards, but now he was there looking so daunted by her
(he kept looking away to the side) she didn't feel that he deserved
the apology for some reason. She almost wanted to insult him or
to tell him to sort himself out somehow, to make him more of
what she had wanted him to be.

'He was with me and then he was gone. I don't know where.'
She looked up and down the street and into the square. He made
to speak but stopped and gestured something to explain his inabil-
ity to do so. 'I need to look for my brother.' She turned
self-consciously. She had hardly taken a step when he grabbed out
at her as though she was a wallet falling over the side of a boat.

'I needed to see you. I was hoping you would be here, in London.
I needed to see you. I wanted to explain about Abu Omar and to
find out whether you knew . . . Has your brother said anything to
you? Did he tell you the history?'

'About Abu Omar? Why would Rashid know anything?'

'No, not Rashid. Sabri.'

The low evening light passing between buildings was straight in
her eyes. He became a fuzzy-edged form in front of it.

'I'm looking for *Rashid*.'

'I know, and you'll find him. He must have gone off. Leave him for now. He'll turn up.'

A couple walked past them laughing, the woman saying something with an air of contempt. Iman could not make out what it was.

'What about Sabri?'

'Let's go somewhere else.' When he smiled she could see he had a tooth missing on the right-hand side, towards the back. She could see now, gathered around his eyes and mouth and streaked across his forehead, evidence that he was much older than Rashid and herself. They could be as much as a generation apart, but the similarity to Rashid was definitely there. He looked down the street away from the square. 'I don't really want to stay here.' He checked around him. 'There's a place that I'd like you to see. There are things that you need to know.'

Above them something had ruptured in the sky and lightning cracked behind them.

'We could go to this place. This way.' He started to guide her then he paused. 'I need to explain a couple of things,' he said, stopping so unexpectedly that a woman behind them rammed her pushchair into the back of his legs. *'Watch it, will you?'*

He guided her along until they were on a broad street with glass ball lamps, fluttering leaves and plane trees with mottled barks.

'There it is.' Ziyyad nodded towards a white hotel that sat huge and luminous on the darkening road, a bulk of iced bullion sprinkled with a thousand and one lights.

'You want to go to that place? That hotel?' Iman recognised its name from a novel she had read at school. It belonged to a world of feathered women and men with slicked-back hair who sliced up the Arab world with sharp pencils after dinner. 'We can't go in there.' She stepped backwards as though pre-empting a push by one of the liveried doormen.

Ziyyad ignored her. He took Iman through the lobby, walking just as he did on the Gaza streets, and did not seem to notice the cloaks of scruffiness that fell over them as soon as they entered the hotel. Tacked on to the back of the building was the bar that he wanted her to see, a glass and wrought-iron structure with mirrored walls and chandeliers. Glass bottles replicated themselves in a glittering cabinet at the back of the bar.

'Here,' Ziyyad said proudly. 'What do you think?'

Garish, thought Iman. *It's been made to look cheap when it isn't.*

'How did you find this place?' she asked.

'They wanted me to stay here,' he spoke as though it explained everything but when he looked at her he could see that it didn't. 'The Authority. They made a reservation here, but when I saw the place I knew I could not take it. I don't want them to be able to say that I accepted any favours. Any privileges.'

They stood at the doorway to the bar. Across the lobby four men with balding heads and ill-fitting suits had just arrived. Ziyyad stared intently at them. He did not move until the men did.

'I have enemies.'

'We all do,' Iman replied.

'And they all pretend to be your friends.'

'Not all of them.'

'Maybe not. But mine are out to get me. Come.' He tried to adopt a different persona, a new smile for a new place. The bar glittered at them, ostentatious and uncared for. The hotel was not theirs, but she did not know whose it was. It could, she supposed, be theirs for an evening if they wanted it to.

It wasn't until they approached the table that she realised how closely they had been standing and walking together since they met on the side street. She hadn't consciously intended to, but it was as if she was compelled to step into his steps, to keep the space around the two of them tight, contained. They sat at a table and it seemed extraordinary to her to do so with him. She half-expected the weirdness of it to be picked up by the other people in there, but the drunken businessmen '*I told him no more than three mill and he went ahead with six,*' and disconsolate tourist families '*We can do the Aquarium after the show, or shall we just go back to Oxford Street?*' were unable to see it.

'Your family are well?' He finally broke into the silence.

'My family? They're fine.' She almost said, *and yours?* and then couldn't think of anything else as she realised how bad it would have been had she done so. 'I saw the end of your talk,' she said. 'I arrived in the square as you ended.'

'I need to explain that.' There was a goofiness to his closed-lipped smile. It didn't match the tunnelling that went on behind his eyes, as though something somewhere had been cast adrift.

He ordered her a fruit cocktail as she couldn't be bothered with the menu, and tea for himself. When her drink arrived she found herself contemplating the straw that stood erect at the centre of the layer of paper umbrellas, cherries and chopped pineapple on the drink's surface.

'What do you need to explain?'

'I had an episode back there when I was giving my talk. I'm OK now, but I have these moments . . . crowds, blood. I'm phobic, apparently. It's been a long time since it last happened. I was fine when I was speaking, because I was looking up so I could not see the people. And then I had this strong desire to look down. And suddenly all these faces around me, waiting.' He grimaced. 'It's over now.'

'You've always had this?'

'Since I was a child. It was when my parents—'

'My father knew your parents.'

'Really?' He brightened momentarily. 'Where? Beirut, I suppose.'

'They read too much for his liking.'

'Read, talked and partied is what I remember.' Again, the

missing tooth at the back of his mouth. A line of vein across his temple that one could trace along with a fingertip. 'Listen, Iman, I need to explain about that day, about Abu Omar—'

'Abu Omar?' Iman hadn't wanted him to raise their former neighbour or anything about that day again.

She would have rather let Abu Omar slip for a moment as they sat in that glassy place. The closeness and the strangeness of where they came from wrapped around them like a thick rug, but she didn't want it between them. She was fed up with voicing her views, giving her position. His shoulders were beautiful. There was rain coming down on the glass roof above them. She put the cherries into her mouth and tried to discreetly remove the stones with a cupped hand and he looked at her as though her doing this was curious and charming. He concentrated so much on her wrist that she became quite self-conscious about it. She found herself looking at it as though it was something quite new. She didn't want to have Abu Omar and his sorrowful gut brought into the uniqueness of being there.

'What about Abu Omar?' she asked dutifully.

'He was instrumental . . .' Ziyyad started. 'We have proof that he was instrumental—'

But her phone rang and it was Khalil telling her about Rashid and she didn't get to hear any more than that.

Chapter 38

The corridor outside Rashid's cell was filled with the anger of drunks. A woman's high heels dragged backwards down it. *You fucking waankerrs* . . .

It was remembering that he had left his window slightly open that morning that made Rashid feel a plunging sense of absence and desperation at being in the cell. In his room, it would be dark now. The sheets on the bed would be cold and the computer would be blipping to itself as the messages piled up on to its screen. There would be an orange light from the street. It was those transformative hours of the evening as night came about that he relished most in that room.

It was all there waiting for him. But he would not be going back, maybe not tonight, maybe not ever. He would become just another story of a detention, a deportation, a rendition: another story of injustice and illegality to be deleted as junk. That was how it was to end for him, on a piss-stinking mattress in an underground cell of a London police station with hookers and drunks. If he had known that this was how it would end. *If he had known.*

Lisa. He had screwed up with Lisa. If he had not drunk so much beer at the restaurant, it would have been different. He would not have so much as *thought* about asking her sister out; he knew now that that was where things had started to go wrong. The small things he remembered now: the way she edited his essays with her red pen and straight back, the time she had stitched up his bag where the buckle had come undone, how she pushed her chin up as her hair fell back across the pillows and down the side of the bed, that time together on the stairwell. He hugged at his legs but they were stiff, bony things that no one would want.

The noise of slamming cell doors punched at his gut. Winded him. A round-up. All the Arabs in London. It was all over. There were grass stains on his knee from looking for the lighter he had dropped under the bench outside the Public Records Office that afternoon. They were signs from a different life. His mother smiling with the gun. They had not got her. She had done things – hijacked a plane for fuck's sake – and they had not got her, and he had not even done anything and yet it was all over for him.

You fucking . . . the shouting started up again. Songs from the demonstration came from somewhere transformed into ancient chants by the acoustics of metal doors and shiny walls.

'Mr Mujahed.' *Moojaheed.* One of the officers had slid back the tile-sized opening in the door. 'We have now been able to verify your identity and due to that, we are able to downgrade the basis of your arrest from that of a Serious Arrestable Offence to an Arrestable Offence. This change of status, which has arisen due to a clarification of your identity, which appears to have initially been mistaken for that of another person, wanted by the police for more serious offences, means that—' The eye had now been replaced by a mouth.

'I can go?'

'Oh no, my son. You cannot go.' The officer sounded almost gleeful. 'Because upon your person you were discovered to have – in your possession – a significant amount of cannabis resin. You even signed for it on your arrival.' Rashid didn't know how, but he had completely forgotten about it. 'That would be marijuana,' continued the officer. 'We are therefore holding you on suspicion of being in possession of a Class C drug with intent to supply. You have requested the duty and the duty is on her way, although she seems to be taking her own sweet time due to the fact that they got all excited in her offices when they thought you were here as a terrorist suspect and they were going to send the partner, but now it is only a drugs and immigration matter they are sending a rep instead.'

The eyes appeared in the hole, pale popping eyes that moved slowly towards Rashid.

'Only a junior mind, probably fresh out of nappies. Sometimes do more harm than good, so what do you think? You can go ahead with the interview without her right now if you choose to. Your choice, mind, but we may need to stick some others in your cell, if you see what I mean. Could disturb your peace and quiet, so if you want to get going, we are happy to go ahead now. At your service and Her Majesty's pleasure, so to speak.'

Would youse shut it? The woman's voice yelled across the corridor at the revolutionary chanter. 'Damn right,' joined the officer. *Pigs* replied the voice. 'Fucking shut it,' the officer boiled up and exploded, 'or I'll fucking shut you up.'

'I'll wait for the lawyer, thank you.' Rashid was standing now. *Thank you?* It was pathetic.

'Suit yourself, if that's what you really want. Could be a wait though.' The officer slammed the window shut.

Chapter 39

It was Lisa on the phone. A Lisa so breathless with consternation that it made her voice almost unrecognisable. Khalil excused himself from Eva to stand with the phone by the window of Eva's flat.

'It's Rashid. They've arrested him. He left a message but I was tied up with everything. You see, my phone was off because I had a dinner, you know, with . . .' Lisa mentioned the name of an aristocrat and gave another name that sounded very familiar to Khalil. 'You know, the poet?' she asked. 'And I just picked up my messages. He must have been there for *ages.*'

'Where is he?'

'Well, that's the thing.' She named a police station that sounded familiar to Khalil and faintly ominous. 'That's the police station where they interrogate terrorist suspects. They must think . . . Maybe they know about the family or . . . your activities.'

'Perhaps you ought to be more careful what you say down the phone. Our "activities" are just connected to a human rights organisation.' Khalil looked up at Eva who was pretending not to listen.

'Of course, *your human rights activities.* I mean, you never know. Everyone is a suspect now. We must go immediately. Shall I meet you there?'

'He didn't say what they arrested him for?'

'No. He said he had no idea.' There seemed to be tears in her that were somewhere just below the excitement, or excitement just below the tears. 'He needs a lawyer and I just don't know *who* because I only know QCs. Excellent QCs but it's no good for a police station.'

'I'll meet you by the front entrance, then?'

'He wanted me to tell Iman. Can you let her know?'

Eva watched Khalil as he called Iman and put the phone back in his pocket. She continued watching him as he sat down. He unpacked some leaflets and books from his rucksack and stood up to leave.

'As you will have gathered, they've arrested Rashid. We don't know what for. I am going down to the police station. I don't know how long it's going to take.' He shrugged at his bags on the floor. 'I'll leave these here. Sorry about this.'

Eva watched Khalil put his things away. She did not know any of them at all really and now one of them had been arrested. She tried not to eye Khalil's bags while he was there. She waited until Khalil had left before unzipping his black sports bag. It was half-empty and sagged in the middle. Inside was a pair of stripy old men's pyjamas, two books (the one he'd shown her and another one on the absurd in Italian cinema), a toothbrush wrapped in a plastic sandwich bag, a T-shirt and a pair of underpants.

She pushed back the door to Iman's room. She had never been in there before. The bed left a tiny L-shaped corridor around it, about a foot wide. A postcard of a fortress in Spain was stuck above Iman's bed, a tiny flag waved on a matchstick next to a blue goblet with a gold trim. Eva opened the cupboards and found a row of new clothes, far more dressy than the jeans Iman normally wore. Most of them still had their labels attached to them.

There was a stack of books next to the bed. Eva edged along and picked one up. Leather-bound and old, it was filled with Arabic script. In her mind Eva saw robed men rocking their heads on desert mountains, guns across their laps. She saw execution videos and a crowd of men beating their chests with their hands, cutting their backs with whips. She picked up another. The same. Same script. Religious-looking books. She shuddered at a line of verse by an anonymous poet of the Umayyad period which, had she been able to decipher it, would have read:

'My little boy's smell is all lavender
Is every little boy like him, or hasn't anyone given birth before me?'

Chapter 40

The mat at the entrance to the police station reception was of a fuzzy synthetic material. It was sodden with the rain that came in when outside smokers kept it open while carrying on conversations with others inside. Leaves and cigarettes were mushed on to its bristles. Khalil watched Lisa walk up the outside ramp, swaying and clumping and pushing her way past the drunken friends and families in sweatpants and gold chains who were smoking under the porch.

Lisa acted as though she had not seen Khalil and went straight to reception. 'I am here for Rashid Mujahed.'

'Take a seat then, love. We're not done with him yet.'

'Where is he?'

'I believe he has just gone into interview.'

'Interview? Why has he only just gone into interview? How long have you been holding him? Has he been charged? Why have you held him so long? Has he got legal representation?'

'All right, miss, if you take a seat I'll phone the custody downstairs and find out for you. You a relative? A friend? What exactly?'

'I'm a friend. His girlfriend, actually.'

'Well, I know he's got the duty with him for starters. The rest I can find out.'

'A duty solicitor? What firm are they from?'

'Hang on, love. Take a seat.'

'No, I'm fine right here.' Lisa tapped with her nails on the counter, waiting as the policewoman picked up the phone and dialled a number.

'Right, right,' the officer intoned down the phone. 'Got ya.' She was scribbling little notes that Lisa could not see although she was pressed right up against the glass. Lisa pulled her hair out from the back of her mackintosh.

'All right, love, he was booked in at 16.20, made his telephone call at 17.50 and asked to see the solicitor at 18.43. The duty took her time only arriving at 20.48, at which point in time the relevant officers were tied up with other interviews, hence the delay in interview time to 21.32. The firm that the duty is from is Watkinson Farley and the duty's name is David Farley. No. That's who it was going to be but then it changed to Annabelle Prieston, Police Station Representative.'

'She's not a solicitor?'

'No, like I say, she's a rep. All the same as far as we're concerned.'

'And the delay? He comes in at 4.20 and does not get to ask for legal representation for more than an hour. Why is that? Where was he then?'

'Well, he was down in the cells. I imagine that that delay was caused because the officers arrested him on suspicion of one charge and then, following a search, decided to question him on the basis of another one. That's all the custody was able to tell me. Now, would you like to take a seat?'

Lisa looked around the room, watched by everyone in it, until she acknowledged that she had seen Khalil and, feigning surprise, came over to him. He moved the chip carton and the page of a free newspaper advertising mobile phone packages off the chair next to him.

'Apparently he was arrested on suspicion of one thing but now they are interviewing him in relation to a charge connected to something they found in a search. What do you think?' she whispered conspiratorially, although the waiting room had all clearly heard the policewoman relaying the report on Rashid. 'What do you think he might've had on him?'

'I have no idea. I've not seen the bastard for ages. I spent most of the day trying to find him in his room and then at Iman's flat. We'd arranged to meet up at the demonstration but he disappeared before I even got to talk to him.'

'He wasn't at the hall of residence this morning?' Lisa asked.

'No. Wasn't he at yours last night?'

'Oh, no. It's not like that. We haven't actually seen that much of each other recently. We . . . I . . . have just been so busy organising the demo and the talks and everything. What did you think, by the way?' Lisa asked.

'I thought it was excellent. I missed quite a bit looking for Rashid, but what I saw was fine. Turnout was great. Who recommended Ayyoubi?'

'He was good, wasn't he? Just weird the way he ended his speech, didn't you think? His party recommended him. I actually wanted one of the big spokesmen types, you know, the ones you see on TV all the time, but they couldn't do it and put his name forward. I thought it worked quite well in the end.' The moulded plastic chair squeaked under Lisa's bottom as she pushed herself back into it, keeping her bag on her lap.

Rashid and Lisa had run out of things to say to each other long before Iman arrived, her hair streaming with rain.

Iman didn't know what Lisa was doing there. Rashid had told her that he had hardly seen her since he had taken her sister out to a concert, months before, although they had spoken on the phone about work issues, speakers for the demonstration and things like that. Lisa did not seem delighted to see Iman. The two women greeted each other grudgingly.

'What could he have on him that would show up in a search?' Iman asked Khalil in Arabic after he answered her questions. Iman could feel Lisa shift uncomfortably at the change in language.

'No idea,' replied Khalil, switching back into English. 'Where were you, anyway? I was waiting for you at your flat.'

'I met someone I knew. We went for a drink.' Iman tried to make it sound like something she did regularly.

'Who?' Khalil asked, 'did you meet for a drink?'

'Who did I meet?'

'Unless it's personal that is . . .'

'I was with Ziyyad Ayyoubi.'

'What did you think of him?' Lisa butted in before Khalil had a chance to express his surprise. 'He was good, don't you think? I was just saying that we weren't sure initially, because we wanted one of the big cheeses to speak, but they insisted on Ziyyad so we agreed. I thought he was quite charismatic. He's a friend of yours?' Lisa spoke with a mixture of reverence, jealousy and petty dislike.

'Who exactly did recommend him, Lisa?' asked Iman.

'I think it was whatshisname? Abu? With the big moustache and bald head?'

'The spokesman?' Iman gave a name.

'That's the one.' She nodded. 'Ayyoubi's a friend of yours, is he?' Lisa asked again.

'I met him once before I left,' Iman said. Her hair, which was still wet, sprayed everything around her when she turned her head.

They could make out the sound of several keys unlocking the door that led down to the interview rooms and the cells. The owner of a loud androgynous voice that was shouting down a mobile was approaching the waiting room. Iman, Khalil, Lisa and the rest of the room stared as the speaker stepped into the room and took it over. She was several feet wide and dressed in a floppy crêpe fabric, her neck strung with low-carat gold chains, her hair dyed into soft orange curls that exaggerated the age of her face. She reminded Iman of a stuffed cushion with a small dog's pointed face coming out of one side that they had at the nursery in Gaza. The children called it Foofee.

The Foofee woman settled quickly on Iman and Khalil. 'You here for Rashid Mujahed, then?' she asked, but before they had a chance to reply, Lisa was talking to the woman – standing up she reached the other woman's shoulder height – lowering her voice and saying something about the broadening of the terrorism laws and how she knew, if it ever came to that, there was a QC who she was sure she could get to act.

'Don't think it will come to that this time, love. All right then, who should I talk to. You all with him, then?' the woman asked.

Lisa sat down, her bag back on her lap. Iman and Khalil stared in awe at the commanding tower of flesh and fabric standing before them.

The woman wiped her brow. 'Humid, isn't it? Rain hasn't shifted it at all.' She sat opposite them, taking up two seats, the cheeks of her bottom divided by the moulding between the chairs. 'Right, OK, so what's happened is, they arrested your friend. Is he . . .?'

'Boyfriend,' said Lisa.

'Brother,' said Iman.

'Friend,' said Khalil.

'All right. Whatever. I'm Annabelle Prieston, right? I represented Rashid Mujahed during his interview. I was his legal representative. What happened was Rashid was arrested this afternoon by the Terrorism Unit in a case of mistaken identity. Apparently they were looking for someone else from the same place as him who is said to be in London at the moment. The other person was being watched during the demonstration but they weren't watching hard enough and they arrested your friend and brought him here by mistake. Then they did some checks and found out they had the wrong guy. Right?'

The woman flicked through her notes. Her handwriting was very tight and sloped backwards menacingly.

'Why didn't they release him, then?' Lisa asked.

'They would have, except for the fact that your friend, brother, boyfriend, whatever, had a not insubstantial amount of a Class C divided into two separate packages which the police chose not to overlook.'

'Class C?' Khalil and Iman asked at the same time. Lisa was holding her bag tightly against her stomach as if trying to protect herself from a punch.

'Marijuana. Dope. Hash. Black. Whatever you want to call it.'

'Grass?' asked Iman.

'Well, no. Actually, technically, yes, as far as the law is concerned, but grass is actually the leaves, whereas this was the black, the resin, the hash block. Now, thing is, you get found with this divided and they'll do you for possession with intent to supply, a much more serious offence than simple possession. Added to this,' she lowered her voice, as she led up to the best bit, 'the fact that Rashid had a) signed for the stuff on the custody sheet when he was booked in and b) actually told the officers that he was going to give the other block to a roommate at uni.'

Annabelle's eyes widened and she sat back against the wall, before leaning forwards again – she could see her audience were not quite getting it.

'Even just passing a joint to someone is intent to supply, see, so by him saying that, he had basically confessed to the more serious crime. Right?'

Iman and Khalil focussed hard on Annabelle.

'But I managed to get that discounted, because at the time there was no legal rep around and he had been arrested for something totally different. In the end I got him off on a caution.' Iman and Khalil continued to stare at Annabelle, forcing her to spell it out.

'It's a bloody good result – a caution – considering how much dope he had on him. May affect his immigration status. You need to check on that. It's not my field, but he won't need to go to court or anything. No criminal record.'

'What's a caution?' Iman and Khalil asked together.

'Think of it like a warning. Right. He got a warning; if he does something like this again he'll be in trouble, but for now he's free to go.'

'Where is he?' asked Iman.

'He's just getting his stuff together. He'll be here any minute.' Annabelle looked disgruntled.

'What do you mean that it might affect his immigration status?' asked Khalil. 'He needs to be here until September for his course.'

'Like I said, I don't know, but he might need to go home sooner than that.'

'But he's on a scholarship,' Iman said.

'Like I said, it's not my area. Here.' She handed over a card. 'Give the immigration section at my firm a call in the morning, all right? They might be able to help him out although I doubt whether he'll get Legal Aid. Right. I'm off now.'

'You don't need to wait for him to come up?' Iman asked, taking on Lisa's interrogative role now that Lisa had fallen silent.

'He'll be up any second, and I've got a GBH down south now.' She stood in front of them.

'Well, thank you.' Khalil stood up before Iman did; he realised that that was what this vast woman seemed to want from him. The rep nodded before leaving the premises.

'*Drugs!*' Lisa was muttering, disgusted. 'If I had known it was just some hash that he was in here for . . .'

Khalil was turning the card over, looking at the name of the immigration solicitor when Rashid arrived. Rashid only seemed to see one of them. '*Lisa!*' he cried. She stood up as Rashid came towards them.

'You all right, then?' Iman asked Rashid.

'Sure,' said Rashid, still looking pleased by the sight of Lisa, who now held her laptop bag to the side of her body.

'I didn't think you'd come.' He walked closer to her and held her arms. 'You know, Lisa, down there, in that cell. It was so . . . I felt so, you know, lonely, and I was thinking . . . I've been so stupid. I've really missed you. I didn't think you'd come—'

'I probably wouldn't have come if I had known it was just for some minor dope charge.'

Rashid was holding some of the bits and pieces from his pocket in a see-through plastic bag that dangled against Lisa's upper arm.

'What did you say?' Rashid dropped his hold on Lisa's arms.

'I said I wouldn't have come down here if I knew that it was just about some hash that you had on you. I thought you had been arrested for some terrorism offence or something. I was at dinner with Lord C. and I rushed off. I told them all that it was really serious and now it turns out it's just some caution for a piece of dope.'

A look was building up in Rashid's face that made Iman want to pull Lisa – even Lisa – away from him.

'You're disappointed, is that it? Disappointed? What is it that you wanted me to do, exactly?' Rashid started out with not a small amount of malice in his voice. 'Blow up Buckingham Palace? Would that get your attention? Is that what you want? Strap myself to some explosives? Is that it? What do you want from me?' Rashid's voice was raised now.

'All right. All right. You lot. Move it outside. No domestics in here. Out you go.' The policewoman was standing by the door, holding it wide and ushering them out. 'That's it then for tonight and leave Buckingham Palace out of it and all.'

The rain had stopped, but it was cold and the wind had picked up. Outside they were no longer performing for anyone, nor were they enclosed and the tension momentarily seemed to drop away. But Rashid's fury was still with him and his English crumbled with the strain of it.

'Do you know, I've had it with you.' His accent became stronger and as his pronounciation weakened Lisa became more resolute. She stood with her bag over her shoulder, her arms across her chest, her jacket puffed out under it. The manifest effect of her stance was one of rebuttal and indignation.

'I don't have time for this, OK, Rashid?' Lisa retorted. 'I've been sitting here waiting for over an hour. I thought you really were in trouble and I thought I could help, but you're not, so there's no point in me hanging around. I'm off, all right?'

To Rashid it felt as though the wind isolated him on the street. It seemed to require him to shout, as though he was on a stage and it was a crowd not the wind that roared past his ears.

'Of course you don't have time for this. You only have time for the brown and the destitute – victim types, isn't it? You do what? The politically repressed only? I don't know why it took me so long to see it.'

'How *dare* you? How dare *you*?' Lisa started. 'After all I've done! And you! You're just . . . so ungrateful!' she screamed. 'The lot of you!'

Khalil and Iman had formed a wall next to Rashid and they watched her walk off. Khalil put his arm around Rashid's shoulders and Iman came up close to him.

'You really gave it to her.'

'He really did,' said Khalil.

'Oh, leave me alone. I'm sick of this, all of this. I don't want to be politically engaged, OK? I don't want it. I'm not like you two, or Mama or Sabri or even Baba; I just want out. All right? Out of the whole damn shit. Did you see that? That . . . that *bitch* would have been happier to have me locked up on some trumped-up

248

charge for the next twenty years. Then she really would have loved me.'

'Come on, Rashid, come on. I haven't seen you for months. Let's go and just, I don't know, spend time together. I missed you *ya zalame*, really.'

'I'm not in the mood; just leave me alone. I have nothing to say on any of the things you want to talk about. Leave me out of it, all right?'

And with that Rashid walked off into the darkness, fishing his cigarettes out of his plastic bag of belongings, lighting one by a streetlight and letting the smoke get whisked away up into the sky above him.

PART V

THE GAZAN SEA

Two months later

Chapter 41

Gloria was dead and his mother had killed her. Each time Rashid looked at the burnt-out oily-looking stump of his marijuana plant he cursed his mother. And he could not stop looking at it. The stump meant one thing and one thing only. His mother didn't care for him. Not one bit. He didn't give a shit whether she was a hijacking legend or not. She managed to look after every other tree, plant, root or vegetable in the vicinity of their apartment, but his cherished Gloria had been neglected and had died from that neglect. It was unforgivable. There were even yellowed cigarette butts, squeezed flat by desperate fingers, sticking out of the soil. He swore at her unconvincingly in his mind. He heard her voice and the scrape of the metal outdoor table being brought around the edge of the house, as it was every morning, and could not swear at her any more. All he really wanted was for her to ask him how he was, but who would admit to that?

'Asleep, of course,' he could hear her saying. He was surprised that Sabri had so much as asked. Rashid looked around the room from where he lay. His most precious belongings, including branches of Gloria's remains (it would not have taken much, just a bit of water, a bit of sun, a bit of love), were arrayed on the floor around him in black plastic bags that blocked his way as he tried to move around, rustling and crunching horribly when he lost his footing. He had already crushed four CD cases that way and there were wires everywhere, coming out of his computer and his stereo. He had not been able to get his computer up and running yet, because his desk for some (unconvincing) reason had been left upstairs. Another *lie*. In place of where his desk should have been was a new freezer, still wrapped in plastic, which belonged to one of the families camped upstairs in their old apartment; it would be stored there, he was told, until such a time as their house was rebuilt.

If it were ever rebuilt. The building work kept slumping with the cuts in the concrete supply. And at the amount it cost, his mother kept saying, you would think that it was ground out of diamonds. He would be gone before the freezer was.

And there was that boy, too, Sabri's little prodigy, Wael, the middle grandson of Abu Omar. The boy was so principled, so dedicated to the cause that he had refused to leave with his family and had been taken in by Sabri who had decided, in his great benevolence, out of the largesse of his omnipotent magnanimity, on a *de facto* adoption of the little shit. The squit of a boy must have had at least six stomachs, the amount his mother cooked for him. 'We'd developed a relationship over the years,' Sabri had said of the boy, 'an understanding.' What understanding? Rashid wondered. Sabri had barely gone downstairs. Did they communicate out of the window? 'He's the same age that Naji would have been,' Sabri kept saying. But that didn't matter either to Rashid, because it was irrelevant crap. The Strip was full of boys of the age that Naji would have been. It was bursting at the seams with them: an unbalanced demographic disaster. What did Sabri need this boy for? To snoop on him probably, Rashid thought. He had spotted the boy down by the disused playground the last time he had gone out to score. 'Greetings, *Ammo* Rashid,' the little bugger had said when he realised that Rashid had seen him. At least they had the decency to put the kid upstairs and give Rashid a room on their floor. A room with a bubble-wrapped freezer in the middle of it, but a room no less. He should count himself lucky.

The weather was perfect, but useless to him in all its perfection. It was far better if it was all lousy. He registered the sounds of his mother wheeling Sabri into the garden along the path. A tray outside clattered with its pot and saucer on it. The smell of coffee came into Rashid's room with the jasmine garden air.

Rashid's visa (he could not be bothered to check it was in his passport; he knew it was there) was to Canada and for resettlement (a term that annoyed him, with its presumption that he had been settled in the first place). It was, according to everyone and their mother, exceptional, thrilling and amazing that Rashid had managed to get the visa, but nothing about it thrilled or amazed Rashid, nor did he feel remotely exceptional. When he was out, in London, he had had no choice but to return. Now that he was back, he had no choice but to leave. And so it was.

'. . . that Mahmoudi boy,' he could hear his mother whispering, '. . . known informer . . .' but the breeze rustling in the bougainvillea made him miss whatever acidic response it was that Sabri offered back. It didn't matter; he knew they were still talking about him. He was a fish swimming in a bowl with a crowd of people gawping at him while tapping on the glass. Everything he did was seen, watched, and reported on. There was no getting away from it. He should tell his mother. He looked across at his plant's blackened stem and could not quite curse her, not with her so close and audible. But she should know that had she bothered to look after his plant he would not have needed to go and seek out the services of Ahmed Mahmoudi. That was their doing, their neglect. The breakfast conversation was back to reports of new checkpoints, the extent of the closure, of dwindling fuel supplies, the fighting with the Islamist groups. The usual stuff.

Iman had come back the day before. Although she had been away for months, all they had been interested in, as far as Rashid could tell, was her experience at the borders. 'Tell me,' their mother had asked, several times over, 'it was the bearded man who went through the papers not the woman with short hair?'

Rashid had waited for Iman's return, counted the days, expecting it to lift him out of the place where he had fallen, but her flushed excitement (he could not believe it was just about being back; something had happened to her in London, he was sure of it) had left him exactly where he had been, if not further down. When he had asked her why she had come back, as she could have stayed longer in London if she had wanted to, she had replied, 'But I don't exist there,' laughing as though that was incredibly obvious, too. *How could you even ask, Rashid?* was her look.

His father had cut him off as well. As soon as he heard what Rashid had got the police caution for, he'd spluttered fury down the phone. *Drugs? Drugs? I send the boy to London for drugs?* And stopped Rashid's allowance. *With immediate effect, you hear? Nothing more from me!* Iman had given him a little money, enough to pay Ahmed Mahmoudi this time, but after that he had no idea. No idea at all. He could not believe he was expected to stay in Gaza broke and sober. There could not be a worse reality that he could think of. Stoned, it was almost manageable. Sober, it was a nightmare of hideous proportions.

'Rashid?' Iman tapped at the door before she entered stepping over the bags, balancing a glass of tea on its saucer. He moved his legs to make space for her on the end of his bed and conducted his side of the conversation in silence for as long as he could.

'Mama says that they closed Sindibad's?'

[nod]

'Are you going to carry on at the Centre with Khalil?'

[shrug]

'Are you really going to Canada?'

[nod]

256

'But what will you do there?'

[shrug]

Iman rubbed her feet against the printed synthetic blanket and traced her big toe along the brown line of a rose petal print until Rashid spoke.

'Mama thinks I'd be better off in prison,' he said, clearing his throat. 'Do you think so, too? It seems that the women around me want me locked up. Nothing according to them would do me better than a stint in jail.' He blew at his tea, but it was too hot and made his eyes water.

'Forget Lisa. Forget her, Rashid. And of course Mama doesn't want you to go to prison.'

'I just heard her saying it to Sabri, that it was an experience I would have gained from, like he did, like Jamal, that fieldworker, is currently gaining from – well, according to her at least.' He slurped noisily. 'But, you know, I'm not that sure that being tied up and shoved into a cupboard with a sack over my head would further my self-improvement.' He slurped again. 'Thanks for the tea, *habibti*.'

'What will you do in Canada?' Iman asked after they had stared up at the ceiling for a while following the banging and pattering of children's feet above them. They were a strange breed of children up there, Rashid thought. They all seemed to run on the heels of their feet.

'Work,' he shrugged again. 'Work.' He straightened himself out against the wall and hoped that she would not ask *what* he would work *as* because all he could think of, even on a good day, was of packing bags in a supermarket. In his envisioned life in Canada he wore a large black puffer jacket, even when he tried to see himself eating breakfast or sleeping. He saw himself living in a room in an apartment building composed of stacked columns of such rooms, where the neighbours would hide behind their doors when he went in or out so that they would not have to speak to him and where the nights were full of the muffled screams of sex, drink and battery. The puffer jacket that he wore in this future life got larger and larger with time, until he was swollen like a blimp bumbling along a deserted snowy street of an anonymous North American city, his head protruding dark and oily like Gloria's stump.

'I found out about Mama and Baba,' Iman whispered. 'Sabri told me.'

'Did he?' Rashid didn't look up at Iman who was keen to register some interest from him. 'Did Mama talk about her past with you, too? Because no one's mentioned anything to me.'

'No, no,' Iman continued. 'But they're connected, the two things: Mama's *activities*, the *hijacking*,' Iman was almost breathless with excitement, 'and the divorce.'

'I see.' Rashid tried to appear as though he was far more interested in the bougainvillea leaves that were making intricate patterns of shade and sparkle on the wall in front of him.

'Don't pretend you're not interested, because I know you are. Besides, it's a *great* story and I can't tell anyone else so you can at least *act* like you're listening.'

'Sure.' When Iman had sat on the blanket Rashid's toes had been under the edge of her leg. She had not moved and he didn't want her to.

'Baba apparently didn't even *know* that she was in the Front. They've gone, right?' She whispered nodding at the window to which Rashid shrugged so she carried on whispering. 'When Sabri was a baby she left him with Baba in Beirut, saying that she had to visit a sick aunt in Jordan, and came back two weeks later with her face all bandaged up and wearing a brace on her teeth. She told him that she had fallen and had an operation. You see, the Front's hijackings, her hijackings, had put Baba's party into a total spin. They had not been told that they were going to happen so Baba was really busy with his party in meetings trying to sort things out.'

Rashid was listening but trying hard not to show how keenly he was doing so. He was never told anything. There were still murmurs coming from outside, the sounds of a tray being cleared away.

'When the bandages come off she's got a different nose and without the braces her teeth are straight; the gap's gone. When he asks about this she says something about it being part of the *operation*. He doesn't really query her. Are you listening to this, Rashid?'

Rashid had finished his tea and was watching the last brown drop of it dribble down the edge of the glass on to the saucer as he held it upside down. He looked up at her, giving her enough for her to carry on.

'Apparently around that time there is a lot of discussion within the party about The Sparrow and the hijacking operations and at one conference Baba stands up and declares to the whole conference that the Front really does need to let the key people within the Outside Leadership know when they are about to carry out an operation.

'Then he says, "The Sparrow can't just go off and do these things and catch us all unprepared," and the conference goes silent. Everyone. Then someone quips in and says, "I know. It's like not knowing what your wife is up to when your back's turned!" and they all roar with laughter at this. Baba laughs too but, you know, Baba doesn't think there's anything to it, although he doesn't understand why they find it *quite* so funny.'

Iman pauses. There's the sound of a collared dove outside tooting out a morse-like message, *to-to-toooot-to to-toooot*.

'When did he find out, then?' Rashid asked, pulling at a twist of blanket fringe.

'Not for ages. Not until the Peace Deal. Imagine? It's over twenty years later, when he finds out. You know Baba objected to a lot of the terms of the agreement. Well, he gets into an argument with some of the agreement's supporters, including Khalil's father,

259

Hamad Helou, about why they shouldn't agree to the terms, and he turns to him, Hamad Helou that is, and says, "Remember how close we were before, Jibril, during the days of Beirut when the operations of the Front were going on," to which Baba nods and doesn't really get where he's going even when he says, "You've clipped Jihan's wings, I see? No dramatics from her for a long time." Poor Baba, he just doesn't understand. This isn't enough for Hamad Helou who then spells it out to him, that Mama is The Sparrow and that a number of people within the Outside Leadership have known for years. He made out that it was every-one except Baba, although that can't be true, because if it was it would have leaked by now.'

'Poor Baba,' Rashid said. 'I can't believe he didn't know.'

'It seems Hamad Helou told him just to get him out of the way, he knew it would humiliate him. Anyway, of course, Baba went nuts. Mama said, "I thought you knew. I told you I had been in an operation," and he says, "Look, woman, you say operation I think you mean a hospital one not a military one!"' Iman looked at Rashid. 'It's almost funny, no? After that he just leaves. *Khalas.* Finished. Gets us all passports to move to Gaza then leaves her, leaves us, leaves the Leadership. Says the embarrassment is too much. Hence the Gulf and Suzi and everything.'

A jet screamed across the sky, a roar followed by a *keeaoww!* that split the sky apart. The TV was turned up so high in the living room that it was audible in Rashid's bedroom, '. . . *the Israeli leadership straining under popular pressure is resolved to pursue the military option against . . .*'

'Mama thinks there's going to be a hit tonight,' Iman said, star-ing out of the pane of the window that had lost its blackout paper.

'Bring it on. Bring it on,' Rashid replied passing his tea glass back to Iman.

Did Iman not realise how much it hurt that these things were kept from him, or that Sabri confided in her, but not in him, that his mother talked about him outside his window as though he was dead? How painful it all was now that there was no Gloria to ease any of this? And that it was so much worse now that he knew that a way out was no longer a way out, but a way followed around by the same guilt of being disengaged, somewhere different where no one understood you and your value was nothing? Did she not realise that it was choking him up and driving him mad that he could neither be in it nor out?

'Bring it on,' he said again, waving his hand at the sky.

'Oh, shut up, Rashid. I'm sick of you like this already. You're intolerable.' Iman hit out at Rashid's bent legs but connected with the cup and saucer instead which fell towards the floor. Rashid caught the cup just before it hit the tiles; Iman clamped her hand down on the saucer to stop it from sliding off the cover before she punched at her brother's arm with all her force.

'*Oww!* What is it? What's that for?'

'Get up, Rashid. Get up. Get washed. Shave that stubble off. You smell and you're ugly with a beard.'

'I thought it rather suited me.'

'Well, it doesn't. It's hideous. Look.' She held up Rashid's passport to him, showing him a clean-shaven version of himself. 'Far better.' She looked at the photo again. 'You look older in this picture.'

'All right, I'll get up. OK. Just stop being all, I don't know, *bouncy.* It's distasteful. What happened to you in London? Is it that English guy, the one who is going to provide all that funding? Is it him? Are you – what? – in love with him?'

'That's just typical. Typical. Just because some man wants to work with me, you have to make out that his interest could only be sexual.' Despite the force of her denial, Iman was unable to look at Rashid directly.

'So, you're a partner for peace but not for love. Is that what you're telling me?' Rashid asked.

'It's just so damn easy to be cynical and mock every effort. So easy, and everyone gets off thinking that they could do so much better than the people who are trying, except they're never even doing a damn thing, just criticising, criticising.'

'All right, all right. Calm down. It's great. I'm not trying to knock it. Tell me, what are you doing with the funding?'

Iman stood for a while, long enough to feel self-conscious before she sat down again on the end of the bed.

'I'm not sure exactly. Not about everything. But we are definitely going to fund the centre for the handicapped, get their offices moved, and provide more facilities. Then a women's centre, maybe a crèche. There's so much, Rashid. Don't give me that look like – I know what you're thinking. That they're just palliatives, right? But every little bit helps – is important. Maybe we can do something with the Centre too. Maybe they'll fund some of the positions there?'

She looked over at Rashid, her eyebrows raised in a question. Rashid scratched at the hair around the front of his neck.

'Are you offering me a job or something?'

'It's possible. But that's not the reason I came in here. I came to tell you that you need to get your suit and shoes fixed up for the wedding tomorrow night.'

Rashid groaned.

'Whose wedding?' he asked.

'The Atif boy.'

'What Atif boy?'

'You know, the Chairwoman's son, the one with the watery eyes and the limp handshake.'

'That could be any one of the boys from the Beach District.'

'You have to go,' Iman insisted.

'I'm not going.'

'You are. You have to. Mama says she'll push you and the bed you're in to get you there if she has to. You *know* who's going to be there. You have to go. Mama's put the suit out. She means what she says.'

'That suit won't even fit me.'

'Who cares? She's put the suit on a hanger by the front door and the shoes are in a bag. The suit needs dry-cleaning and the shoes need the heels done. You can go to Abu-whatshisname for that.'

'Abdulla.'

'That's the one. *Yallah!* Come on. Get up. I'm coming back in five minutes and I'll expect you to be dressed. It's depressing this room.'

With Iman gone, Rashid sent a text message, smoked a cigarette, got the reply he wanted, got up, kicked at some of the bags, resolved to get his desk back that day, remembered he was leaving, decided to forget it, found a clean towel outside his door, and got into the shower. Abu Omar's flat, being on the ground floor, had the one advantage of increased water pressure.

Chapter 42

'Just look at the stitching.' Abu Faris, the owner of the dry-cleaners, ran his finger along the inside of the jacket, against the red silk lining. His workers, of whom there were far too many, stood in a semicircle behind him. Abu Faris padded over to the cash till to find some half-moon glasses in a tray of pins and paper labels and returned to the suit that was laid out over the counter as carefully as a prepared corpse. 'Beautiful,' he breathed, then lifted up the inner neck of the jacket close to his nose to decipher the swirling silver stitch. 'Paris,' he said and whistled a low, reverent note just audible over the spurts of steam and chemicals coming from upstairs, his head shaking in wonderment. The human arc agreed dutifully. They hugged up to their employer as he lifted up the label for their benefit. 'I would recommend the Super Deluxe Clean for this, sir.' Abu Faris proffered his professional opinion with sincerity. His querulous finger pointed at a number on a handwritten price list that had been covered over with yellow sticky-backed plastic. Rashid was about to take the owner's recommendation when he saw the price and balked.

'Just do the cheapest clean you've got,' Rashid said.

Abu Faris stroked the legs of the outfit in sympathy at its neglect. It was Sabri's wedding suit: wide-striped, shoulder-padded and double-breasted. It was fit for a monkey, Rashid thought, in a bow tie. Rashid was taller and slighter than Sabri had been and the idea of wearing anything that would show so much sock, to Rashid, was just simply vulgar.

'Tomorrow, after ten, God willing.' Abu Faris did not look up at

Rashid as he departed; the cheap clean was evidently contemptible to him. Rashid left Abu Faris holding up the jacket, showing off the hang of the fabric to his employees, as he twirled it with the grace of a flamenco dancer, a hand on each shoulder.

The shoe repairman, Abu Abdulla, was not there. His window was shuttered up and deserted. The nearest shop sold spices in virulent autumnal colours heaped in plastic tubs. Dried leaves burst out of the top of sacks. The shop's wares were arranged outside on upturned buckets and fruit boxes and protected by a cluster of parasols. Rashid had to stoop under them to see anyone.

'Abu Abdulla?' he asked after greetings had been exchanged with the owner, who had been hiding behind a multi-coloured wall of handheld foil windmills.

'What of him?' the man asked.

'I want to get my shoes done.'

'Oh. That one. He's gone.' The shop owner got up and adjusted his waistband, which was already too high, so that he could look Rashid square in the face. 'He left to get some materials for his shop from Egypt and wasn't allowed back. Gone.'

'Who are you talking about?' a customer asked.

'Abu Abdulla.'

'Oh, he's gone,' the customer confirmed.

'What's all that on your face?' the owner enquired peering closely at Rashid.

'Nothing. I shaved,' Rashid said touching the raw skin around his jaw. There was at least one cut and several hive-ish rashes that were coming up.

'Did a terrible job of it, *ya zalame*. You need a new razor? Come inside and take a look.' The owner opened his hand towards the dark interior of his shop where a couple of tins sat on each shelf in front of a row of exercise books with upturned corners.

'No. Thanks.' Rashid stepped away from the shop backwards,

his neck bent, bumping his head into a cluster of tied-up loofahs as he came out from the roof of parasols. The other customer was watching him closely.

'Vaseline,' the man advised, 'before bed. Then warm towels like this.' He patted his face as a barber would when applying the final cologne.

Ahmed Mahmoudi was not at the agreed meeting place by the children's playground. Rashid sat on the low wall to wait. The ginger cat he was trying to get to come closer to him scampered away as a message from Khalil bleeped in his pocket. Khalil was at Rashid's house already. *Fifteen minutes*, Rashid replied. He persuaded the cat to return and waited for Mahmoudi. It was quiet and there was no one he knew, or even recognised, walking down the street. For a moment, he found himself thinking that he had been in that park before, with Sabri, that Sabri had pushed him on the swings, but that was impossible. Sabri had never been with him at the age when he was being pushed on swings. He was thinking of a mythical older brother, a fantastical childhood.

The discerning personality of the ginger cat made Rashid determined to befriend it. Once he had gained the cat's trust, the cat came forth with an unbounded amount of affection towards Rashid, ramming its head into his leg, purring like a small motorbike.

On the opposite corner, two men stood by the photography shop under a picture of the laughing baby in a big-eared bear suit. He recognised them; the most immediately identifiable was the fighter with the thick moustache and pockmarked skin from the day of Abu Omar's arrest. The younger man he was finding it harder to place. The pock-faced one was indicating down the road towards the line of cars with his head, his gun strapped across his back, while the younger boy was nodding and smiling.

He was hardly a man, just a scraggy boy really, enthusiastic but crafty looking, probably no older than sixteen. He was restless, moving from foot to foot, checking out the road, up and down; his head too large, his hair scruffy and matted. He had worn-out tennis shoes on, pumps not trainers, that may once have been red, and Rashid focussed on the shoes as a key to the boy's identity until finally he got who he was – the carrot boy (but in shoes this time), the phone card peddler from the café. The boy had grown a foot since Rashid had last seen him. He was almost Rashid's height now.

The Stalin man left and the boy, despite the fact that he had given no prior indication that he had seen Rashid, made his way straight over to him. The radical nature of the cat's transformation caused Rashid to smile up to the carrot boy as he arrived as though he was party to the new bond that Rashid had formed with the creature. The boy did not seem to see the cat.

'Mr Mahmoudi asked me to tell you that he is unable to meet you at the present time. He will be free at around four o'clock this afternoon.'

Looking down the deserted road, the boy cleaned out something from the skin curling over the top of his ear.

'You work with him now? Is that who you are? I remember you. You were the boy—' Rashid started, about to say, *carrot boy*.

'I know. We met. I know. You paid for my breakfast.' The boy carried on looking down the road at the row of cars, then up at the tops of the buildings as though searching for something on their roofs. 'What's in there?' he asked, nudging at Rashid's bag with the tip of his foot.

'Shoes,' Rashid said.

'Shoes?' the boy asked. 'What type of shoes?'

'Take a look,' Rashid said. 'Feel free.' The boy surveyed the quiet road one more time before sitting down next to Rashid. That side of the road was sunny and the cat was rubbing the top of its head against Rashid's leg as though trying to push him from the low wall. It was purring ridiculously.

'*Shuuf! Sho helou!* Look how nice!' the boy said as he took the shoes out. They were brogues with pointed toes and punctured leatherwork. *Wilson's Bootmakers, London, since 1848* it said on the inside of the shoes. The tips had curved metal crescents underneath them but the heels were worn down, asymmetrically slanted by an uneven tread. Rashid picked one up and looked at the size. As he had suspected, they were one and a half sizes too big.

'They were my brother's.'

'And he gave them to you?' The boy appeared envious, awed.

'He doesn't need them. Just listen to this cat!' Rashid had his fingers buried in the fur of the cat's neck. 'The whole street must be able to hear it!' The cat rolled on to its back, its head still rubbing against Rashid's leg, its white mussed-up stomach exposed. The boy was running his finger along the leatherwork, touching the metal beads at the end of the laces. 'Try them if you want,' Rashid offered.

'*Aan jad?* Seriously?' and with his excitement the boy's youth could not be concealed. He did not ask again, he placed his shoes to his side and slipped his scrawny feet into the brogues.

'Too wide,' Rashid said, looking over. Startled by the sound of the boy tapping the metal toes of the shoes on the paving stones, the cat sprung to its feet and disappeared around a corner.

'No, they fit perfectly.' The boy clipped the metal toepieces together and stood up.

Rashid remembered Khalil was due at their place. 'Keep them,' he said, handing the empty bag to the boy. 'They're yours.'

'Hey, thanks!' the boy shouted as Rashid moved off. 'Thanks!' he yelled again as Rashid turned to disappear behind the corner that the boy had come from.

Forget the wedding, Rashid thought as he stepped over the puddles and broken earth on the way to his house. *Forget it*, he was thinking as he heard a *crack crack!* The report of a gun somewhere to his left. A flurry of pigeons lifted up in panic and flapped around each other above their rooftop cages, as though they had been propelled upwards, forgotten how to fly, and were now caught in an invisible balloon tied to the roof and unable to leave. He stood and looked in their direction until they had settled back into their gridded cubes on the skyline. Nothing followed the gunfire. A car started somewhere. The sea roared then shushed itself quiet.

Chapter 43

Sabri thought that he must have been getting soft. He was finding that he was quite enjoying this Khalil Helou's company. He told Khalil about how his book had to be revised, and about how he had found out who the informer was who had been instrumental in the attack on him and his family. At least he said as much as he was allowed to say, how he had always had his suspicions. The TV was on and whenever the news turned to them – it was normally just anticipating that night's attack, but sometimes there would be something new, a different angle on the recent violence, some fresh analysis – they had that to discuss, too. It had all been quite pleasant and he had been glad that Rashid had been kept tied up with whatever useless business it was that kept him out of the house, so that he could have Khalil to himself. Mama brought them tea and pistachio *maamoul*; Iman came in and out with tape for the windows.

Sabri had just got on to the subject of his time in prison, when the news channel switched from a report from the south, where most of the demolitions were taking place, to an interview with the Western volunteers down there. They were about to form a human shield to protect some of the houses. Sabri had paused for a little, then continued as he, for one, had seen interviews like this before. But as the camera turned to one volunteer, Khalil stood up and quite abruptly indicated that Sabri should stop. No, worse, that Sabri should basically *shut up*. He had waved his hand up and down in front of Sabri's face.

'Eva!' Khalil had finally said when the girl had stopped talking. And what a strange, androgynous girl she was, with her wispy hair and weak eyes all screwed up and twitchy in front of the camera. Her name with the description *Medical Student, Volunteer* ran in white letters across the bottom of the screen. Khalil had put his jacket on, wavered around his chair hopelessly, as though negotiating something with it, then said, 'I'm getting her and bringing her back. They might kill her down there. The bulldozers. They don't care any more what skin colour or passport these volunteers have; they'll kill her down there. I'll bring her here.'

'You know her?'

'From London. Yes. Yes. We met. We talked. Yes. I told her about the situation.' Khalil opened the palm of his hand, removed the remains of the *maamoul* that he had mashed into it, placed them on a saucer and walked out of the room.

Sabri looked back at the TV screen where the girl who was the cause of Khalil's distress could be seen lumbering (the woman walked like she had just crossed the Sahara on a donkey) over the remains of a bulldozed house in an oversized fluorescent overall. He didn't know what it was with those boys and their girls from London; Sabri could not see it himself. He wheeled himself over to the window where he had left his notepad and binoculars in hopeful, but pointless preparation for the night's attacks; he could only see smoke from the ground floor. He looked over the notes of the previous night and waited.

'*Aaaay!*' he suddenly found himself screaming. '*Aaaay!*' with an outrage he didn't know he had left in him, as a man climbed over the back wall and into their garden. The man – some kind of fighter, there was a gun on his back but he couldn't see his face – bent himself double to less than the height of the bottom of the windows as he crept around the side of their house. '*Aaaay!*' Sabri screamed again.

By this time Iman and his mother were already calling. 'What? You fell, Sabri? What is it?' and came to find him jammed into the doorway (he had not had the chance to take the arms down on his chair and Iman had closed one of the double doors), swearing and cursing everyone to hell. He started trying to describe the man but before he had a chance to do so, they could make out the sound of someone knocking hard and fast at their front door.

'Umm Sabri?' said the voice behind the door. 'Iman?'

'Who is it?' Sabri's mother whispered at Sabri. 'Do you know?'

'No, but he climbed in over the back wall.' Sabri looked at his mother and his sister's faces watching the shape of the figure that they could see crouched down through the opaque panes of the front entrance. 'He's armed.'

'I'll go.' His mother went to the door. 'Who is it?'

'Ziyyad Ayyoubi,' the voice said. 'Umm Sabri, sorry to trouble you. I've been shot. I need to come in.'

'Mona and Khaled's boy?' Sabri's mother asked, going to the door. 'Is that possible?'

'Ziyyad!' Iman stood back as her mother pulled the locks across and the figure stumbled into their house.

'This is not how I expected to meet my avenger,' Sabri said looking at Ziyyad once they had him seated in the living room.

'What do you mean, your avenger?' Iman felt shamed and worried by Ziyyad being there, so close to Sabri, as though his presence alone exposed a secret union between them. 'You know him? Avenger? Sabri? What are you talking about?'

'I think Sabri is trying to tell you what I wanted to explain to you in London,' Ziyyad began, 'about Abu Omar.'

He was far paler now than he had been on the day of Seif El Din's assassination. Iman's mother indicated that they should move him on to a seat that she was hastily covering with an old bed sheet.

'What about Abu Omar?' Iman was looking at her brother as she helped her mother with the sheet.

272

'The man enabled them to take my family. And my legs. We know now that it was his information—' Sabri said.

'You knew this and you didn't tell me?' Iman was looking at Ziyyad.

'I wanted to, but we didn't get the chance,' Ziyyad started again.

'You shouldn't talk,' their mother said. 'Be still. I have some of Sabri's painkillers. They'll knock you out.'

Sabri felt uncomfortable when others rushed around him. Iman had gone out to get rid of any traces of blood leading up to the house. They had drawn the curtains, removed Ziyyad's blood-soaked jacket and hung it on the back of a chair, put his gun in a corner by the door and then brought in sponges with hot soapy water and syringes for the painkillers.

'I can do those,' Sabri said, taking the drugs and unwrapping a syringe from its paper, easing it full from the bottle (how pleasurable the whole process was, just to think of the release of it filled him with such desire it verged on the erotic). 'Do you know who it was?' he said to Ziyyad. 'Who shot you?'

'I'm pretty certain he was from my party, I could almost swear it, but he was some distance away, which is why they didn't get me as well as they wanted to.'

Ziyyad adjusted in his seat with difficulty. Iman standing at his side was trying to dampen his forehead with a flannel. Their mother left the room to get some bandages. Ziyyad clamped Iman's hand tight, so much so that her fingers were bunched over each other. He was squeezing her hand so hard that Sabri half-expected his sister to scream, but instead she seemed to become invigorated by the pressure. Her face had taken on an expression that Sabri was not familiar with seeing in her and it made him look away. He turned back to Ziyyad.

'Do you know why they were trying to get you?' Sabri asked as their mother came back into the room. The injection was ready but if he were to administer it, the man might get knocked out completely. It was better to know before the man was completely gone who was out to get him.

'I think . . . no, I know, that the other side – the Israelis – want rid of me, that's for sure. It's been the case for a long time. This is not the first time they've tried. The difference is that before,' he was wincing at Sabri now, 'my party would protect me.'

Their mother indicated that Iman should help lean Ziyyad forwards. Once the shirt was removed she cleaned around the wound with cotton wool.

'Look, see, one of them missed. It's just a scratch. But there's a bullet still in there, lodged against the hipbone. It's not very dangerous but we need to get it out.' Their mother pressed close to the wound with the heel of her hand to slow the bleeding. 'You should not have jumped over that wall; you've lost too much blood for such a wound.'

Ziyyad tightened his lips; his face was shiny and jaundiced under the overhead light. Sabri put the syringe in its kidney-shaped tray and wheeled over. Iman came around for a better look. Ziyyad continued to stare above their heads to the curtain rail that had come loose from the wall. The dusk call to prayer could be heard outside and a small cluster of birds fluttered up from their perches on the bougainvillea, chirping.

'Anyone know where Rashid has got to?' their mother asked.

'I should've thought it through,' Ziyyad said. 'I really didn't think they'd go this far, but I'd been upsetting them, one way or another. I won a popular vote within the party on a couple of things and then – maybe this is what did it – I started saying that we had to run a cleaner shop, that there should be greater financial accountability. I was not trying to discredit anyone, you understand. I just wanted to point out that our opponents were

274

getting so much mileage out of these allegations of corruption.'

'That would have done it,' their mother said vehemently. 'Can't stand between them and their money.'

'I'm sorry to have come here, Auntie. I am sorry to bring this into your house. I didn't know where I could go. I left my car on the main street and I was going to take it, then I thought that they might have tampered with it or something. Wired it up . . .' He strained again. His left hand hung over the side of the chair, slightly bloodied, at a distance from him. 'Would you mind?' he asked, looking at Iman indicating for her to wash it.

'I've been meaning to apologise to all of you, and especially to Rashid, because I heard that his arrest in London was meant for me.'

'Nonsense,' their mother said. 'Rubbish. He got himself into his own mess.'

Sabri caught Iman tracing the tip of her finger along the scratches from the bougainvillea thorns that had come up like rows of red machine stitching on Zayyid's arm. What exactly had happened with these two in London?

'No. I believe it was a tip-off from someone in my party. I'm sure that was the whole reason they sent me to London. It probably explains why the Israelis were so ready to grant me an exit visa. They just messed up and got Rashid instead.'

'You do look quite alike,' Sabri said.

'Rashid's thinner,' their mother said, 'but I can see some resemblance. Here, take this,' she said handing him some mint tea after stirring several spoons of sugar into it, 'then it's time for the painkillers.'

Sabri gave the injection with care, but also with jealousy for the release that it brought.

'He's scared of blood,' Iman whispered after Ziyyad passed out in the chair. 'Phobic. And of crowds.'

'Nonsense,' retorted their mother. 'A man like him, never.'

275

Chapter 44

Things always took longer than expected – most people accepted that – but Khalil had obviously decided he could not wait and was already running off somewhere when Rashid arrived. By the time Rashid reached the wall of the house, Khalil was out of shouting distance, intent on getting away. Khalil's red tracksuit bottoms (he wore these when he wished to look *shaabi*, like a simple man, one of the people) were moving off towards the sea. The tracksuit bottoms put Rashid off the idea of chasing him. Rashid had just reached his front door when a message bleeped, telling him that Ahmed Mahmoudi was now ready to meet, and so he retraced his steps back towards the town.

But something was going on. He knew that when he turned around; the smell of it came to him. The sense of it had been in his body since the sound of the gunshots, but it was clearer now. Something had happened. Such knowledge communicated itself imperceptibly, but absolutely. He felt he had lost this special Palestinian capability when he was outside in London, but within hours of being back, it had come back too, this ability to know that something had happened, was going to happen, was in the offing. This was both past and future. He looked towards where the gunshots had come from. The pigeons had settled back into their cages. The sun was streaking the sky with red as it set. A drone buzzed overhead, to the north. Otherwise, he could not see anything. There was nothing visible.

But something was definitely up.

Ahmed Mahmoudi was not there. Rashid sat for a while under the playground sign with its faded lettering, *Brotherhood Park*. He walked up and down the row of shuttered shops and considered the parked cars in front of him; they were in the same place as before, none of them had moved. It wasn't surprising; only the leaders, fighters and ambulance drivers had petrol.

He looked for the ginger cat along the wall and then continued his search in the deserted playground but found only geckos and a heavy-faced tom with a bent tail. The street was quiet and, crouching in the wild grass of the playground, he thought he could see the carrot boy bent low behind the cars, but then he was gone. There was no sign of the cat. Mahmoudi was not there and the sky was being zipped up with drones.

Abruptly and from nowhere, Ahmed Mahmoudi announced his arrival with a whistle that emulated a bird's warble. He stood at the corner of the road dressed in the style that he had developed long before Rashid had known – or known of – him: an open blazer against a T-shirt, pointed lace-ups in a light shade of tan, sunglasses on his nose, his head or around his neck. There was a likeable air of a Rio beach about his outfits, of music videos with people in white linen, glasses twinkling on jetties, of boats with blue wind in their sails and bikinis on their decks. But his voice, nasal and menacing, cut through this impression each and every time.

He was typing something into the keypad of his phone. 'Who were you hiding from over there?' Mahmoudi asked, indicating the playground with his nose. 'Hiding or watching, which was it?' He didn't look up as he spoke.

Rashid thought about the foolishness of the cat hunt and weighed it up against the alternative assumptions.

'I was looking for a cat, a gingerish cat,' Rashid said, laughing slightly. Damn it. The man was as slimy as they came, his fingernails long enough to make a tapping sound against the metal phone cover as he communicated something long and complex to someone distant (or perhaps uncomfortably near?), *tap, tap, tap.*

'It's cats now, is it? Not girls, just cats.' He looked up at Rashid, altering his face to show Rashid the undulating horizontal line of stain crossing his teeth. His smile cracked at the sore on the side of his mouth. 'You should be careful – there's a lot going on at the moment. You shouldn't be wandering about, acting all suspicious.'

'I heard gunshots earlier, near here.' Inside his pocket, Rashid turned the notes over in his hand, he just needed a small tab of the stuff, the equivalent of an eighth; he should have enough money for that. He would make it last for as long as possible; then he would try and find someone else or he would be out of there. He would not use Mahmoudi again.

'That would have been Ayyoubi.'

'Ziyyad Ayyoubi? What, making an arrest or something?' Rashid remembered the gun swaying on the slightly stooped back of the fighter, the tying up of Abu Omar's hands.

'No, no. It was to *get* Ayyoubi.' Again, Rashid noticed the tidal wave of scum across his teeth and a slight tick around the dealer's eyes. 'Man's got enemies,' Mahmoudi said, anticipating Rashid's unformulated question. He took out a see-through plastic bag filled with *bizer* and started cracking the seeds between his front teeth. He dangled them close to Rashid, who lifted his head, *No. No thanks.*

'They killed him?' Rashid asked, trying hard to act as though he couldn't care less.

'Here it is.' Mahmoudi took out a wrap in cellophane from his inside pocket and held it against the palm of his hand with his thumb by his side. His other hand was still busy feeding his mouth *bizer* and in the movements of his mouth the rabid anxieties of Ahmed Mahmoudi became all too apparent.

Rashid repeated himself, trying to keep the almost personal sense of offence out of his voice. 'They killed Ayyoubi?'

'No, but they will. They got him, but he's not dead; it should not be hard to track him down.' In the distance, up by the boundary fence, some tank shells thudded on to the ground, a helicopter juddered low over them. 'They'll try again. Do his car or something. So you should watch yourself, because it's parked just around here. What is it? Are you doubting what I say? It's not as if he can leave this place now, is it? Of course they'll get him. Listen, you want this or not?'

Mahmoudi moved his arm out straight from the shoulder to draw attention to his closed hand; Rashid reached over to take the wrap and swapped it over with the money.

'See you when? Next week.' Ahmed Mahmoudi turned his back slightly, placing the *bizer* back into his jacket pocket, and counted out the notes in the shadows. 'You'll probably need me by then, huh?' Rashid could tell just by the feel of it that he had not been given the quantity that they had agreed on.

It was dark, with only the one streetlight working and the shadows were long and ill-defined. Rashid slipped the hash into his back pocket. Screw the wedding, he thought again, and anyway, if the bastards struck as heavily as they were expected to (there were even two gunships off the coast), well then, with any luck, the wedding would probably be cancelled anyway.

Chapter 45

The television in the living room was never turned off, or even down. A broadcast continued: '. . . *the Islamist groups who have taken over de facto control over this area of the Gaza Strip are vowing revenge following the incursion by tanks and bulldozers and the subsequent demolition of over sixty homes by the Israeli forces . . .*'

'Anarchy,' said Sabri. 'We're getting torn apart. They're getting exactly what they wanted.'

'Divide and rule,' Iman said in a voice softer than her usual one as she was still dabbing at the skin around Ziyyad's bullet wound with disinfectant.

'And how we let them!' Sabri exclaimed. 'There's the shame of it. There have always been examples of it, of how we killed off our brightest and best because they cast others in a bad light, but not to this extent. Trying to get rid of a man like this, we can't even remember who the enemy is any more.'

He went over to the shelves and started smoking. Not a regular smoker, when Sabri did smoke, he tended to make a great show of it, never leaving the thing alone, tap, tap, tapping the cigarette against the edge of the ashtray, puffing smoke up to the ceiling in a great dramatic sigh.

'Do you think you should smoke around him?' Iman asked, gesturing at Ziyyad.

'Eh?' her brother replied. 'Why not?'

'Just like Baba,' she giggled. '*Eh? Eh?*' She was imitating him when the knocking started on the door. 'Probably Rashid's forgotten his key again,' she said.

But it was not Rashid; it was Khalil and Eva. Sabri had managed to remember Eva's name and had told Iman that it was Eva whom Khalil had met in London, but it was not until Iman saw Eva, her Eva, standing there that she came close to believing that she was there, in Gaza, in her house.

Meeting them at the door, Iman blocked them from moving further into the apartment. She had closed the double doors to the sitting room behind her. However, the lock had come loose and the double doors creaked apart behind Iman as she tried to explain to Khalil, in Arabic, why he should take Eva somewhere else.

'What's wrong with that man?' Eva said, breaking Iman off. She was pointing behind her into the living room to where Ziyyad lay comatose and half-naked in front of the television.

'Nothing. Nothing,' Iman said.

'But maybe I can help. I'm a medical student; you know that. Do you want me to take a look at him?'

'Yes,' Iman's mother, who had come out of the kitchen to see their most recent guests, said. 'Yes, we do. Don't we, Iman?' She took Eva over to the purple sink that stood in the corridor against wallpaper depicting beech trees in the spring. 'I have been trying to find a doctor to come over but I was running out of ideas. The only man I could trust has left the country and the others? Well, you never know; there are so many who are willing to talk. He has a bullet inside him, you see. We need to get it out. Not deep, it got stuck against the hipbone. It's shallow, but it can't stay there.' Iman's mother guided Eva towards the basin in the corridor.

'I see.' Eva had tied her hair back tight with an elastic band behind her head. She was washing and washing her hands, soap and fingers running around after each other in the dark toothpaste-splattered basin. 'You know I'm not a qualified doctor. I'm just a medical student.'

'No matter. You'll do. It's not deep. Here, clean your hands with the bandage. We have lots of bandages, they're old but they're sterile, from my son.' She indicated Sabri to Eva with the nod of her head; he was examining Eva while pretending to be absorbed by the news. 'We have more bandages. I've sterilised these already with detergent on a flame.' Their mother held out two narrow metal crochet hooks to Eva and held her fat, dry thumb up in front of Eva's face and cut across it with the forefinger of her other hand. 'Only this far down. I've sterilised the needle already for the stitching.'

It was easier once Eva was in front of him, looking into the wound, with the light in place. She had done worse things before. In London, she had been instructed to remove all kinds of objects from patients' rectal passages: coke bottles, vibrators and potatoes. That was worse. This was a clean, shallow wound, not unlike a tightly pursed mouth, with the bullet, a shiny little tube pointing up at her. The scraps of fabric were harder, but she was able to pick them out with tweezers. Once out, the suturing was always pleasurable; she knew she had a neat hand and this wound closed up perfectly.

In the south she had seen the effect of the dum dum bullets, their ends cut so that they would scatter inside the body. It was starting to get to her, the dirtiness of it all, but at that point in time, dabbing disinfectant on to the delicately sown wound of an unconscious patient, it was offset many, many times over. Khalil fed greedily from Eva's look of satisfaction. Sabri's mother claimed the victory as her own. 'See, I told you that we could do it!' she said, moving back on to the sofa after she had looked closely at the stitching and picked up the bullet, twisting it around under the light.

No one spoke for some time until the advertisements followed the news: *Now New! New! Detergent for You!* a family sang over a sparkling alpine kitchen. *Ping!* went the sparkles! *Ping!* went the stars on the floor.

'Managed to get a lift both down and back,' Khalil said, 'I'm glad we didn't have to leave it any longer. It's getting rough down there.' Khalil broke the silence that seemed to have come about due to the awkwardness between the two women.

'When did you come here?'

'How did he get shot?' Iman and Eva asked each other two different questions at the same time while the television family went forth into the snow-capped mountains. Iman waited for an answer rather than giving one.

'When did you come here?' she asked again.

'It seems like for ever, but it was only ten days ago. I've volunteered for three months. It's been crazy. Tonight we meant to stay but it went mad. They say it was sixty houses they knocked down, but we think it was more – they did the whole area. It looks like they did that around here, too? I just can't believe they get away with it. We meant to stay in one of the threatened houses tonight but yesterday one of us, this young Jewish girl, Irene, she got shot at. She's fine, but none of us had ever been shot at before, and then Khalil came and convinced our organisers to stop; they were pretty much there already. We kind of knew that there was nothing we could do.' Eva stopped talking. It was as though she didn't know where she was.

'Are you all right?' Iman asked, goading herself into a guise of friendship with this girl that she found awkward to put on, after all the time spent criticising her at close quarters. But it seemed like this was a different girl in many ways.

'I feel completely overwhelmed,' Eva started. 'Utterly overwhelmed. We were so happy last Tuesday. I can't forget that feeling, like nothing I have ever had: the closeness we, the volunteers, all felt together and with the families. We kept smiling at each other and hugging each other, as if we needed to confirm with each other what we had gone through, how good it felt. I can never forget that evening, the memory of it will be sacred until I die; nothing I ever did before compares with that. It scares me that I could've lived without coming close to ever feeling that.'

Sabri had gestured to Khalil that he and Eva should take the two-seater sofa and Khalil had guided Eva towards it. She did not seem to notice that she had sat down.

'And that was only Tuesday, but it seems so long ago, so long ago. I don't think I've slept since then. The noise of the bulldozers – you don't understand – well, you do, but it's new for me, it just rolls through my head all the time, I can't sleep. On Tuesday all we did, and it seems almost pathetic now, but we stopped two houses being demolished, we all stood in front of them and chanted and managed to get the soldiers to back off (but they are not soldiers, they are *boys* – can you believe how young they are? They say they listen to music in their headsets while they ride around in those bulldozers. Is that true?). And it was like we were crazy-drunk. We felt so good after that, but now they've gone too. The houses we saved, they've been demolished. I'm talking too much, aren't I? I'm sorry, but I just can't get it straight in my head.'

'It's not something that you ever get "straight in your head,"' Sabri said, turning away from the television screen to look at Eva. 'It is too wrong to be justified, too screwed up to be straightened out. If you force yourself to understand it in any way that leads you to justify it then you are fucked and we are lost.'

'Yes, sure,' Eva nodded eagerly. 'Absolutely. Got it.'

Chapter 46

Rashid had gone down to the beach, trying to find somewhere to have a smoke, now that the roof was out of bounds to him. But it had not felt safe down by the shore at all. There were trucks of armed men speeding over the tarmac and bumping over the sand dunes. Open trucks overloaded with men in uniforms, their guns spiked up at the sky, some masked, some bearded, some ridiculously young but all restless (restless, jubilant, both), and all of them spoiling for something, some release from it all. Some attack on the other. Rashid had smoked fast and deep behind the wooden pavilion where sweets and footballs were sold during the day, smoked too fast and he was not as used to it as he had been. The effect was bad: a desperate, bleary body and an overly anxious brain.

It came over him suddenly as an extended epiphany:

that the trucks were only speeding so that they could find him, Rashid;

that there were armed men everywhere looking for him, Rashid;

that every car shadow held a man crouched with their guns readied, searching for him, Rashid;

that the cars parked down the side of the beach were all wired up, waiting (again) for him to touch them so that they could blast him, Rashid, into the sky in a chute of flames.

The dunes hid tanks and bulldozers; each helicopter searched for him with its beam; the gunships pointed at him and him alone, Rashid.

Rashid had found himself walking fast, bent and angular, his eyes watery with the sea wind, teary with blown sand. He walked with his shoulders held low, in a silly attempt to make himself small. There was a rainy spray spitting at him and the wind that carried it tugged at his clothes, pushed him back as he came to the crest of the dunes, wriggling like a stranded eel. The house was miles from him across a treacherous terrain that he had lost faith in crossing. He felt himself ant-like and squashable beneath the weight of the swarmy sky.

How he got home, he was not sure, but he did it. He had done it. And once there, he held on to the door handles to his home offering a prayer of gratitude to them and to God (whom he found at times like this) while cursing Mahmoudi's spiked shit to hell. But when no one in the living room looked up as he came through the door, it made him wonder whether he was there after all, and then he saw that his body was there already, splayed backwards over a chair, stripped down to the waist, drugged, half-naked with his jeans covered in blood.

He, Rashid, was dead. His body was lying out in front of the TV in a state of undress. He was dead but they were talking about someone else. *Typical*, he thought, *typical*.

'His parents were assassinated in Beirut,' Iman was explaining to a Western woman sitting with her back to the door. 'Intellectuals. Both of them.'

'He's fought for the cause all his life. A man of integrity. The type we need more of,' Sabri added.

'A hero you could say.' Sabri's mother directed this at the passed-out Ziyyad. 'Could be my own, don't you think? Looks like he could be my son, no?'

'The son you never had,' Rashid said, but his mouth was dry and the scene was so surreal he didn't know whether his words had been spoken or dreamt. He didn't understand how, in a couple of hours, his house could be so changed. His sister fawning over a man lying with his jaw hanging open on a bed sheet; Khalil whispering to a bespectacled white girl (and he had told Khalil all about English girls after Lisa; he had figured it all out and yet Khalil apparently had not listened to a word of it).

'Ah, Rashid.' His mother eventually noticed him. He was there. 'This is Ziyyad Ayyoubi.'

'He's been shot by his own people,' Sabri added.

'We're looking after him,' his mother continued. 'He's a brave man.'

'Wonderful,' Rashid said. 'Wonderful.' And he wandered into the corridor and leant over the basin. He splashed water over his face and picked the sand out of the corners of his eyes, rubbing them before snorting water up into his nose from the palm of his hand and blowing it out while holding the bridge. He did this several times until he started feeling a post-swim tingle of water going down the wrong way somewhere in his nasal passages and realised that Khalil was standing behind him.

'You OK?' Khalil asked.

'Sure,' Rashid said, drying his hands on his trousers and his face on a piece of bandage left next to the basin. 'Sure. Just hungry. Really, really hungry. You want to eat?'

Over a plate of *bamya* and rice in the kitchen, Rashid discovered that Khalil had brilliantly discovered two heroes in one afternoon, one of either sex: Eva ('*So brave! I mean what's it to her? She could've got killed!*') and Ziyyad ('*Did you know his parents were assassinated? And they tried to get him too? A gifted leader, I understand.*'). He had apparently also formed a solid friendship with Sabri of the type Rashid had never had ('*I never knew that it was Abu Omar who had informed on Sabri. Why're you looking at me like that? Didn't you know? He just told me.*').

Wonderful. Wonderful. Rashid had approved but didn't look up from his bowl. That was it. Rashid decided he hated all forms of hero worship. All forms of secrecy. He realised that he had had it with the farce of family and that romantic relationships should be banned (*'What d'you think? It looks like Iman has struck something up with Ziyyad, don't you think?'*). The *bamya* was all slime; someone had picked out all the okra, all the meat; it was a tasteless tomato soup with loose vegetable fibres that he had to force himself to ingest. On the sideboard was one of his mother's trays for Sabri. *Bet he got meat,* thought Rashid. It was the worst *bamya* Rashid had ever had, despite his hunger, despite the joint. His mother had probably had him in mind when she made it; she'd spooned it full of her own disdain.

Khalil was watching him. There had been a way, before, that Khalil used to look at him, that Rashid always tried not to register on a conscious level. A look that when he caught it, he wished he had not. More than love, even. He had never dwelt on it before and had preferred to pretend that it was not there. But now it was gone, Rashid missed it more than he would have believed possible.

Chapter 47

There was no place for Rashid in the other room. They had formed a ring of seats and had positioned the unconscious Ayyoubi at its head.

He could hear Sabri's radio: '... *vowing to continue its aerial attacks on Palestinian territories. The Israeli officials spoke of fierce reprisals following Sunday's failed rocket attack ...*'

Rashid sat alone in his bedroom, his computer at his feet on the tiles in a mangle of plugs and wiring, its screen dusty and dumb. There was no one he wished to hear from now. No news that he wanted to receive.

A group laugh burst out from the sitting room and he found himself standing very close to the window, so close that night coldness touched at his cheeks. He rolled his forehead against the chilled, bare pane.

He was not stoned any more. He was not even fuggy.

His family must have been in his room looking for something while he was out; his shirts had been pulled out of a bag on to his unmade bed. The sweatshirt Lisa used to wear was spread out flat and empty in the centre of his bed. Rashid sat with his passport open and thumbed through it, as though it was a religious text, a path to salvation. They must have been looking for a shirt for Ayyoubi.

Raised voices in agreement came from them now, and then another laugh. The sound of Khalil's goat-like bray even cut through the argument going on between the neighbours upstairs and over the TV news broadcasts and the screams of the neighbour's kids.

It was then that it came to him, what he needed to do. It suddenly all became clear to him.

Rashid stood up and looked at the bed, the clothes, and the bags on the floor. He looked down at his computer. He stared at the photograph in his passport. It all confirmed what had come to him, the solution that had been revealed to him.

And once he found it (his destiny), he became wired with a sensitivity to his surroundings that he had never previously experienced. The decision seemed so obvious, once found, it closed down all other choices absolutely.

A jet plane burnt through the sky above with a low wail and a heavy thud juddered the house into silence leaving only the rise and fall of the commentators' broadcast voices.

Rashid felt above it, high up, above it all.

Wired with purpose.

Reborn.

Chapter 48

He strutted a bit once he was past the wasteland and away from the house. The gun hanging across his back gave him the zest to do so, gave him a purpose: to belong. Rashid headed towards the place where he had been so afraid, down to the seafront, stepping over spangles of barbed wire and collapsed fencing as he went. But it was quieter down there than it had been. No trucks of men roared past and his play for visibility was not picked up on. There was no one there. Even the sky was quieter. He could hear a drone buzz, but when he stopped to listen that was all he could hear. A gunship stood in the moonlit sea, stuck like a rig.

He crossed back towards the town, taking a different route along the edges of some farmland; the greenhouse plastic crackled and flapped in the wind and the earth was rutted in the ancient ways of Iraq, of Egypt. The moon illuminated it all with its fullness and across a field a porch light warmed the doorway of a house into an orange cube. How wondrous at this time of night this place was; even the deep, thick smell of manure was rich in its dankness. Rashid felt he could see and feel everything twice, with a heightened perception, a touched-up brightness, a childlike sense of wonderment and awe.

He ignored the helicopters circling over to the south, the clouds whirling like smoke in the shafts of light shooting down from their nostrils. Instead, he looked straight above him at the night clouds, high puffs of them stuck on to a moving dome pricked with stars beyond which was a fine muddled net of whiteness.

Occasionally a jet would crash through it all: *Keeooww*, a wild pre-emptive scream followed by a thud, a blast and the kind of horror he had no desire to think about.

Walking with the intention that he now had made him freer than he could believe possible. When he remembered what it was that he had resolved to do – something far better than anything else that he had ever done – his heart reverberated with massive pride and then shrank into itself, scared. His face became hard and insensate as did his hands, but this was a different kind of fear; it was a calculated, necessary one and he could force himself into its pace, into a liberated step he never thought he would have.

The key had been in the pocket of the jacket, as he knew it would be. There was a small pendant with it, a turquoise eye on a string to protect the bearer from *hasad*, the evil eye, to stave off the envious. The key had the name of the car model and registration number on it, as he had hoped. It was enough; he would be able to find the car.

The town was deserted, lines of hard walls and metal shutters padlocked to the ground. The rubber from Rashid's soles squeezed against the paving stones. He was coming up to the corner of the street, with the main road next to the playground in front of him, when a wave of it, the fear, came over him, almost uncontainable this time until he set it firm in his jaw, in his hands which now held the gun up, pointing straight at the sky, up in front of him. Nothing moved, but he could hear somewhere the cry of a baby in a room and the *tunnanana tunnanana* of the drumroll which introduced the beginning of the news. The precarious street lighting that still worked spat in its casing. He had never been there when it was so dark. Across the road, one of the signs boasting European funding swayed forwards out of the playground, catching a streak of light on its painted letters, the space behind it flat as a black card.

A *click*. First one, then a couple together. *Click, click, click*, fast like a marble finding its way down a run. He turned to where he thought it was coming from, but the street stopped dead after the lamp post, its light dull, grey on the dusty roofs of the cars. Then he saw a figure. Not that little sneak of Sabri's, Abu Omar's grandson, that Wael from upstairs? *Click!* He turned back again, but there was nothing. Even the baby had stopped crying.

Chapter 49

Eva had fallen asleep in the middle of a long sentence filled with question marks and qualifying clauses. She had been given, despite her insistence that she should not, Iman's bed and Iman was on a mattress on the floor. It was like camping under a flyover; the planes roared and thudded; the helicopters circled. And through it all Eva snored, small sniffly snores, her mouth slightly open. Her hair spread out in sticky wisps around her head.

The snoring became more obvious as the planes became less frequent; it rose in flurries of snuffles and fell into troughs of baby snorts. Above, with the departure of the planes, Iman could hear children being settled to sleep, moved on to blankets in the centre of their rooms, away from the windows. If she lay on her front she could feel her heart.

She was wide awake. More awake than she had ever been. More happy than she could remember, so happy that she could not trust it at all. It was going to be taken from her; someone would just come in and take it from her.

They would get him.

Iman sat up to listen.

They would take him from her. Probably now, his enemies were searching for him and someone would inform on him. Her neighbours would have no idea what other members of his party wanted from him, that they wanted him harmed. They weren't to know that. They could say, 'Yes, yes, Ayyoubi. We saw him, didn't we?' (She could hear them say it.) 'That way, he went over towards the

Mujahed house, over there.' They could break in to find him, smash panels in the front door, slide the locks across, and drag him out. She got out of bed. She should check outside for bloodstains again; there was one splotch of it that kept coming back to her, on a fallen cement pillar in the wasteland that he must have stepped over. Not all the blood had come out when she had tried to smear it away with her foot without drawing attention to herself. His enemies would see it and come over the wall, like he had.

The corridor smelt of cardamom, disinfectant and cigarettes. A strip of fluorescence lit the hall above the basin catching the Russian beech trees plastered on the wall behind it. She stepped down towards the living room, where the double doors hung open. Khalil was asleep on a sofa, his feet bare and hairy, poking out from under a blanket, his shoes tucked into a corner, the socks rolled up inside them. And he, Ziyyad, was still there, also covered partly with a blanket, his head tilted to the side, resting on the back of the sofa. She crept into the room and turned on the table lamp so that she could see him better.

The tablecloth was decorated in a loopy pattern made up of fine synthetic tubing and satin trim. Small imitation crystal drop- lets hung off it over the side of the table. It was old and dust had darkened the undersides of the tubing, dulled the trim; it had been coloured with children's pens and branded with the rings of sauce- pans too hot for it, but it was not the stains that Iman found herself wondering at, but at Rashid's passport, lying open at the page of his Canadian visa. Someone had placed a book of Myres' across the pages to keep them open.

She thought that she should, perhaps, remove Ziyyad's shoes. It couldn't be comfortable to sleep with shoes on. She untied them and loosened them hole by hole. Rashid probably needed some- thing more for his visa and he had put out the passport for that, so that they could remind him in the morning. She tugged at the heel of the right shoe and eased it off, spilling out some sand on to the floor, and started on the other foot. She should have washed his feet before he passed out, but then her family would have known, would have guessed she was not the type to wash strange men's feet.

But Rashid had said the visa was ready. He had emphasised that that was *it*; he even had an exit visa. She rolled off the socks, dark socks that smelt of Rashid's room, a familiar smell of unkempt man, but even that was not distasteful; she liked the element of need about it. She tucked the socks into the shoes after rolling them up the way Khalil did (he was so funny about his feet, his socks, his shoes, his clothes, so particular). She wanted something more to do, something caring and nurturing for this wounded fighter. She would place them away from him, by the table next to his jacket. But the green jacket was not on the chair where they had left it. It was not in the kitchen either, or hanging up by the front entrance.

Iman checked Rashid's room. Pulled the sheets off the bed. She had known it. She had sensed it. He was gone.

She stood by the front door and checked the locks, the upper and the lower bolt had been pulled across but the door had also been locked from outside with a key. She rubbed her forehead with two fingers hard.

She was missing something, something so obvious.

The passport, the jacket. The passport, the jacket.

Rashid's passport, Ziyyad's jacket.

Iman swallowed twice, breathed a couple of times, quick, quick, found herself walking in a small circle, but still she could not get it, her head was screwed tight. She went back to the doorway and looked for it. The gun was not there and she felt her hands, feet and stomach go cold and solid with fright.

She could not run well in her mother's *thoub*. It was a bad choice, too long, too narrow, but she had grabbed at it and the scarf from a chair in the kitchen, pulled it on over her pyjamas and found the spare keys in a drawer (how long these things took. It was ridiculous! What if there was a fire? She would tell her mother). And then out into the darkness, just the moonlight caught in the ridges of the mud, picking up the old white of the tents, the painted walls of destroyed homes and she could hear him now, almost like he was shouting it, but at the time it had been a mumble and they had just ignored it, because it was Rashid after all (which was probably it, really, the reason, if you thought about it), Rashid standing by the door saying, 'The son you never had,' in that self-pitying way he would sometimes adopt. Stupid.

You would not. You could not.

She found herself cajoling him, teasing him in her head, the sound of the words falling with her feet against the hard sandy surface she had now reached. *You would not! You could not! You would . . .* But that was probably a big part of it. Of why he would. She could not say that. She had to say something else when she stopped him (because of course she would stop him). She would say, 'It's enough that you tried,' or, 'You were ready to do it. That's enough.' The last one was better and she could say, 'He can look after himself,' but that didn't convince even her and she found that she had to stop, because her breathing was too heavy, her head was full of blood and she didn't know what she wanted (*who she wanted?*) any more and a sick, hateful part of her wanted it done with, so that it was no longer her responsibility to act. *Go on, kill yourself, you fool.* I don't care. Her face was wet, wet, wet. Enough. She had had enough.

She started running again, but in a way it was more like a running fall, stumbling over the earth somehow, anyhow, and she was still running when she heard the car start on the main road and the thing explode like a meteor hitting the earth, flames leaping up to lick at the sky behind the buildings just there, right there in front of her.

Chapter 50

Although the course of his family's life had largely been determined by them and despite the fact that he had seen more of them
and listened to more of them than most people would ever care to,
Rashid had never actually *used* a gun. He released the safety catch
of the one he now had (he knew that much from television), and
put the leather strap across the back of his neck, since the sound
behind him (*click! click!* there it was again), or possibly above him,
had started. His finger was in place, and surely the rest, he thought,
was obvious, just a question of applying pressure.

A plane passed and then the street was completely silent again:
no televisions, no babies, and no clicking sounds. And with the
silence came the smells of rotting rubbish and cooked rice.

'Hey! Ayyoubi!' the voice had called out from the shadows at
the side of the wall. 'Hey!'

Whoever it was shouting was not more than two steps behind
him. The voice was croaky but young. Rashid was further from the
street lamp now, at least half his face would be in the shadows. He
stopped and turned slightly. The boy stepped out into the centre
of the road, the lamplight coming in behind him. He was wearing
Sabri's shoes on his sockless feet. A phone hung around his neck
like a security tag.

Rashid could (and he was still holding himself back against the
wall where it was darker) make a run for the car. He could shoot
the boy, as he didn't appear to be armed, but the boy was unlikely
to be alone. But if he could shoot one, then another surely could

not be so hard. He had not anticipated anyone; he had imagined that his choice, and not the execution of it, would be the hardest bit. But the boy was someone who could screw it all up. He could not do it; he could not shoot this boy while he was able to see Sabri's unlaced brogues on those sockless feet. Rashid closed his eyes and moved the gun in front of him, but the boy must have just stepped away from the line of fire, towards him because his voice was now very close, next to Rashid's face.

'Hey. I thought there was something odd. I didn't think you were walking like a man who had been shot,' the boy said pleased at his own deduction. 'What are you doing here? What are you doing in Ayyoubi's clothes, with his gun? Where's Ayyoubi?'

Rashid lowered the gun. Hopeless, even in this, he had failed.

'You could get yourself killed, walking around like that.'

'That was the point,' Rashid said. 'That was the point.'

The boy laughed and started cleaning at his teeth with a finger-nail. 'Easier ways to kill yourself; you don't have to dress up in someone else's clothes to do it.' The kid chewed at the side of his mouth, trying to evaluate the extent of Rashid's deception.

'The point was to let him live,' Rashid said, 'as me.'

The boy laughed again. *Ha!* a cruel stupid laugh. 'Why would you want to do that?'

'It's important that he lives. No one should be trying to get rid of him, particularly not one of us.'

'They say he's a traitor.' The boy hawked out a large bolus of saliva from the back of his throat and propelled it out against the wall with his tongue. 'Where is he, anyway?'

'He's not a traitor.' Rashid was not sure how much the boy would understand, for however bright and darty the kid's eyes were, he and the boy came from very different worlds on the same tiny piece of land. 'Ayyoubi is a hero. He's a leader, see? The only reason the others want him gone is because he made them look bad. He was trying to stop some of the others from stealing the people's money for themselves.'

The boy was looking at Rashid curiously, his finger itching at the entrance of one nostril, one leg lifted up to scratch the other leg. Rashid stepped back a little. Probably the boy had fleas.

'What's it to you?' Rashid continued. He felt a great urgency in the execution of his plan. He had to do this, end like this. It would cancel out everything else. A boy, the carrot boy, could not thwart it. He would not let him. 'Listen, I die. They think Ayyoubi dies. Ayyoubi lives as me, goes away, comes back and saves Palestine. What's it to you? You can pretend you never saw me. You can say, "Hey, yes. It was Ayyoubi. I saw him. He's dead. Job done." Ask them to give you a promotion or payment or whatever it is that you need from them. See? It's easy.' But if he could not trust this boy, there was little point in him going ahead.

The boy continued to watch Rashid who put his hand into his back pocket making the boy pull out his gun and aim it at Rashid's body.

'What are you doing?' The boy had something cruel in him now. Rashid acted as though he had not seen either the look or the gun.

'Calm down, calm down,' Rashid said, bringing his hands in front of him. 'You know, it's good I saw you because I've got something for you. I was hoping to see you, but then this came up, so it was not going to be possible. Here.'

He handed over the dry-cleaning slip to the boy, who turned it over suspiciously.

'What's that?'

'The ticket to a suit of great beauty,' Rashid replied. 'It's being cleaned at Abu Faris' and will be ready tomorrow. You take it. You pick it up. It goes with the shoes.'

'Suit? What kind of suit?' The boy looked at the ticket under the light. It had a stamped number on it, a perforated edge and nothing else.

'How can I explain? It's in the style of what I would call "American Gangster",' Rashid said, catching himself thinking how much he would have enjoyed telling Khalil about this scene. Khalil would have loved the whole set-up, loved it so much that Rashid was no longer certain that he wanted to do anything that robbed him of the chance of telling Khalil about the way things had gone.

'American gangster?' the boy smiled. It was a great term, and Rashid hung the gun over his head so that he could use his hands.

'Ah, American gangster. You don't know this style? Well, the shoulders are *hayk*, like this, broad, at the shoulders with white lines on the fabric coming down and the lining is red silk.' Rashid rubbed his fingers together. 'So soft,' and then he added, 'it was made in Paris, by a very high-class tailor.'

'Paris?' the boy smiled lopsidedly like they were sharing a dirty joke.

'Paris.' Rashid nodded. 'You know, it's very lucky that I met you like this, because I thought it was really your thing.'

Rashid worried that he had gone too far, that he had pushed his luck with this boy, whose eyes were now glazing over while staring hard at Rashid.

'Understand something?' the boy asked. 'You want to understand something? Well, I tell you that this show, this part of it: this is *my* show, *fahem keef?* You see how it is?' He lifted the phone up by the chain that it was attached to around his neck. 'I've got the number in here to do the car, see? So it's my show. But this time, just as, you know, the usual strategy requires, there's someone else too. He's just the lookout, but you should know that he's there.'

'Where exactly?'

'OK, well, we're here, you go straight down here and you hit the playground in front of you, yes? OK, now what you do is . . . the car is to your right when you turn into the main street. It's blue, third car along. Opposite where the car is parked down that small side street next to the playground is the lookout. Now . . .' The boy licked the end of his index finger repeatedly with his tongue, then looked again at Rashid as he rubbed his forefinger and thumb together as if he was about to start counting money. '*Fa*, this Ayyoubi, *batal aanjad?*' he asked. 'He's a hero, really?'

'*Batal aanjad*. He's really a hero,' Rashid confirmed. '*Aanjad*, really,' Rashid said seriously.

'Well, if you're prepared to die for him,' the boy smirked and puffed himself out a bit, '*Ya zalame*, I'd die for no one. Never,' he said proudly. 'Except Palestine, of course.'

'Of course,' Rashid replied. 'I understand.'

'OK,' said the boy, rolling his tongue around the front of his mouth between the gums and the lips as he thought, nodding his head in a way that seemed to indicate some kind of delinquent purpose. '*Shuuf*. See here, here's what you've got to do,' and he told Rashid what it was that Rashid had to do.

'I can trust you, *ya zalame?*' Rashid asked.

'With your life, brother,' the boy said, bending the dry-cleaner's ticket in half and putting it in his back pocket, 'with your life.'

And with that Rashid had agreed to do what it was that the boy had said he had to do.

Chapter 51

It was just around the corner, but it must have been that Iman had not moved for a while from where she stood. She had been frozen somewhere in time and place on a badly lit street on a strip of land in the far corner of the Mediterranean where people fought over something which she could not remember. 'We're two sides of a walnut,' Rashid had said to her. When was that? When she had cried at school in Switzerland frustrated by another move, another loss of friends, another departure of her parents to greater things? Was it in an airport somewhere? On a border? 'We'll never be apart. I'll always be with you.'

The people were coming out of everywhere with the explosion, out of dark houses with torches and candles. There was a cameraman jogging past her with a furry pink boom microphone and a flak jacket and she was being pushed along too with the crowd around the corner to where the flames fed off tangled cars, fuel and the lives of idealistic people. She found herself in the crowd where she was one of the women, one of many dressed like her in *thoubs* and scarves, screaming and crying for the loss of her brother, her brother.

'Ayyoubi!' the scream goes up. 'They killed Ayyoubi!'

'A dead fighter!' someone is crying as the stretcher is carried above her, past her head, but it is not Rashid; she can see the legs, the size of the body, the feet are not his, the shoes are not his.

'From the Authority!' they cry. 'A fighter from the Authority!'

'They wired his car! Ayyoubi was the target!'

'Death to the Islamists!' a cry went up from a boy. 'Up with the Mainstream party of the Authority!'

'I can't stand it any more!' a woman next to Iman wailed, beating her chest. 'I just can't take it any more, not if we are killing ourselves. No! I can't take it! Not after all we've been through.'

'What an explosion! The force of it! No trace of him left from the car! Must've been right under him!'

'Just some of his jacket here. See, the green. I would always recognise that jacket.'

'Rashid.' Everything was pouring from her nose, her eyes; it was messy, red and stinging all around her face and each time she wiped it away with the arm of the *thoub* it was back until she could not see. 'Rashid,' she was wailing now and there was someone behind her, a figure, the bulk of Umm Nidal from the Women's Committee, holding her up.

'You can't find your brother, *habibti*? He probably followed the body, with the other men. Go that way. There, go,' and with that Iman was guided to go back the way she came, with a big warm hand on her back. Not knowing what else there was for her to do or who it was she was to grieve for, Iman joined the crowd mourning the death of the unknown fighter.

Chapter 52

If the boy's plan had involved taking care of the lookout, then it could have been said to have gone according to plan.

The main street had been even darker than the one he had left the boy in. From the moment he turned into it, he could feel the blood pumping in his ears as though he were in an upturned boat on the shore with the sea pounding at it. The moon was still fat and bright in the sky and he felt his way out into the street, *pat, pat,* only so many single steps to the car door, only so much space to cover. He concentrated hard on the practical element of it, and by trying hard to forget all else: this new brightness under his skin, the drugged-out beat of his heart. His breathing that was so heavy it was like someone there, behind him, *huuh, huuh, huuh,* like an obese old man, *huuh,* but it was him; he knew it was him. If he forgot all else and concentrated solely on the line of cars: the dents picked up in the half-light, the bent wing mirrors, the stickers on back windows, the stuffed dogs and leopard-skin fur on the back ledges. He could move forwards, as he usually did, one step before the other, the one foot picking up and coming down, and then the next.

Startled by a foe in the grasses, a cat leapt off the low wall that ran around the playground in an awkward backward twist, as though pulled by a string from its neck. Rashid looked over at it instinctively, without thinking, looked to see whether it was the ginger tabby of that afternoon and by doing so he saw, and was seen, by the fighter, the lookout.

He had expected the lookout to be younger than the boy, or at least smaller. He had not expected him to be the man with the Stalin moustache from the day of Abu Omar's arrest. 'You,' said the man, who was far closer to Rashid than the boy had led him to believe. 'You?' and despite all that Rashid had not expected, he had at least expected it more than this man had and it was this advantage of shock – a two-second, perhaps a five-second advantage – which had allowed Rashid to think, 'But this must be how you do it,' and to pull down the trigger, aiming the implement at the man's gut protruding like a question mark towards him. That had been all that was needed before something jumped away from Rashid with a bloody-minded resolve and then whipped back at him with an awful thwack that made him stumble. He was thrown against the car, a side mirror cracking at his hipbone and the look-out was down.

One second, maybe two, the jacket was off and thrown into the car, the gun too. Inside with the door open, he cranked the window down, down. The beating pulse coming now from his face; it was rushed with blood; his head centred his world. The shot would have been heard. Beyond the rushing layer of sea about his head there were voices coming from the houses. Rashid closed the car door and leant in through the window. It was a question of the boy, the question of the reliability of the boy, the triggering of the device with the boy's phone. He turned the key in the ignition to make it more real. *Now!* his body and his head screamed, running towards the corner, heading away from the car, down towards the small alley, to somewhere tight and secret. *Now!* it screamed again as he reached the turn. *Do it now, boy. Press it!* And then the blast came like the door of heaven slamming behind him and he was lifted off his feet like a cat, thrown forwards, headlong, like an inanimate thing, on to broken paving stones, wet leaflets and fragments of glass.

Chapter 53

The silly fucker had got him right there, in the heart, and he was done for, the lookout knew it. He had fallen on to one leg and then the other one just closed in all by itself. It was as though the raft he had been standing on had been tugged from under him away from where he was leaving life to rush up and down his body under his skin in waves like a sheep with a slit throat, rush up and down and out of him until it left him all together. It was all dark below and wet with a stickiness that he didn't expect and it is only his son that the fighter thinks of now, not the other fighters and the meetings and the jealousy of that man Ayyoubi who had it all so easy and had never wanted for a thing in his life. He does not think of his mother or his father or the tent he had been born into, which had been so low that you could not step into it without lowering your head, or his father's second wife who had made sure his father left them there when he had moved out of the camp. He does not think of these things, but just of his boy for whom he had wanted it all to be better, for whom no act was too small or too low for him to carry out. He thought only of the boy's soft-skinned arm on his neck and the swoop of his trusting eyelashes, for that was what it was all for, but he thinks no longer as he is turning now under these waters, caught by a current in these new depths that let his body rock back and forth giving him only the consolation they can afford.

Chapter 54

And how wonderful it was then to run, to feel the mechanism of his body moving how he wanted it to, finding within it a fuel and propulsion that he had not known he had. The synchronicity of mind and body amazing him as he hopped from side to side, along alleys creviced by a run of water in their centre: how he could do this while barely slowing himself down, how he could leap at the end of it all over the cut-up earth, fallen pillars and tent strings of the wasteland that was theirs, how he could feel his heart propelling him forwards with a love of chance, of risk, of the opportunities for tomorrow. And he loved it all: the light of the moon on the sea, the blinking, blackness of the water with the gunboats turned away for the night, for it was his night and their presence in it was not required. And he's running in such long strides now – a beat, a beat and another – that he is flying high above it all, up, over, out of it all; flying all the way until he reaches the sea.

Acknowledgements

I would like to thank the following friends, relatives, writing professionals and institutions for taking the time to read my work and to provide advice, encouragement and support over the years: Ghassan Abu Sitta, Layla Al Maleh, Omar Al Qattan, Mitchell Albert, Lorraine Bacchus, Samia Bano, Shameen Bashir, Brenna Bhandar, the British Council, Gaenor Bruce, Emily Burnham, Clem Cairns, Caroline Cederwell, Cathy Costain, Steve Cragg, Amy Cramer, Claire, Dina, Hani, Hassan Salah, Nadia, Salma, Samira and Taysir Dabbagh, Wafa Darwish, Mick Delap, Khaled El Ali, Azza El Hassan, English PEN, Bernardine Evaristo, Fish Publishing, Emanuel Garboua, Haris Gazdar, Vanessa Gebbie, Carlo Gebler, Maggie Gee, Zeina B. Ghandour, Jo Glanville, Francisco Goldman, Katia Hadidian, Annie Hickson, David Holmes, International PEN, Randa Jarrar, Mike Jones, Frederic Joseph, Dina Kasrawi, Kavi Kittani, Rahat Kurd, Maha Ladki, Daniel Machover, Eloise Marshall, Lena Masri, Scott McGaraghan, Abdullah, Lulwa, Linda, Naser, Samir and Jumana Mutawi, Nadia Naqib, Tessa O'Neil, the late Harold Pinter, Christine Pohlmann, Adil Rahman, Caroline Rooney, Jacob Ross, Dana Sajdi, Tope Saraki, Stacy Stobl, Tales of the Decongested, Catherine Viala, Sue Said Wardell, The West Cork Literary Festival, Sarah Leah Whitson and Josh Zimmer.

Special thanks to the following friends and relatives who provided particularly thoughtful and detailed comments on earlier drafts of this novel: Paloma Baeza, Nadia Capy Osgood,

Felicity Cunliffe-Lister, Claire Dabbagh, Nadia Dabbagh, Izzat Darwazeh, Christine Habbard, Graham Harfield, Elias Nasrallah and James Richard.

I am also greatly indebted to the enthusiasm and support that I had from Kate Jones, whose sudden death in February 2008 was a shock and a loss to so many. Many thanks also to Amanda (Binky) Urban at ICM and to Margaret Halton for their advice and encouragement.

I have a stupendous agent. Karolina Sutton at Curtis Brown could not do more in terms of understanding and furthering my aspirations for both the style and subject matter of my work. Her editorial comments on *Out of It* were incisive and invaluable. This book would have been a lesser one without them. She has always believed in me and always protected my interests and for that I am extremely grateful. Many thanks, Karolina, for everything.

A very special thank you goes to Ahdaf Soueif for praising and promoting my work as well as for making the publication of this novel possible. Her support of individual Palestinian writers, as well as her work with the Palestinian Festival of Literature (PalFest), is critical for those of us who write about a crisis that many would prefer nothing more to be heard about. Her writing is also an inspiration: *In the Eye of the Sun* changed my life in a way that few books have come close to doing.

Thanks also to Bloomsbury Qatar Foundation Publishing, most notably to Andy Smart, Seif Salmawy, Jehan Marei for selecting this novel and to Kathy Rooney and Safaa Mraish for working on taking it through to publication, with special thanks to Jehan for her editorial comments.

At Bloomsbury Publishing, I would firstly like to thank the reader Wala' Qasiah from Hebron who upon finishing *Out of It* told Alexandra Pringle, 'But this is what it's like.' Thank you Wala'. That was important and meant a lot.

I am also indebted to Clare Hey for her eye for detail, detective and editorial skills in general, to Erica Jarnes for editorial work and for seeing the text through to publication, to Alexa von Hirschberg for being so enthusiastic, to Greg Heinimann for taking my idea for a cover and making it beautiful, to Jonathan Ring for being a patient photographer with a restless subject and mainly, of course, to Alexandra Pringle who did nothing less than realise a personal (but very specific) dream by backing this novel.

Thanks to the Bashir family of Somerset Avenue, Karachi, for their extraordinary hospitality when I stayed with them to work on edits in January, and to the O'Neils of Yateem Gardens, Bahrain, for letting me have use of their house for the same purpose the following month.

On a (more) personal note, special thanks to my children, Miro and Maia, for being fabulous, funny, warm and mad, to Ranjanie Nirmala Devi John, without whose unflaggingly high standards and dedication to my family much less would be possible, to Zeina B. Ghandour for giving me a notepad and telling me to just do it, and to Abdullah Mutawi, father of my children, ex-husband and friend.

A NOTE ON THE AUTHOR

Selma Dabbagh is a British Palestinian writer based in
London. Her short stories have been included in a number
of anthologies, including those published by Granta and
the British Council. She was the English PEN nominee for
the International PEN David T.K. Wong Award.
Out of It is her first novel.

A NOTE ON THE TYPE

The text of this book is set in Linotype Goudy Old
Style. It was designed by Frederic Goudy (1865–1947),
an American designer whose types were very popular
during his lifetime, and particularly fashionable in
the 1940s. He was also a craftsman who cut the metal
patterns for his type designs, engraved matrices
and cast type.

The design for Goudy Old Style is based on Goudy
Roman, with which it shares a 'hand-wrought'
appearance and asymmetrical serifs, but unlike
Goudy Roman its capitals are modelled on
Renaissance lettering.